Civil Rights in the
Texas Borderlands

Civil Rights in the Texas Borderlands

Dr. Lawrence A. Nixon and Black Activism

WILL GUZMÁN

UNIVERSITY OF ILLINOIS PRESS

Urbana, Chicago, and Springfield

First Illinois paperback, 2016
© 2015 by the Board of Trustees
of the University of Illinois
All rights reserved
Manufactured in the United States of America
1 2 3 4 5 C P 5 4 3 2 1
♾ This book is printed on acid-free paper.

Library of Congress Control Number: 2015903878
ISBN: 978-0-252-03892-1 (hardcover)
ISBN: 978-0-252-09688-4 (e-book)
ISBN: 978-0-252-08206-1 (paperback)

Contents

Illustrations

Notes on Usage

The terms "African American," "Black," or "New World African" will be used interchangeably in this biography to refer to former African captives who were enslaved in the United States and colonies of European powers in the Americas. Terms such as "Negro" or "colored" are used when required in proper context or the quoting of sources. I agree with scholar Jeffrey Perry in that because many Black activists and intellectuals during Lawrence A. Nixon's lifetime "struggled to capitalize the 'N' in 'Negro' as both a statement of pride *and* as a challenge to white supremacy," it makes sense to likewise capitalize the "B" in "Black" "when it is used as its equivalent" but that "there is no similarly compelling basis for capitalizing the 'w' in 'white.'"[1]

"Afro-Latina/o" is a contemporary word used by activists and scholars to describe individuals of African descent who are born in Africa (such as Equatorial Guinea or Angola), the Americas, or the Iberian Peninsula and speak Spanish or Portuguese or have been acculturated into Spanish or Portuguese culture or both. The term "Afro-Latino," and similar terms such as "Afro-Caribbean" and "Afro-Latin America," announce a reclamation of, and sense of pride in, African heritages as well as a social and political connection with others throughout the African diaspora that is grounded in the legacies of slavery, segregation, discrimination, and racial violence. The term "Afro-Latina/o" also complicates homogenizing uses of Latina/o and definitions of Latinas/os as a mixed-race constituency.[2]

"Chicana/o" is a term used to describe both Mexican immigrants and Mexican Americans. To say of a Mexican American woman that she is Chicano may be "taken as emphasizing an identity with Chicano culture in general," while to say she is Chicana may "suggest a feminist perspective on that identity."[3]

"Mexican," "Mexicano," and "Mexican immigrant" are used interchangeably when describing those born in Mexico who reside temporarily in the United States. "Mexican American" is used to describe those born in the United States and those who change their citizenship status.[4]

"Latina/o" is used to describe "persons or communities of Latin American origin." "Hispanic" in this study encompasses "all Spanish-speaking peoples in both hemispheres," although I am aware of the possible negative political implications of both "Latina/o" and "Hispanic" depending on one's geography or politics.[5]

"Anglo" is used to distinguish a white non-Hispanic from a person of Hispanic heritage. In parts of the United States with large Hispanic populations, such as the Southwest in general and El Paso in particular, an American of Polish, Irish, or German heritage might be termed an "Anglo." However, in parts of the country where the Hispanic population is small, or in areas where ethnic distinctions among European groups remain strong, the word "Anglo" has little currency as a general term for non-Hispanic whites.[6]

Abbreviations

EPPL-SW	El Paso, Texas, Public Library—downtown branch, Southwest Collection
FOIPA	Freedom of Information and Privacy Act
HUAC	House Committee on Un-American Activities
IOH-UTEP	Institute of Oral History at University of Texas–El Paso
LANP-LBJL	Lawrence Aaron Nixon Papers, Lyndon Baines Johnson Library, Austin, Texas
LOCMD	Library of Congress, Manuscript Division, Washington, D.C.
NAACP	National Association for the Advancement of Colored People
NARA-DC	National Archives and Records Administration, Washington, D.C.
N/MFP	Nixon/McIver Family Papers, Albuquerque, New Mexico
USDJ-FBI-DC	United States Department of Justice, Federal Bureau of Investigation, Washington, D.C.

Lawrence A. Nixon Chronology

Event	Year
Born in Marshall, Harrison County, Texas	1883
Moves to New Orleans, Orleans Parrish, Louisiana	1886
Moves back to Marshall, Harrison County, Texas	1893
Graduates from Wiley College in Marshall, Texas	1902
Graduates from Meharry Medical School in Nashville, Tennessee	1906
Moves to Cameron, Milam County, Texas	1906
Marries first wife, Esther Josephine Calvin	1907
Witnesses the lynching of Alex Johnson	1907
Birth of son, Lawrence Joseph Nixon	1909
Moves to El Paso, El Paso County, Texas	1910
Death of father, Charles Blanton Nixon	1910
Mexican Revolution	1910
Helps establish the El Paso NAACP	1914
Death of Esther Josephine Calvin from influenza	1919
Intervenes to prevent sharecropper Henry Lowry from being lynched	1921
Texas Terrell Election Law revised, Blacks barred from Democratic primary	1923
Becomes life member of the NAACP	1927
L. A. Nixon v. Champ C. Herndon and Charles V. Porras	1927
L. A. Nixon v. James C. Condon and Charles H. Kolle	1932

Civil Rights in the
Texas Borderlands

Introduction

Tale of a Doctor, History of a Land

Until lions have their own historians,
tales of the hunt shall always glorify the hunter.

Igbo Proverb

The accomplishments of Dr. Lawrence Aaron Nixon were similar to those of other courageous Black Texan leaders.[1] Nixon, along with Lula B. White of Houston, Juanita J. Craft of Dallas, Claude W. Black Jr. of San Antonio, and Warneta and Volma Overton of Austin, was instrumental in advancing race relations at the local level and ensuring that the United States lived up to the principles of its constitution.[2] The arena in which he and these other activists fought was inhospitable, and much more deserves to be said regarding Nixon's personal contribution within the larger context of borderlands history, African Americans in the West, and the engagement of the Black professional class in so-called racial uplift during the pre–civil rights movement.[3]

Nixon was an African American physician and civil rights activist who lived in El Paso, Texas, from 1910 until his death in 1966. Born in Marshall, Texas, in 1883, Nixon graduated from Wiley College in 1902 and Meharry Medical College in 1906. He then established a medical office in Cameron, Texas, in 1907, but the racial climate in central Texas was terrible, and so he moved to El Paso in hopes of a better life. Nixon's community involvement flourished in this border city. He helped establish a local branch of the NAACP and also took part in trying to prevent Henry Lowry's abduction by a lynch mob. Additionally, Nixon attempted to integrate the local public pool and engaged in an effort to establish an all-Black hospital. Furthermore, he joined the liberal Southern Conference for Human Welfare (SCHW) despite rumors of its communist ties. If Nixon had not done anything else during this four-decade period, his life story would still be worthy of a biographical treatment because of the challenges he endured, the obstacles he overcame, the achievements he obtained, and the impact he had on his community. Yet Nixon's courage, independence from the white economy, and the backing of the NAACP allowed him to contest the 1923 Texas Terrell Law, which barred African Americans from participating in a Democratic primary election. By testing this unjust law, Nixon set in motion a twenty-year struggle during which he was the plaintiff in two important Supreme Court cases, *Nixon v. Herndon* (1927) and *Nixon v. Condon* (1932), that successfully challenged Texas's all-white Democratic primary. Despite these legal successes, sadly, Texas continued to prevent Blacks from voting in the Democratic Party primary. However, Nixon's efforts established the legal precedent that ultimately dismantled all-white primaries throughout the entire South in the famous *Smith v. Allwright* Supreme Court decision in 1944. This biography unearths previously unknown information about his life, reminds readers of his legal victories and their eventual ratification, and analyzes how his life unfolded and his achievements were obtained.

The southwest borderlands, as writer Américo Paredes defines it, is a "historically determined geo-political zone of military, linguistic, and cultural conflict," a place that is difficult to understand without first having some idea of the phenomenon of a frontier.[4] Historians Jane M. Rausch and David J. Weber, in their 1994 *Where Cultures Meet*, define frontiers as "places where cultures contend with one another . . . to produce a dynamic that is unique to time and place," representing "both place and process, linked inextricably."[5] When we speak of the popular concept of the U.S. western frontier, we speak of a land seemingly without limit, a land of opportunity, a land of desert, cacti, and panoramic sunsets. It was once viewed as an exotic place full of danger and mystique, a place where the Spanish were heroes. However, in the 1960s and 1970s, scholars of borderlands began to understand the vital need to shed light on the "others" in the arena of the western frontier, mainly those who had been traditionally left out of the history books: Native Americans and Chicanas/os. "The Mexican-American side of the story," Julian Samora, Joe Bernal, and Albert Peña noted in 1979, "has finally been brought to the attention of other Americans." As historian Patricia Limerick observes, "The inclusion of these new angles of vision added vitality and depth to Western American history" and to borderlands history as well.[6] The intellectual thrust of "the borderlands" and the frontier West that Limerick and her cohort describe is "mutually distinct and simultaneously overlapping." Both Limerick's and Frederick Jackson Turner's western frontier promote and critique "a fairly unique 'U.S.-Anglo' construct rooted in westward

1. Lawrence A. Nixon, ca. late 1890s or early 1900s. Courtesy of the Edna A. (Nixon) McIver family collection.

expansion." The Spanish empire viewed northern Mexico "as a buffer where cultural collateral was acceptable to lose, while the U.S. viewed the frontier as the crucible of civilization, democracy, and American character." Thus, the borderlands is where the Spanish buffer and the U.S. western frontier "collided," and "the results over time are ambiguous, complicated."[7]

This culturally complex area is where Lawrence Nixon's life unfolds. Although he was not Mexican or Native American, his is a story of the borderlands and western America because it provides a "new angle of vision" that adds "vitality and depth" to the idea of what it means to be an American. Lawrence Nixon was born in a border county (Harrison County, Texas), educated in border cities (New Orleans, Louisiana; Marshall, Texas; and Memphis, Tennessee), established a medical practice in central Texas (Cameron, Milam County), and lived for over fifty years in the southwestern border city of El Paso. Geographically, literally, and physically, his was a border life.[8]

Nixon's life also represents a borderlands existence metaphorically. For literary critic Blake Allmendinger, the "frontier line," an idea modeled on Samira Kawash's suggestion that "the color line metaphorizes racial distinction as spatial division" in which the historic "idea of race has a long-standing relation to the idea of geography," refers to "the border between 'civilization' and 'savagery,' represented by whites and indigenous peoples, respectively."[9] Lawrence Nixon lived a life on the edge of the metropole: he was a Democrat in an era when most Black men were Republicans; he was highly educated and medically trained in an era when few people attended college; he challenged the status quo when most avoided conflict because of the potential violent reprisals; he moved to the Southwest in an era when most African Americans moved to the Northeast or north Midwest.[10] He was a Black man living in a city where Blacks were a distinct minority and Mexican and Mexican Americans were in the majority.[11] And finally, he was a Black man living on an international boundary. This speaks to his worldview and sensibilities, clearly a borderlands-as-metaphor experience.

As a Black man in the United States, Lawrence Nixon, to borrow Paredes's words, was exposed to constant "cultural conflict" merely for being who he was: "unapologetically Black," which in the minds of some was the antithesis of being an American.[12] Unfortunately, the Turnerian narrative, as historian George Lipsitz has stated, "does not prepare us to think about the Americans who crossed the Pacific rather than the Atlantic, or about the people who did not come to America . . . but instead had America come to them with the brutality and sadism of conquest, slavery, and genocide."[13] Nixon's ancestors were part of the latter group, brought to this country by force and in chains. Nixon lived in a highly segregated, racist, and violent society that deemed him an intellectual and biological inferior and that denied him his humanity, his citizenship, and his manhood.[14] Nixon was aware of this, noting in 1932 that it was possible for a Black person at times to "be acclaimed because of the excellence of his brute power where it is almost impossible for him to receive notice for achievements of intellect or character. The Negro with a vision is indeed a lonely mortal!"[15]

"A Racial Frontier": African Americans in the U.S. West

In his book *In Search of the Racial Frontier*, Quintard Taylor describes what he calls "the rich, complex, tradition of black western history." This book is one response to Taylor's request for historians to look at the Black West for the more comprehensive story of the African American experience it has to tell. Nixon's life in El Paso, Texas, illustrates both the Black West's "regional distinctiveness and its continuity with the legacy of African American history in the rest of the nation." Nixon's life is also an example of the diversity of the Black past and "the existence of multiple African American historical traditions."[16]

The Black community of El Paso, which was a border city, a southern city, a western city, and a city that was not racially inclusive, found itself caught between hope and despair. Again Taylor gives us the central paradigm in the history of Blacks in the West:

> Did the West represent the last best hope for nineteenth and twentieth century African Americans? Was it a racial frontier beyond which lay the potential for an egalitarian society? Or did the region fail to match the unobtainable promise imposed upon it by legions of boosters, to provide both political freedom and economic opportunity? Perhaps black Americans, in their desire to escape the repression of the East and South, simply exaggerated the possibilities in the region. Did western distinctiveness apply to race? Such questions defy easy, immediate answers.[17]

The western frontier did not turn out to offer the future southern Blacks had hoped for. Southern Blacks found themselves in a region that was no different than the rest of the nation in its ongoing yet slanted obsession with race. In *"It's Your Misfortune and None of My Own": A History of the American West*, Richard White remarks that "in coming west, African Americans had . . . voted with their feet against legal segregation and the south only to find themselves subject to de facto segregation in the West."[18] In the conclusion of *In Search of the Racial Frontier*, Taylor asks, "was the West a racial frontier beyond which lay the potential for an egalitarian society?" In response, Taylor claims that even when allowing for "subregional, cultural, or gender differences and the presence of some Euro-Americans supportive of racial equality," many scholars, including those who have studied white western racial attitudes, answer "no" to the question.[19] Nixon's life experiences in El Paso validate this conclusion, because El Paso engaged in Jim Crow practices as mandated by state laws and social norms.

In *Bound for Freedom: Black Los Angeles in Jim Crow America*, Douglas Flamming describes racism against African Americans during the first half of the nineteenth century in the southwestern city of Los Angeles as manifesting itself in three distinct forms. These forms were not particular to Los Angeles, however, but in fact evident in many communities across the nation and indeed in El Paso during Nixon's lifetime. First, and perhaps the least important of the three, was public insult designed to denigrate Black people, which demonstrated the power whites held over Blacks (of course, there are many racial and ethnic slurs in the English lexicon, so African Americans were not singled out). For example, for a Black Pullman porter to be called "George" or "boy" by a white child or adult, particularly in a public arena, was a reminder of the powerlessness of Black men in direct relation to those with institutional power. Many Black Pullman porters and waiters "winced when they heard 'George.' Not responding was grounds for dismissal. Answering meant admitting they had no name of their own, no identity as an individual." "Boy" and "George" were verbal assaults that nostalgically referenced the time when African captives were forced to accept the names given to them by plantation owners.[20] Calling Black men "George" or "Boy" was a subtle but powerful way for whites to say "We're on top and there's nothing you can do about it."[21]

The second form of racism that Flamming describes is "structural, or institutional, inequalities," which was the "one most often targeted by civil rights activists." What many Black people wanted was real, substantive equal opportunity: socially, politically, legally, and perhaps most importantly economically. The institutional forces that perpetuated racism included Jim Crow laws, or state-sanctioned racial apartheid, extralegal law enforcement in the form of lynchings, a bias within the criminal justice system that led to an inordinate number of Blacks being arrested and sentenced, the one-party South, the curtailing of voter registration and voting through the use of such tactics such as violence, intimidation, poll taxes, the grandfather clause, and literacy tests. In addition to being confronted with these institutional manifestations of crass racism, African Americans were denied economic and educational opportunities. Most whites simply did not hire Blacks in meaningful and highly valued positions. Flamming reminds us that when African Americans "were employed, they were usually hired last, fired first, and paid less, than their white counterparts—and all this too, was a legal institutional barrier" to African American advancement.[22] Nixon challenged this structural or institutional racism by involving himself in the battle to dismantle the all-white Democratic primary, laying claim to a rich legacy of defiance among African Americans.

The third kind of racism that Flamming discusses is the assumption of Black inferiority.[23] Some whites in the West assumed that African Americans, "as an undifferentiated group, were criminal, violent, dirty, ignorant, lazy, loud, unsanitary, oversexed, carefree, and unambitious." When Anglos in the West met African Americans that "obviously did not fit the stereotype, they classified those blacks as 'exceptional'—the exception that proved the rule—thereby preserving their presumption of black inferiority." Stereotypes, as Black cultural critic Hazel Carby asserts, are designed not to represent a reality "but to function as a disguise, or mystification, of objective social relations."[24] Nixon must have experienced all three forms of racism, but his reactions to them were such that he was able to survive, to thrive, and earn respect. This book explores this in further detail.

"Racial Uplift": Black Professionals and the Pre–Civil Rights Movement

In the seminal "Black Professionals and Race Consciousness: Origins of the Civil Rights Movement, 1890–1950," Darlene Clark Hine encourages historians to "identify and revisit other foundational moments and deeply to penetrate the layers of our country's past in order to bring into the bright light of history all those whose struggles and resistance made freedom more than a dream." Clearly Lawrence Nixon's Supreme Court cases were foundational moments in African American history. This study attempts to answer Clark Hine's call by placing Nixon's contributions to the civil rights movement in a broader context and demonstrating how it paved the way for future resistance. Nixon's story allows people to understand "the proto–civil rights movements," which Clark Hine correctly points out is "fundamental to the reconstruction of the origins of the classic civil rights movement of the late 1950s and 1960s." The pre–civil rights movement paved the way for all future actions, and as Clark Hine shows us, "the formation of parallel organizations . . . proved to be far more radical, far more capable of nurturing resistance, than anyone could have anticipated in the closing decade of the nineteenth century and opening decades of the twentieth."[25] While there is no evidence to suggest that Nixon was a member of the National Medical Association (NMA), he was part of the Lone Star State Medical, Dental, and Pharmaceutical Association History, which was the state-level affiliate of the NMA.[26] Additionally, Nixon was part of the Black professional class as a physician, and throughout the late 1920s and early 1930s he attempted to establish an all-Black hospital in El Paso, which, had it come to fruition, would have been instrumental in cultivating more future Black doctors and establishing a sense of pride within the African American community in the Southwest. It was also during this time period that the Black community, as Clark Hine tells us, "produced a class of professional men and women, who would meet the race's survival needs, promote its uplift, develop its advancement agenda, and provide a crucial link with the struggles of the mid-twentieth-century for first-class citizenship." Although largely an unknown figure outside of Texas, Nixon belongs in the company of his generation's most notable civil rights activists in the West, Southwest, and beyond.[27]

Historian Edward Beardsley challenges historians to think differently about erroneous perceptions of the Black middle class in the first half of the twentieth century. "Supposedly, this group was so eager for white acceptance and so fearful of being lumped with the mass of 'shiftless' blacks, that it turned its back on the poor and virtually repudiated its own membership in the race."[28] I take up Beardsley's challenge and show how Nixon refused to turn his back on the race. Nixon's long-standing crusade for freedom also illustrates historian Carter G. Woodson's assessment of the role the Black professional classes played in the struggles for African American dignity, respect, and equality: "In organizing the people . . . and in stimulating their effort to battle for their rights the Negro physician has contributed more than any other class, with the possible exception of the Negro lawyer, toward enlarging the domain of individual liberty and securing for a despised element a hearing at the bar of public opinion."[29]

Flamming suggests that professional middle-class Blacks sought to combat "white presumption of black inferiority" by becoming what he refers to as "super citizens," hoping thereby to dispel those negative assumptions.[30] As a member of the African American community in El Paso, was Lawrence Nixon a super citizen? It appears that way, especially when one considers that he was well liked and had few enemies. No one is on record of having a disparaging remark to say about Nixon, although surely he was not perfect. He was dignified, composed, and soft spoken in public, but was this public persona part of his personality or was it a tactical strategy to disarm his enemies and protect himself and his family from the stings and blows of white supremacy, domination, and control? For Blacks of the middle class, Flamming writes, "the quest for civil rights was not a 'movement' or a set of dramatic movements; it was a way of life." Lawrence Nixon and others of his generation, race, region, and class—despite their outward appearances—"were not soft-spoken in their demands for equal rights or their denunciations of racism, and they were anything but escapists."[31]

As Clark Hine notes, in creating a nurturing environment, the actions of the Black professional class may have appeared "to imply acquiescence in segregation," but Black institutions "never silenced internal dissent. Ideological tensions between parallelism and integrationism haunted black discourse throughout the twentieth century." Ironically, Black professionals such as Lawrence Nixon "identified the Achilles' heel of white supremacy: Segregation provided Blacks the chance, indeed, the imperative, to develop a range of distinct institutions that they controlled," which allowed them to exploit "that fundamental weakness in the 'separate but equal' system permitted by the U.S. Supreme Court's 1896 decision in *Plessy v. Ferguson*."[32]

2. Lawrence A. Nixon, ca. 1915.
Courtesy of the Edna A. (Nixon) McIver
family collection.

There have been very few books written about Black doctors and their con-
tributions to advance the race, particularly during the era in which Nixon lived.
Books such as Florence Ridlon's *A Black Physician's Struggle for Civil Rights*, Linda
Royster Beito and David T. Beito's *Black Maverick*, Thomas J. Ward's *Black Physi-
cians in the Jim Crow South*, Gilbert R. Mason and James Patterson Smith's *Beaches,
Blood, and Ballots*, Barbara R. Cotton's *Non Verbal Opera = Not Words but Works*,
Sonnie Wellington Hereford and Jack D. Ellis's *Beside the Troubled Waters: A Black
Doctor Remembers Life, Medicine, and the Civil Rights in an Alabama Town*, and Hugh
Pearson's *Under the Knife* provide rich information about the medical and civil
rights contributions of various Black physicians, including Theodore R. Howard of Mound Bayou, Mississippi, and Chicago; Edward Mazique of Washington, DC; Joseph H. Griffin of Tallahassee; and Gilbert Mason of Biloxi, Mississippi. But none of the individuals showcased in these books lived in the West
or Southwest, and all four physicians gained prominence or began their civil
rights activism after the 1950s.[33] Nixon was born and came of age after federal
troops withdrew from the South in 1877, a period that historian Rayford Logan
calls "the nadir" because of the horrible conditions most Black people endured

endured and the deteriorating state of race relations.[34] *Civil Rights in the Texas Borderlands* provides one of the few biographies of a Black physician in the civil rights struggle during the first half of the twentieth century and of a Black doctor in the West or Southwest. Ward's *Black Physicians in the Jim Crow South* is an excellent overview of many southern doctors scattered throughout the region and their plight during the Jim Crow era, although not a biography of any one particular physician. Nixon's story compels us to rethink the literature on Black doctors and their communities, activism, and patients.[35] This book places the saga of Nixon and his activism in context with the larger historical narrative and explores specifically the impact of his life and legacy.

CHAPTER 1

Marshall, Texas, 1883–1909

> One of the worst sections in all this round world
> for any Negro to live in.
> William Pickens, ca. 1914–1915

Lawrence Aaron Nixon grew up after the presidential compromise of 1877—a time in U.S. history when violence by whites against Blacks was rampant and when resurgent white power, especially in the South, steadily circumscribed the constitutional rights of African Americans.[1] This era was a period of social unrest and political upheaval, during which race relations deteriorated dramatically. Black people and their interests were placed on the sacrificial altar of political expediency by many whites within the Republican party in exchange for the removal of federal troops from the South, sectional harmony, and the expansion of big business and global imperialism.

Lawrence A. Nixon's Family Genealogy

Nixon was born on February 9, 1883, to Jennie Valerie Engledow and Charles Blanton Nixon in Marshall, Texas.[2] He was the couple's oldest child. He had two sisters—Annie Lucillia Nixon, born in March 1885, and Alfaretta Sally Nixon, born March 1887—and two brothers—Hallie P. Nixon, whose birth date is unknown, and Charles Jeff Nixon, born April 1889, the youngest member of the family.[3] Hallie died at the age of two, and Annie died in March 1944.[4]

Much of the information about Lawrence Nixon's family that follows here was provided by two living relatives: Edna Nixon McIver, Nixon's seventy-five-year-old daughter who currently lives in Albuquerque, New Mexico, and

Lawrence A. Walker, Nixon's eighty-nine-year-old nephew who currently lives in Graham, North Carolina. The information that Walker shared was gathered by his mother, Alfaretta S. Nixon Walker (Nixon's sister), who compiled a large amount of the family's history in the 1950s. Lawrence A. Nixon's genealogy can be traced back to Africa. According to family lore, his paternal grandfather, Charles Neil Nixon, was an African captive who was brought to Georgia directly from the continent.[5] Alfaretta Walker writes that her grandfather talked of being "from the Bush tribe," which could mean a number of things. He may have been a member of the Bushongo of the Kuba Kingdom, who inhabited the Congo basin region.[6] He may have been a San, Bushmen, or more appropriately a Kwe, Nharon, Hai, !Khu, or !Xo, ethnic groups who live across Namibia, Botswana, and South Africa, although this is statistically improbable, since more than 90 percent of enslaved Africans taken to the Americas were from the West African coast—Mauritania to Angola.[7] Perhaps Nixon's grandfather simply could have been referring to the fact that he came from the rural "country," a deep forest region, or a forgotten area of the African interior.

Although primary documents have been difficult to uncover, there is a strong likelihood that Nixon's grandfather was indeed a native African. Scholars have estimated that "between 1790 and 1810, about 194,000" Africans were captured and forcefully brought to the United States. Of this number, "more than 90,000 were newly transported African captives," who were traded through Charleston, South Carolina, and Savannah, Georgia. Approximately "63,000 stayed near the port of entry, 15,000 in South Carolina and 48,000 in Georgia." The United States Congress outlawed the importation of African captives in 1787, and the law went into effect on 1 January 1808.[8] Despite the ban on importing Africans, "illegal slaving vessels" continued to bring in "perhaps 7,000 more Africans . . . during the next decade," of which "Georgia took about 2,000."[9] Decades after the ban, in the 1880 census, Nixon's grandfather gave his age as fifty-four, meaning he was born in 1826.[10] From this information we can deduce that he obviously was not within the group of two thousand Africans that arrived in Georgia between 1808 and 1820, nor the group of forty-eight thousand African captives who arrived prior to 1808. However, according to family memoirs, he did live in Georgia during slavery, and so it is possible traders in African captives illegally smuggled the elder Nixon into the United States sometime after the 1830s, decades after the official ban. Southerners would brazenly violate this federal law by continuing to import African captives well into the late 1850s and early 1860s.[11]

Charles N. Nixon had four wives. Alfaretta, Nixon's granddaughter, describes her grandfather as being "dark," with "busy [bushy] hair, prominent nose, and thin lips."[12] While held in bondage, Charles N. Nixon had large families with his first two wives, about whom little is known. Nixon's descendants say that he was eventually sold off by plantation owners and that he never saw his families again.[13] This was a traumatic and frequent occurrence among African captives in the Americas, particularly in the southern United States. Logic would seem to have dictated that it was in the best interest of plantation owners to secure loyalty, maintain cohesion, and create a sense of normalcy and stability by *not* splitting up Black families by selling off valued loved ones. Yet the fact is most plantation owners wanted to "maximize labor productivity and slave-trading profits," and so African captives and their families were "sold, moved, and relocated . . . in reaction to economic pressures," not in accordance with emotional sensibilities, moral righteousness, or an ethical worldview based on reciprocity, respect, or dignity.[14]

Charles N. Nixon's third wife, Marguerite Macfarland, a Virginian, was an African captive who was "said to be a Lee," according to family records, meaning she was owned by the infamous Robert E. Lee, general of the Confederate Army.[15] Between 1857 and 1862, Lee owned more than two hundred African captives, nearly all of whom he freed on 29 December 1862.[16] Many Black families, particularly in Virginia, took the surname Lee after General Richard Henry Lee, the American Revolutionary war hero and an ancestor of Robert E. Lee.[17] Family documents indicate that Marguerite Macfarland boasted of a Lee connection, but she obviously did not adopt the Lee name upon freedom. In the family records, Macfarland is described as having been "short of stature," with "white skin" and "long brown hair and blue eyes." She bore three children with Charles N. Nixon: Charlie (Lawrence Nixon's father), Adeline, and Caroline.[18] Although Marguerite Macfarland was dead at the time of the 1880 U.S. census, her European features were pronounced enough for the enumerator to classify her and Charles N. Nixon's three children as "mulatto."[19] Their son Charlie would go on to have five children of his own, including Lawrence A. Nixon.[20]

Charles N. Nixon had an additional five children with his fourth wife, Ann Nixon. She is described in the 1880 census as a thirty-two-year-old mulatto who is "keeping house." Their children are listed in the census as Andrew (thirteen), Sarah (ten), Savannah (seven), Edward (four), and Lawrence (eight months).[21] Interestingly, Charles N. Nixon and his parents are said to have been born in Virginia according to this 1880 census, which would contradict Alfaretta S. Walker's account in her family history. There are many possible explanations for this. For one, the census enumerator could have been mistaken in documenting the information. For another, it may be that the elder Nixon did not find out about his African roots until years later or was ashamed of his direct African lineage. It's also possible he felt the enumerator would not believe him if he said he was born in Africa, since it was against the law for Africans to be imported into the United States after 1807. Although unlikely, another possibility is that Nixon fabricated the story for the amusement of his grandchildren, who then unwittingly passed it on to future generations as fact. Charles N. Nixon died of heart disease sometime in the 1890s; he would have been in his mid- to late sixties or early seventies.

In a 1952 letter to Walter White, NAACP executive secretary at the time, Lawrence A. Nixon wrote, "My father [Charles B. Nixon] was ten years of age at the end of slavery," making his father's birth year approximately 1855. However, if one subtracts his stated age at the time of the 1880 census, he would have been born in 1858. His mother, Jennie Valerie Engledow, was born in March 1865 ("the 'year of surrender' as she used to say"), making her only a few weeks old when the Civil War ended. On 19 January 1881, in Marshal, Texas, the Reverend Elder Luke officiated over the wedding of Nixon's parents.[22] His father was twenty-two (according to the census method of determining his year of birth) and his mother was fifteen.[23] In 1883, their first son, Lawrence Aaron Nixon, was born.

Pullman Porter: Life on the Railroad

The 1880 census has Charles B. Nixon's occupation as "servant," and though it does not indicate an employer, we know he was employed by the Texas and Pacific Railway Company.[24] Steady employment with the railroad must have given Charles B. Nixon some confidence in his financial ability to support a family. According to Lawrence Nixon,

> When my father married my mother, he owned his own home [in Marshall, Texas], the house where my older sister and I were born. All the years of his adult life he worked for the same corporation, the Texas and Pacific Railroad Co.—as a laborer when the road was building and later, up to the time of his death, on the General Manager's private car.[25]

Railroad employment provided income to thousands of Black men (and to a lesser extent Black women), allowing them to make a vital contribution to the economic health of African American communities in both the North and the South.[26] George Pullman started the Pullman Palace Car Company in 1862. Soon after, the company became the largest employer in the nation of African American men, primarily the South's formerly enslaved.[27]

The security, stability, and mobility that railway employment offered its workers cannot be overstated during this time period, particularly for most Black men who were prevented from traveling during the antebellum days. Traveling symbolized freedom.[28] However, it was because they had been enslaved that George Pullman hired African American men to serve the mostly white customers on his cars.[29] This helped to perpetuate the notion that Black men were nonthreatening, jovial, and submissive servants who relished serving whites and fulfilling their every request.[30] In 1916, fifty-one years after slavery's demise, Louis S. Hungerford, Pullman Company president, stated that their "training" in the South made former African captives a good fit for service in the train cars.

However, southern Blacks were not acquiescent because they loved the life of servility or enjoyed bowing to white customers. Prior to the Civil War, and even after, many whites failed to recognize that the Black men who did behave docilely were actually engaging in a form of resistance and survival.[31] They clearly were "wearing the mask" and "putting on Mr. Charlie" so as to extract a small slice of pleasures such as food or favors and amusement, or simply to go another day having avoided the whip or lash.[32] Pullman porters perpetuated this same behavior in order to survive in their work environments and win additional tips from whites. Additionally, many African American porters "embraced the role of courtesy in their work, carefully drawing the distinction between politeness and servility." Politeness marked them as gentlemen, "the aristocracy of Negro labor," while servility "undermined their struggle for fair treatment from employers and passengers." The *Pullman Porters' Review*, a Pullman Company publication, portrayed porters as courteous gentlemen, not servants: "By courtesy is not meant obeisance, bowing, etc., . . . [but] politeness which comes from the Latin verb, 'polite' to polish, to be finished, to be well bred, a smooth, refined, sober and polished gentility."[33] Although there was a fine line between adopting the mannerism of the genteel Victorian age and slavish behavior so as to extract tips, the line was there, and unfortunately, it was blurred in the minds of some Blacks and whites.

By working on the trains, Black men hoped to secure middle-class status within their respective communities. During the first half of the twentieth century, the Black middle class mostly sprang from blue-collar occupations, and most of those who held white-collar jobs knew the "stitching on those collars was noticeably weak." The idea of the middle class for most African American families during the late nineteenth and early twentieth centuries was less about "wealth" than about "values, lifestyle, and aspiration. They believed in the sanctity of home, family, and church; placed a premium on self-discipline, and education; had a penchant for thrift, savings, and acquiring real estate. They were strivers and joiners." And although "economic racism blunted their financial ambitions, they had faith in the promise of upward mobility for themselves and their children."[34] This is what being employed in the railroad industry afforded the Nixon family and so many other African Americans during this time.

Despite the rigors and drudgery of the jobs themselves, it would be this middle-class and higher social status—relatively speaking—that would give some members of the African American community the disposable time and income to take part in the uplifting of the race and to "assume important leadership positions within" their communities.[35] Ultimately, these railroad employees would become "the civil rights leaders of their era. They themselves seldom used the term *middle class*, which had not become an everyday term in America. Instead they spoke of themselves as the 'better class of Negroes,' or as 'the educated class,' or 'the right sort.'"[36] Working on the railroad put Nixon in the company of those civil rights leaders who were employed within the railroad industry at what has been described by historian Eric Arnesen as "a temporary occupational stage in a life of social advancement."[37] Such leaders include Malcolm X, Harry Haywood, Benjamin Mays, Roy Wilkins, and Thurgood Marshall. Other luminaries were singer Taylor Gordon, writers Claude McKay and Langston Hughes, adventurer Matthew Henson, and Blues legend "Big Bill" Broonzy.[38]

The Nixons in New Orleans

Charles B. Nixon's status as a train employee, particularly as chief steward for the private car of the general manager of the Texas and Pacific Railway, not only afforded him a semblance of status in his own community but also allowed him to travel, see the country, meet new people from other regions, become more cosmopolitan in his worldview, and offer his family opportunities he otherwise might not have been able to.[39] In 1886 or 1887, for example, they temporarily relocated to New Orleans, where Nixon enrolled his children in a private school within the city. In describing his upbringing, Lawrence Nixon explains, "My early childhood was spent in New Orleans, Louisiana. I went to a private school for colored children and lived in a neighborhood composed of colored people and descendants of German and Italian immigrants. It was a clean, thrifty neighborhood and we were all good neighbors." Nixon further elaborates, saying, "I can't imagine a more happy childhood than my two sisters, my brother and I lived. We came up knowing how to work. A great deal of the joy of my boyhood came out of the work I did. My father disliked people who were ashamed to work with their hands."[40] In New Orleans, during these early years of his education, Nixon was influenced by an English woman whose British accent affected his speech pattern and syntax. This "remained with him all his life, for he never spoke with a typical southern accent, but a softly clipped manner of speech" causing people to believe he might be a native of the English-speaking Caribbean.[41] The time in New Orleans was beneficial in other ways: the family expanded by two with the addition of Lawrence Nixon's sister Alfaretta and brother Charlie. After approximately five years, in 1891 or 1892, the Texas and Pacific Railway reassigned Charles B. Nixon back to Marshall.[42]

In 1883, the year of Lawrence Nixon's birth, the U.S. Supreme Court handed down two major decisions that would impact African Americans. In the first, *United States v. Harris*, the court ruled that local and state governments rather than the federal government had the right to punish individuals for violent crimes such as assault and murder. This ruling also declared that the enforcement of the Equal Protection Clause—found within the Fourteenth Amendment of the Constitution and the Civil Rights Act of 1871—applied only to state action and not state inaction. This would have serious implications, since violence by terrorist groups such as lynch mobs and the Ku Klux Klan was rampant during the Reconstruction era.[43] In the second, the *Civil Rights Cases*, the high court deemed the Civil Rights Act of 1875 unconstitutional. This act outlawed racial discrimination in public accommodations, but the court felt that while states were obligated to respect the rights of Black Americans, individual business owners could discriminate.[44] The court's decision also nullified the two Enforcement Acts that were passed by Congress on 31 May 1870 and 20 April 1871.[45] This was the national context in which Nixon was born, and it marked the official end of Reconstruction, at which point southern communities were in the process of being "redeemed."[46]

Life and Political Climate in Marshall, Texas

Marshall was incorporated in 1844 and became the county seat of Harrison County just prior to the Civil War.[47] The 1870 census indicates that the city had a population of 1,920, 44 percent (851) of whom were African American.[48] By 1880, just three years before Lawrence Nixon's birth, the Black population had more than tripled to 2,787, representing nearly 50 percent of the city's population. The number of whites in Marshall increased to 2,837, bringing the total population in 1880 to 5,624.[49] In the 1890 census, African Americans were over 50 percent of the population, comprising 3,673 of the total. Additionally in 1890, the census lists 336 foreign-born individuals and 2 Chinese persons along with the 3,532 whites.[50]

Although whites were clearly a numerical minority in Marshall, albeit a large one, they continued to wield economic and political control over the city and county.[51] This is an important point to stress in light of the views of the "Redeemers," who believed their social and economic status had been jeopardized with the loss of the Civil War and the advent of Reconstruction. The facts do not bear this out, particularly in Harrison County. According to Randolph B. Campbell, "The wealthiest class persisted because while the loss of the Civil War led to the end of slavery, it did not mean confiscation and redistribution of real property" from the former slave owners. The white planter elite in Harrison County held more African captives "*and* land than anyone else in 1860" in Texas. Although the federal government may have eliminated white people's ability to own Africans, it nevertheless left the "landed property largely untouched, and there would be no socioeconomic revolution."[52]

In this period, racism became steadily more institutionalized. Through the first half of the twentieth century, east Texas remained more southern than western demographically and with respect to race relations. The history of the institution of slavery continued to cast a shadow over the region, and racism stood at the heart of the experiences and history of all east Texans, Black and white: "The centrality of these events," according to historian Cary Wintz, "underscores the fundamental connection of African American history to East Texas."[53] As Henry McNeil Turner, Georgia state representative, put it in 1866,

> We have built up your country; we have worked in your fields, and garnered your harvests, for two hundred and fifty years! And what do we ask of you in return? Do we ask you for compensation for the sweat our fathers bore for you—for the tears you have caused, and the hearts you have broken, and the lives you have curtailed, and the blood you have spilled? We ask it not. We are willing to let the dead past bury its dead, but we ask you now for our rights.[54]

Reconstruction was the most violent era in United States history, particularly against African Americans simply because they demanded their rights. Violence against Blacks in the South persisted due in large measure to the aggression of domestic terrorist groups such as the Regulators, the Constitutional Union Guards, the '76 Association, the Council of Safety, the Pulaski Ku Kluxers, the Knights of the Ku Klux Klan, the Knights of the Rising Sun, the Knights of the White Camellia, the White Brotherhood, the White League, the Red Shirts, the Whitecaps, and the Order of Pale Faces.[55] Harrison County in east Texas was no different from the South in general; racial violence and intimidation was widespread there as elsewhere in the region. The planter class in the county retained its power and wealth during the Reconstruction era, and the members of this class frequently resorted to violence against Blacks to reinforce their position.[56] On New Year's Eve 1866 in Marshall, Captain Charles Rand of the Union Army, who at the time was working for the Freeman's Bureau, asserted that the situation for Blacks was terrible. "Yesterday," he wrote, a Black man "presented himself with two bullet holes through him" for no other reason than participating in a Christmas celebration. Rand also noted that outrages were "committed daily with impunity and all pass unnoticed for lack of assistance." Less than two months later, in February 1867, Rand informed his superiors of ten Blacks being murdered by whites in Harrison County. Hoodlums "would kill a f.m. for 75 cents and boast of the action as a laudable one of high minded chivalry." As often was the case in Marshall during Reconstruction, local officials took no action, despite the presence of federal troops in the city.[57]

The Citizen's Party: Everybody's White Folk

By 1878 Marshall was described as "a rapidly advancing" city with "first-class" schools, the elegant Capitol Hotel, a "fine" jail, six churches for whites, four churches for Blacks, and two newspapers, the *Tri-Weekly Herald* and *Messenger*. The increase in the population, which was attributed to the Texas and Pacific Railroad Company relocating its operations to Marshall, accounted for the growth of the city.[58] However, economic growth did not prevent the violent conservative backlash in Marshall that ultimately manifested itself in the political rise of the Citizens' Party of Harrison County, which in 1878 took power from the majority Black Republicans and held on to it for decades. The Citizens' Party lauded itself as a nonpartisan group that supported "racial harmony" and the restoration of "fiscal responsibility and honesty to local government" while stressing that its members were *not* Democrats per se yet labeled their opponents (Republicans) "radicals." The conservative takeover was accomplished by promising Blacks that the Citizens' Party would protect their rights "at least as effectively as did the carpetbaggers and scalawags," which did not prove to be the case.[59] The Citizens' Party also appealed to nonracial issues, such as "how radical taxing and spending threatened the well-being of blacks as well as whites." In addition, as Randolph documents, "the conservatives told blacks that white radical leaders had simply used their votes to take offices and the income from those positions for themselves."[60]

The Citizens' Party's fustian discourse appeared to work on some within the county's majority Black population, particularly Black conservatives in

Marshall such as Jasper Black, who wrote a letter to the editor of the *Tri-Weekly Herald* encouraging African Americans to vote for the Citizens' Party nominees. Other conservative Blacks actually joined the Party and made campaign speeches with its candidates. But the party did not have enough confidence in this support from the African American community in Marshall, so along with the misrepresentations it made or outright lies it told, it also resorted to violence, intimidation, and electoral fraud during the 1878 coup. The party even made the empty promise that Blacks would be recognized "as white folks."[61]

The takeover and subsequent seventy-year reign by the Citizens' Party in Harrison County not only dethroned the local Republican party on the eve of Lawrence A. Nixon's birth but also indicated just how isolated moderate Republicans statewide had become. As Republican losses throughout state government mounted, conservative Democrats quickly gained a foothold, becoming politically entrenched. While many of the white Republicans found other jobs within the party, African Americans drifted into "political limbo, lacking effective political voice until well into the next century."[62] Support for the Republican party slowly waned among African Americans, particularly at the local level, which encouraged Blacks to either become disengaged from the political process or look at alternatives such as the Populist, Progressive, and even Democratic parties as viable options. Despite the political hardships and racially charged violence, between 1865 and 1878, African Americans in Marshall "supported and attended schools, voted, held office and exercised civic responsibilities such as jury service," and they determined the outcome of every election in the county before losing their political strength to the white Citizens' Party.[63] By 1883, the racist assaults launched against Blacks had become so brutal that Harrison County Blacks finally organized their own militia to protect themselves. Local whites, with the help of state forces, crushed this Black initiative.[64]

Pillars Rise Up from Fertile Soil: Nixon and Wiley College

Notwithstanding the political turmoil in Harrison County, the Nixon family returned to Marshall from New Orleans in the early 1890s. Lawrence Nixon enrolled at Wiley College, where he continued his grade- and high school training. He completed his undergraduate degree there in 1902, after which he left for Meharry Medical College in Tennessee.[65] Originally known as Wiley University, Wiley College was founded in 1873 by the Methodist Episcopal Church's Bishop Isaac Wiley and chartered by Freemen's Aid Society of the Methodist Episcopal Church in 1882.[66] Wiley offered its first bachelor's degree in 1888 and changed its name from Wiley University to Wiley College in 1929.[67] It is notable in that it is one of the oldest predominantly Black colleges west of the Mississippi River.[68] The president during the last few years of Nixon's time there, Matthew D. Dogan, who had taught mathematics at Walden University in Nashville between 1890 and 1896, may well have encouraged Lawrence Nixon to attend Meharry to continue his formal training, since Dogan was familiar with the institution, its personnel, and its offerings prior to his arrival at Wiley.[69]

Many historically Black colleges and universities (HBCUs) have traditionally instilled a sense of activism in their students, and Wiley was no exception.[70] HBCUs vary widely in "degree of religious emphasis, student freedom, political tenor, faculty makeup, administrative independence and stability, financial security, academic rigor, explicitness of race-conscious ideology, and class tensions."[71] To understand what and who inspired Lawrence Nixon with a desire to excel and become an engaged and responsible member of the community, we not only have to look at his family, upbringing, and community but also the educational institutions Nixon was a part of, including their teachers and staff.[72] For such a small school, Wiley has produced some notables within the civil rights arena: Emmett J. Scott, James L. Maximilian Farmer Sr., James Farmer Jr., Melvin B. Tolson, and Heman M. Sweatt.[73] Lawrence Nixon is part of that tradition of engagement. On small HBCU campuses, an individual administrator or faculty member such as Tolson could have a tremendous impact on institutional mood and direction as well as on the lives of individuals.[74]

Wiley students, particularly those who graduated in the 1930s and 1940s, called the school the "Harvard west of the Mississippi."[75] This may be because in 1933, under Dogan's leadership, Wiley became the first Black college west of the Mississippi River to be granted the A rating by the Southern Association of Colleges and Secondary Schools.[76] Despite Dogan's successful forty-six-year tenure, there were some who did not hold him in high esteem. For example, in 1937 Wiley students James Farmer and Benjamin Ball attempted to establish a college branch of the National Association for the Advancement of Colored People (NAACP). Across-town rival Bishop College had had a chapter of the civil rights organization for over a year, and students at Wiley felt it was time for them to have one as well.[77] The city of Marshall started an NAACP branch in 1919, but within months it folded due to the Longview race riots in July.[78] Dogan was wary because African Americans outnumbered whites in Marshall and had done so for many decades, and in his view "racial antagonism can more easily develop in sections where Negroes constitute a large part of the population. . . . I support the NAACP financially because I feel it is a fine organization, but up to this time, it has not been thought best by some of us here in Marshall to form a chapter here."[79]

Farmer explains Dogan's attitude:

At the top, on the black side, there was Wiley's president, Dr. Matthew Dogan, D.D., L.L.D., and Professor Pemberton, principal of Central High School. Both were respected by the white world. They knew the town's banker and top businessmen; and that gave them influence with the white world and power in the black. Dogan and Pemberton were buffers between the two worlds; they kept the black one from collision with the white one. In return, they were honored and privileged persons. Yet, they had to respect the etiquette of the caste system: they were called not "Mister," but "Doctor" and "Professor," and there was some grinning and bowing and scraping and foot shuffling. They treated whites like sacred cows in their presence; but behind their backs, they talked about them and laughed at them. It was a classic case of role playing. Many students considered them "Uncle Toms," but that did not define them; they were not owned by the whites, just rented. They were fully conscious of the role they were playing. They served their wards as well as their masters. Pemberton got money from the white school board for the segregated black high school, and Dogan raised a $600,000 endowment for Wiley.[80]

Many students instead preferred the leadership style of individuals such as longtime professor Melvin Tolson, who began his teaching career at Wiley in 1924, nearly twenty years after Nixon's graduation, and who was seen as more assertive, aggressive, unapologetic and outspoken and perhaps more militant. Tolson remained at Wiley until 1947, and his impact was felt for many years. Historian Gail Beil explains that "he inspired one of his students to become a leading civil rights leader in the 1960s, another who successfully sued to integrate the University of Texas School of Law, and others who changed the segregated face of the nation in quieter ways." One of those *not*-so-quiet ways was a 1948 lawsuit filed through the NAACP against the Harrison County Citizens' Party by one of Tolson's students and a classmate of James Farmer: Fred Lewis. The association won the suit in 1950, and Lewis attributed the "courage to take on the white establishment in his home town to Tolson's teachings."[81]

Tolson was asked by Texas governor James Burr V Allred to represent the state at the 4 August 1935 National Negro Day Celebration during the International Exhibition in San Diego, California. Allred told Tolson, "we are glad to have a man of your standing represent Texas, and are quite proud of the name Wiley College has made for itself through its debating team, with you as coach." Along with influencing James L. Farmer Jr. and Fred Lewis, Tolson also taught civil rights activist Heman M. Sweatt and academic, author, and Black power activist-scholar Nathan Hare. Tolson departed Wiley College in 1947 after the institution underwent significant upheavals under President Egbert C. McLeod, leading to a nationally reported student strike.[82]

From Wiley to Meharry

Since his early teenage years Lawrence Nixon had wanted to become a medical doctor.[83] It is not exactly clear what led Nixon to the medical profession, but at various times there were Black medical doctors in Marshall during Nixon's upbringing that he could have admired and wanted to emulate. Mason J. Snowden, Edward Abner, and John Walter Fridia, for example, might have been his role models. Nixon graduated from Wiley College and earned admission into the same medical institution of those doctors he saw in his community as a child: Meharry Medical College.[84] Meharry was established as the Meharry Medical Department of Central Tennessee College. Central Tennessee College became Walden University in 1900, and the medical school acquired the new name of Meharry Medical College of Walden University. In 1905, while Lawrence Nixon was still there, Meharry separated itself from the financially failing Walden University and established itself as a stand-alone nonprofit institution. Then in October 1915 the medical school applied for and received "a charter of incorporation in the name of Meharry Medical College."[85] Nixon 1906's diploma names the institution as Meharry Medical College of Walden University.[86]

An early history of this prestigious college was written by one of its longtime professors, who likely taught Nixon. In 1904, Charles V. Roman became professor of ophthalmology and otolaryngology at Meharry, a position he held until 1931. Also in 1904, Roman was named president of the National Medical Association—the association for African American doctors. For ten years, 1908–1918, he served as editor-in-chief of the *Journal of the National Medical Association*.[87] In addition, Nixon received training from Daniel Hale Williams, the famed surgeon who was a lecturer on clinical and operative surgery at Meharry.[88] Williams, the first Black cardiologist in the United States, is best known for becoming the first African American to perform open-heart surgery successfully in 1893 and for establishing the first integrated hospital in the nation, Chicago's Provident Hospital, in 1891.[89] In 1899, Williams began teaching at Meharry in a series of annual clinics. Williams's classes became very popular not only with students but also with physicians, who traveled from almost every southern state to attend. At Meharry, Williams gave lectures, clinics, and even conducted operations for the benefit of students, patients, and physicians alike.[90] Doctors whom Williams trained at Meharry who would go on to graduate with honors and join the faculty included W. A. Reed, J. A. McMillan, and John Hale Williams.[91] These three physicians also trained Lawrence Nixon during the years he was a student.[92] John Henry Hale, a 1905 Meharry graduate, became a professor immediately after graduating and must have known of Nixon both as a fellow student and from being a professor during Nixon's senior year. Hale would also serve as president of the National Medical Association in 1935, after Roman's tenure ended.[93] Nixon, having established himself as a medical doctor among these men, would go on to run his own practice.

To finance his medical education, Lawrence Nixon secured work as a Pullman porter. In addition, Nixon also worked one summer at a Chicago bar.[94] Charlie Nixon must have been proud of Lawrence's educational aspirations and employment selection. The children of porters or railway workers were "the best affirmation of their esteem for their fathers," as seen by "how many followed them into the sleeping car business."[95] Lawrence Nixon was not planning on making his porter job with the Pullman Company a career as his father had but was merely using the opportunity to get himself through school and occupy his summers with money-earning activities. Yet Charles Nixon could feel comfortable in knowing that if the educational route did not work out for his oldest son, at least Lawrence Nixon already had his foot in the door with the company and could perhaps return in a permanent position if needed.

Nixon graduated from Meharry on April 4, 1906.[96] Of Nixon's sixty-nine–member graduating class, three were Black women, and ten were from Texas. In addition to the sixty-nine classmates from the medical department, there were an additional fifteen dental graduates and ten graduates from the pharmaceutical department, four of whom were Black women.[97] Although no records exist of Nixon's academic performance or social life while attending Meharry (or Wiley College), the well-known school must have prepared Nixon well. Two months after graduating, Nixon took the Texas State Medical examination in Dallas and received a passing score of 76.3 percent. He was among three Meharry graduates who passed the examination that day. A. L. Hunter of Hearne, Texas, had an identical score, and W. H. White of Bastrop, Texas, earned a 75 percent.[98] Five other Meharry classmates did not pass on this particular attempt. Of the 144 would-be doctors who took the test, 42—nearly a third—did not earn the minimum score of 75 percent.[99]

Cameron, Texas

In the fall of 1906, Lawrence Nixon established his medical practice in Cameron, in Milam County in central Texas, approximately two hundred miles southwest of Marshall and fifty miles southeast of Waco.[100] He moved to this small farming community at the urging of an unnamed friend. Nixon writes, "I had never seen the town, but I decided to rely on the judgement of the friend who induced me to go there." He arrived with "fifteen dollars worth of [medical] instruments" and "about thirty dollars" in his pocket. Once there, Nixon quickly became "very much disappointed," partly because he was lonely but also because he "had never before seen [Black] people living in such wretched surroundings." He temporarily returned to Marshall to marry his childhood sweetheart, Esther Josephine Calvin.[101] The wedding took place in Marshall on 23 October 1907.[102] Alfaretta S. Nixon (Lawrence Nixon's sister) and Jessie C. Calvin (Esther J. Calvin's sister) were the bridesmaids and A. L. Hunter and E. E. Nesbitt (both of whom were Nixon's Meharry classmates) were groomsmen.[103] Their only child together, Lawrence Joseph Nixon, was born in Marshall on 4 July 1909.[104] Because they were living in Cameron, the fact that their son was born in Marshall suggests that Esther Nixon went back for the delivery and to be nursed back to health near family and dear friends.

3. Esther Josephine Calvin, first wife of Lawrence A. Nixon, ca. 1900. Courtesy of the Beth Elnita Nixon family collection.

4. Lawrence Joseph Nixon, the first child of Lawrence A. Nixon and Esther Josephine Nixon. Courtesy of the Beth Elnita Nixon family collection.

After graduating from Meharry, Lawrence Nixon could have gone anywhere, and so one has to wonder why Nixon chose Cameron instead of at the very least Marshall, where he would have been near his immediate family and could mature professionally in a place that he intimately knew. He was home grown, and the city would have been proud to embrace him, his educational accomplishments, and his fledging medical practice. The desire to be near friends and family led many southern Black medical school graduates to remain in the South.[105] According to *Black Physicians in the Jim Crow South,*

> Many black doctors were recruited to come south by communities in desperate need of medical care; others believed that their greatest opportunity for financial success lay in the South. A few came south as medical missionaries to care for the region's large and impoverished black population. But perhaps the greatest force that drew black physicians to the South was that it was—despite its prejudice and violence, its poverty and discrimination—*home.*[106]

One reason for not returning to Marshall may have been that the city already had too many Meharry graduates practicing their profession, including Mason J. Snowden (class of 1888), Edward Abner (class of 1893), John Walter Fridia (class of 1895), and W. M. Drake (class of 1905).[107] A safer, if not more calculated, location for his initial practice could have been in the nearby Texas counties of Gregg (55 percent Black), Panola (43 percent Black), or Smith (41 percent Black); the city of Longview (43.7 percent Black); or even Shreveport, Louisiana (49.6 percent Black).[108] These locations, twenty to sixty miles from Marshall, would have allowed Nixon to remain closer to his family. Instead Nixon chose the much farther Cameron, which inadvertently exposed him to atrocious acts of violence against Blacks that would at first silence him and then later make him take a more proactive stance. His leaving the community that nurtured, protected, and insulated him for so many years speaks to his risk taking and courage.

Cameron in 1900 had a total population of 3,341, of which 1,040, or 31 percent, were African American.[109] Agriculture, primarily corn and cotton, was the dominant economic force within the county, with coal mining playing a smaller, but important role. Most residents were sharecroppers, tenant farmers, or coal miners.[110] The Black community was much smaller than in the places Lawrence Nixon had lived before, but Cameron's Black population was sizable enough that he could still have an impact, gain a reputation, and make a name for himself among his own people. Despite having settled down in Cameron by establishing a medical practice and relocating his new wife there, Lawrence Nixon nevertheless ultimately decided to leave.

Central Texas had had a long and storied tradition of racial violence dating back to the mid-nineteenth century.[111] It was this violence that compelled Nixon to leave Cameron and abandon his budding medical practice that he had worked nearly three years to build. Lawrence Nixon's office was in downtown Cameron, not too far from the courthouse. On 4 November 1907, a mob had taken Alex Johnson, an African American, from a jail cell and according to newspaper accounts hanged him from a tree for the alleged crime of "attempting to attack a young girl" (in the account Nixon gave years later, however, Johnson was burned at the stake, not hanged from a tree). News reports indicate that the lynch mob was five hundred strong and refused to give in to pleas from "officers and influential citizens" to allow "the law to take its course." Nixon was at his medical office at the time and remembers "that chairs were placed on the balcony of the two-story building to accommodate the crowds gathered to witness the lynching," while he stayed behind locked doors in his office, "listening to the cries of the dying man."[112]

This indeed was a very traumatic experience for Nixon, who had been in the city for less than a year. As a Black man in the United States, he was accustomed to hearing gory details of lynch mobs. An earshot away, Nixon heard the shouts and agony of Alex Johnson pleading for mercy from an unsympathetic crowd. Whether Johnson was burned at the stake, as Nixon recalls, or died from a noose around his neck, Nixon heard the horrors of his death and the crazed cries of a mad crowd. Nixon did not intervene, for to do so would have invited his own death. Texas governor Thomas Campbell called in the state militia to assist local Cameron officers, but the state guards arrived one hour too late.[113]

Johnson was one of thirty-two people—three Black women, four white men, and twenty-five Black men—lynched that year. The year prior, seventy-two people had been lynched. These figures include only incidents "of unmistakable lynching, leaving out those in which the victims were killed by pursuing posses while resisting capture."[114] In 1909, the same year Nixon's son was born, there would be many more lynchings throughout the country, including Texas. Between 1880 and 1930, only Mississippi and Georgia would surpass Texas in the number of lynchings.[115] This violence was a part of the mindset of Texans; as one white newspaper editor put it, "Lynching becomes chronic and contagious. Boys grow to manhood with the idea, ingrained in them that lynch law is right and proper, and worthy of applause, and they follow the example set them by their fathers."[116] This cultural attitude fostered an arrogance among many white Texans; they asserted that "there is not much danger to any of the Negroes who attend to their business and keep their mouths shut, but there are some who must be checked by some means or other."[117] It was this atmosphere as well as a desire to seek economic opportunities elsewhere that caused many African Americans at the turn of the century to move to other states or into less hostile regions within Texas. As one central Texas newspaper observed in 1902, "The exodus of the colored people from this city still continues. The territories are the mecca and there is hardly a day but a large party does not leave."[118] Less than two weeks after hearing of another lynching in nearby Rosebud (sixteen miles from Cameron), Nixon too became part of this movement, leaving Cameron for El Paso, Texas, on 31 December 1909.[119]

Unfortunately, Nixon could not return to his hometown of Marshall due to the recent racial violence in that city. Between 1897 and 1917, thirteen Black women and men had been lynched in Harrison County.[120] In 1909 alone Marshall witnessed four lynchings within a four-day period in April.[121] William Pickens, who taught at Wiley College for one year (1914–1915) and later became NAACP field secretary, described Marshall as "notorious for frequent and particularly barbaric lynchings" and called the town "one of the worst sections in all this round world . . . for any Negro to live in." Pickens made this statement after nearly being killed twice by whites during his brief one-year stay in the city.[122]

For decades Black doctors in the South feared acts of racial violence against them. In the 1930s, scholar Carter G. Woodson found that more than one in ten Black physicians who established practices in the South eventually left the region "because of the terrorism." Physicians told Woodson that they left not only because of violence and economic difficulties but also "to get away from inferiority-complex Negroes and superiority-complex whites." One doctor told Woodson that he had to leave town for "replying in the affirmative to a white man's question as to whether [he] thought [he] was as good as [the white man] was."[123] Lawrence Nixon too would leave the region and "sharpen his oyster knife" in the dry and dusty border city of the Southwest: El Paso.[124]

CHAPTER 2

The Lure of El Paso, 1910–1919

Through struggle are great men and useful races produced.
Booker T. Washington, 1911

Lawrence Nixon departed Cameron, Texas, on New Year's Eve 1909. He and his good friend LeRoy White loaded their personal belongings, including household and office furniture and a horse and buggy, onto a freight car.[1] It is not clear how LeRoy White and Nixon became friends or where they had met. They could have been childhood friends from Nixon's days in New Orleans or Marshall. Perhaps they met in the city of Cameron during the three years that Nixon lived there or in Nashville while Nixon was a student at Meharry. If they were childhood friends from Marshall, then perhaps Nixon moved to Cameron at White's urging. Nevertheless, the pair made the ten-day 565-mile trek across Texas together and arrived in El Paso in January 1910.[2] They had different paths to follow, but once in El Paso, they both would make it their new and permanent home. Esther and his son would join Nixon in El Paso some months later.

In El Paso, White would become assistant pastor of Shiloh Baptist Church, a government employee at the Stanton Street Bridge, and a barber at a shop owned by George W. Meroney.[3] Lawrence Nixon would practice medicine in El Paso for the next fifty years. It is not clear why Nixon chose to move to El Paso. He had been to El Paso in 1893 when he was about ten years old.[4] His mother had a brother in the city who was a barber, and she and Lawrence visited him, traveling from Marshall on the Texas and Pacific railroad.[5] This initial stay may have left enough of a positive impression on the young Nixon to make him want to return and embark on a new chapter in his life, one in which he would become civically and politically active.

El Paso, Texas

El Paso is Texas's westernmost city, located 564 miles northwest of San Antonio, 617 miles southwest of Dallas, and 43 miles southeast of Las Cruces, New Mexico.[6] The first Europeans, Spanish conquistadors, called it El Paso del Norte due to its natural passageway through the mountains.[7] El Paso's sister city, immediately across the international border of the Rio Grande, is Ciudad Juárez, a former colony of the Spanish crown that used the city as a strategic entry to its towns in New Mexico beginning in 1659.[8] Initially, Ciudad Juárez was also known as El Paso del Norte. However, in July 1888 Lauro Carrillo, the constitutional governor of Chihuahua, decreed the official name change to Ciudad Juárez, which took effect in September of that year.[9] The name comes from one of the few indigenous Mexican presidents, Benito Pablo Juárez García, who took refuge there during the French occupation between 1862 and 1867.[10] Ciudad Juárez has always been strategically useful, even more so after the railroads' arrival in the 1880s, which solidified the city as an important entryway for the exchange of people, culture, services, and commodities between Mexico and the United States.[11]

In 1849 army major Jefferson Van Horne and his troops reached El Paso, where they established Fort Bliss, a new military post.[12] It would remain an important strategic military asset and a strong economic force in the El Paso area throughout Lawrence Nixon's stay in the city.[13] The military installation is named after William "Perfect Bliss" Smith, who fought the Cherokees and the Seminoles in Florida and participated in the American invasion of Mexico from 1846 to 1848.[14] Despite the fact that only a very tiny minority of El Paso's residents owned African captives, in February 1861, El Pasoans voted almost unanimously to support secession and formally join the Confederate States of America in the effort to preserve the institution of slavery.[15] The 1860 United States census indicates that there were fifteen African captives in El Paso, along with fourteen free African Americans.[16] Also, at least five officers and other soldiers brought African captives with them to Fort Bliss during the Civil War.[17] Sympathies with the South in general and support for the Confederacy in particular would remain strong throughout the war.[18] However, the Confederacy failed to claim all of New Mexico and Arizona under the expedition of General Henry Sibley, and Fort Bliss surrendered peacefully to Union forces. When

Confederate soldiers returned to El Paso in 1862, they found that union troops under General Carleton had already reclaimed the city.[19] El Paso remained in Union hands for the duration of the war, and although the city was occupied by both Union and Confederate forces, it saw little combat.

By the mid-1800s, El Paso had became a western boomtown known as Six Shooter Capital and Sin City, owing to its lawlessness and many saloons, dance halls, gambling establishments, and brothels.[20] The railroads arrived in the early 1880s. The Southern Pacific was the first railroad company to enter El Paso in May 1881. The following month El Paso welcomed the Atchison, Topeka and Santa Fe. The Texas and Pacific, the railway that Lawrence Nixon's father worked for from the early 1880s to 1910, arrived in El Paso in January 1882.[21] One San Antonio newspaper reported in 1881 that "the scene at El Paso just now beggars description. The fact that three railroads are practically there has caused a world of people of all classes, nations and colors to rush to this new center."[22] This included different ethnic groups and many Mexicans from different classes and hues. A visitor to El Paso in the early 1890s commented:

> El Paso is part Mexican and part American. The Mexicans and a great many of the Chinamen live in adobe houses. . . . When I speak of Mexicans, you must remember that they are of all kinds and types, from a tawny yellow . . . to the deep red of the Indian, and even as black as a Congo negro. And right here you have them all in a bunch. Then there are tourists representing all the States in and out of the Union. As a cosmopolitan crowd, there is nothing to beat it.[23]

The Afro-Mexican presence in El Paso was pronounced enough for author and nineteenth-century Southwest traveler Rudolf Eickemeyer to remark on "a Mexican soldier in dark blue uniform, himself as black as the ace of spades," who "walks to and fro in front of the gate, and a set of ragged urchins keep him company."[24]

A fourth major railway, Galveston, Harrisburg and San Antonio, entered the city in 1883.[25] One commentator described it as "one of the best constructed and most efficiently operated railways in the State," adding that it constituted "an important link in the great Southern Pacific Transcontinental Railway system, one of the most powerful and successful railway systems in the world."[26] The Mexican Central Railroad started its service from Mexico City to El Paso in 1884. This main line connected the north and south of Mexico, which began passenger service from Mexico City to Ciudad Porfirio Díaz in the northeastern state of Coahuila in 1884. By 1894, the Mexican Central Railroad lines had reached the most populous states of Mexico in the central plateau.[27] The *Lone Star*, one of El

Paso's first dailies, commented that the city was now connected with the "Paris of America"—Mexico City—and encouraged increased trade with Mexico. His-torian Monica Perales perceptively notes that the newly established train paths "reinforced old connections and traversed the same routes previously traveled on foot and by mule train."[28] For the Southwest, the railroads symbolized a new American era dominated by a modernizing economy that would make El Paso a railroad, mining, ranching, and labor center. The railroads became major em-ployers of labor in El Paso, hiring thousands of Mexican immigrants to work in construction and on maintenance crews throughout the Southwest.[29]

The population of El Paso County grew from 15,678 in 1890, nearly a decade after the arrival of the first railroad, to 24,886 in 1900, after all four railroads had been well established. By 1930, El Paso's population reached 131,957. Such growth is attributed to El Paso's regional, national, and international rising economic importance. It was a hub for railroad transportation; it was close to the mining areas of Mexico, New Mexico, and Arizona; it was a gateway into Mexico; and it had a thriving ranching industry—all of which required a large supply of cheap Mexican labor.[30] Another factor in El Paso's boom-ing population was the 1916 completion of Elephant Butte Dam near Truth or Consequences, New Mexico. The dike allowed the El Paso area to develop and flourish by making a consistent water supply available for manufacturing and farming (including cotton) as well as by providing much-needed electricity to residents.[31] Additionally, an influx of Mexican refugees fleeing the disruption of the Mexican Revolution contributed heavily to El Paso's population growth after 1910.[32]

These profound changes meant a new prosperity and greater job variety for African Americans. Not only did African Americans find work as barbers, laun-dresses, maids, janitors, schoolteachers, and mail carriers, but, as the town grew into an important transportation center, many Black families arrived as railroad employees. On the trains they worked as day-coach porters, dining-car waiters, chefs, and sleeping-car porters. The day-coach porters made the shorter three-hundred-mile runs to Tucson, Albuquerque, and Sanderson, Texas, while the sleeping-car porters made the longer trips to California, working a 240-hour month with no days off.[33] In addition to providing services on the train, Black porters also worked as brakemen who jumped off the trains to switch tracks and to help direct the flow of traffic.[34] In the rail yard, Black men were employed as yard laborers, car repairmen and cleaners, boilermakers and cleaners, and locomotive inspectors. Jobs connected with the boilermaker were the most highly sought in the yard.[35]

The Segundo Barrio: Mexicanos' Ellis Island

Just a year after Nixon's arrival in El Paso, the Mexican Revolution began, and the city found itself thrust into the national spotlight due to its geographic importance and economic influence. The Mexican Revolution was an outgrowth of the oppression the poor and various indigenous groups had experienced for many decades. The uprising became, as historian Gerald Horne describes, "a rending upheaval of mass movements marked by profound anticlericalism, far-reaching land reform, deep seated hostility to United States imperialism, and democratic promise." Nearly one million people died either in combat or of starvation and disease, dropping Mexico's population from over 15 million in 1910 to 14.3 million in 1921. Between 300,000 and 1 million Mexicans fled to the United States, dramatically swelling the immigrant populations already there.[36]

These were the economic and social circumstances that prevailed in the city when Nixon established his medical practice at 101 South Campbell Street, across the street from the courthouse. Nixon's office was nearby that of Chinese physician Ng Che Hok, who practiced at 105 North Campbell Street.[37] According to the 1917 city directory, Nixon moved his medical practice to 106½ South Campbell and lived at 3114 Oro; his brother Charles Nixon, meanwhile, was a janitor at the St. Regis Apartments. Lawrence eventually ended up moving and opening up an office a few blocks away in an area that was in the city's Second Ward. Also known as the Segundo Barrio, it was largely a Mexican and Mexican American enclave,

5. Lawrence A. Nixon home and medical office at 2029 Myrtle Avenue in El Paso, Texas, ca. 1920s. Courtesy of the Edna A. (Nixon) McIver family collection.

yet according to resident and author Gloria López-Stafford, "a small percentage of the barrio's population was of other ethnicities, as indicated by some of the unusual surnames" of the people who lived there. However, "they usually spoke Spanish as fluently as any Mexican."[38] Lawrence Nixon had no qualms about acquiring a new tongue. He learned to speak Spanish fluently, which enabled him to communicate more effectively with his clients and also to write prescriptions in Spanish for his Spanish-speaking patients. Flora Wolf and Henry O. Flipper were other prominent Spanish-speaking African Americans who lived in this neighborhood. Wolf, also known as Florida J. Wolfe or "Lady Flo," the elegant and genteel heiress to the Delaval James Beresford fortune, lived seven blocks from Nixon at 417 South Ochoa Street. In 1910, Flora Wolf was listed in the census as a thirty-nine-year-old Black woman who was born in Virginia, as were both of her parents. As her physician, Lawrence Nixon signed Wolf's death certificate in May 1913 when she died of tuberculosis.[39] Henry O. Flipper, the first African American cadet to graduate from the United States Military Academy at West Point, lived at 202 or 212 Third Street, nearly ten blocks from Nixon's home, and was employed as an office clerk at the local "Colored" YMCA.[40] The Segundo Barrio also housed the all-Black Douglass School and Second Baptist Church (located at the end of Virginia Street). The church was listed under the heading "Colored Churches" in *Coles*, the El Paso city directory during this time.[41]

The Segundo Barrio was "a kind of Ellis Island for Mexicans" before they migrated to other parts of the United States. Some felt that the neighborhood was a "little Mexico in the city of the pass, in the elbow of the state of Texas, at the bottom of the United States."[42] Local lore has it that this unique district is where the term "Chicano" originated. Mike Romo, longtime resident and League of United Latin American Citizens member, remembered, "they called all of us down in the Second Ward pochos. We would combine Chihuahua and Mexicano together and came up with the word Chicano." "Chicana/o" may have initially been used in a derogatory way to describe the poorest of Mexicans and Mexican Americans in the United States, yet Mexican American students and activists in the 1960s and 1970s reclaimed it "as a term of ethnic pride, capitalizing it as an ethnonym and building a political and artistic movement around it that still endures."[43]

El Paso's Douglass School

The segregated Douglass School, initially named Franklin School, was an important fixture and institution in El Paso's small Black community. Black education in El Paso was established in March 1883 under the leadership of Andrew

Morelock. The school's seven pupils first met at the home of Joseph Snick and then, beginning in 1885, at a church building on Seventh Street.[44] The school was renamed Douglass School in 1883 to honor Frederick Douglass (ca. 1818–1895), one of the most prominent figures in U.S. history—well-known abolitionist, women's suffragist, editor, orator, author, statesman, and reformer.[45] In 1886, Alfred C. Murphy became the new principal, and Douglass School moved to a new structure on the corner of Fourth and Kansas and was formally adopted into the city's public school system. By 1900 enrollment was 87 and in 1909 it was 260. The school moved again in 1920 to 101 South Eucalyptus Street. The Douglass School was home to several important principals, including W. R. Taylor, William Coleman (1908–1927), William Oliver Bundy (1927–1937), Olalee McCall, Emmanuel Campbell (1944–1952), William Marshall (1952), and Edwin W. Mangram (1952–1956).[46] Under the leadership of William O. Bundy, Douglass School incorporated a course on Black history into its curriculum for the first time.[47] In 1956, Douglass permanently closed, and its building was torn down due to federal and state integration policies.[48]

Bernice Love Wiggins, born in 1897, was one of the school's many accomplished graduates who wrote poetry that was published in the *El Paso Herald*, *Chicago Defender*, and the *Houston Informer*. The "Shakespeare of Harlem," Langston Hughes, visited El Paso in April 1932 and remarked, "I think I am the only Negro poet who has ever given a program in the frontier town."[49] Clearly, he must not have met or known of Texas's Bernice Love Wiggins, whose poetry, similar to that of Hughes, focused on the ordinary Black community.[50] Wiggins received her primary and secondary education at Douglass, which so influenced her that she dedicated a volume of poems she published in 1925, *Tuneful Tales*, to Douglass teacher Alice Lydia McGowan and asked longtime Douglass principal William Coleman to write the introduction.[51]

Zephyr Chisom Carter was also another early and prominent graduate of Douglass School. She was born in El Paso in 1891, graduated Douglass in 1909, and graduated Howard University in 1913. While at Howard University she helped establish the well-known Delta Sigma Theta Sorority along with twenty-one other Black women at Howard. The sorority ultimately became one of the largest Black women's organizations in the nation, if not the world. Carter joined Vashti Turley Murphy, Winona Cargile Alexander, and Madree Penn White as members of the Howard branch of the NAACP. The *Crisis* described Carter as the "leading spirit in the organization." Other Douglass School graduates that would enroll at Howard University include William Perry Coleman, Arthur Earl Burke, and Vernon Collins.[52]

Coleman was a teacher and principal who was born in Georgia in 1870, attended Valdosta Academy, and earned his undergraduate degree from Brown University in 1897 and his DDS from Howard in 1920. He was a professor of modern languages at Benedict College and assistant principal at Colored High School in Fort Worth, and in 1907, he became principal of Douglass School.[53]

Lawrence A. Nixon's first child and only son, Lawrence Joseph Nixon, graduated from El Paso's Douglass High School in 1926 and then attended the University of California at Berkeley. Lawrence J. Nixon ultimately settled in Pittsburgh, Pennsylvania, in the late 1920s or early 1930s, where he became a master printer-machinist within the linotype department of the famed liberal *Pittsburgh Courier*. He worked for the *Courier* for over twenty-one years and for the *Pittsburgh Post Gazette/Press* for thirteen years.[54] At its height, the *Pittsburgh Courier* was one of the most popular national African American newspapers, and it influenced public opinion on a range of political and economic issues.[55]

Douglass also served as an important venue for community activities such as a meeting place and "gallimaufry" for various community organizations such as the Rio Grande chapter of the Colored Disabled Veterans, Alpha Social Club, Phyllis Wheatley Women's Club, the Nathaniel Dett Musical Club, the YWCA Girl Reserves, and the Wiley Club.[56] The Wiley Club was an alumni group of which Lawrence A. Nixon was the local president, and he hosted the famous Wiley College debate team at the auditorium of the school when it competed against the University of New Mexico on 22 March 1935.[57] The Wiley Forensic Society included students Henrietta Bell Wells, Hobart Jarrett, and James L. Farmer Jr., who were coached by well-known and respected professor Melvin B. Tolson. Ten days after the Douglass School debate against University of New Mexico, Wiley College debated and defeated the University of Southern California—reigning debate national champions—in front of an interracial audience of over two thousand at Bovard Auditorium on the Trojan campus.[58] No doubt Tolson must have shared his excitement of this upcoming USC match with Lawrence Nixon during the Douglass event. And surely Nixon must have met members of the Wiley team, who themselves would have an impact on the civil rights movement.

El Paso and African Americans

Life in the western half of the United States was not the racial utopia that many believed it would be. Although Lawrence Nixon had fled Cameron due to its hostility toward Blacks, he had no illusions that locations farther west would be much better. However, many African American leaders felt the West would be a more hospitable racial environment for Blacks. In 1913 W. E. B. Du Bois visited the western states of Texas, California, and Washington. Du Bois was a pioneering sociologist, historian, novelist, playwright, cultural critic, international spokesperson for peace and the rights of the oppressed, and preeminent American intellectual of the twentieth century who committed his life to articulating what African Americans wanted, to demonstrating the significance of Black culture before the world, and to combating racial and social injustice. He helped form both the Niagara Movement and the NAACP and fostered several pan-African congresses. He founded the *Crisis* and served as its editor for twenty-four years and also sat at the helm of other progressive journals.[59] In an editorial touting the West, he described Black people of the western region of the United States as "colored folk" who "are educated; not college-bred, but out of the shackles of dense ignorance; they have pushed, for their very coming so far westward proves it; and, above all, they are a part of the greater group and they know it."[60]

Du Bois was not the only Black leader who held the West in high regard. Some years later in 1925, when visiting Colorado and other western states as national secretary for the NAACP, James Weldon Johnson proclaimed that the region provided more prospects for Blacks "than any other section of the country." "I cannot attempt to analyze the reasons for this," he added, "but the fact remains that there is more opportunity for my race, and less prejudice against it in this section of the country than anywhere else in the United States."[61] Yet this was not always the impression that Blacks in the West had. One major western city daily in 1897 commented that "there is room for only a limited number of colored people here." The relatively few African Americans did not pose an immediate economic and political threat, but the newspaper warned, "overstep that limit and there comes a clash in which the colored many must suffer. The few that are here do vastly better than they would do if their number were increased a hundredfold."[62]

El Paso County had a "Negro" population of 377 in 1890 and 620 in 1900. By 1910, the year of Lawrence Nixon's arrival, the total Black population in the county had more than doubled to 1,562. Of this figure 768 were men and 794 were women; 1,196 of the total were classified as "Black" and 366 as "mulatto." There was a total population in the county of 52,599, which meant that Blacks were 2.97 percent of the overall population.[63] The city of El Paso had a Black population of 1,452 in 1910.[64] Yet the small number of African Americans in El Paso did not mean they were not a threat to the status quo or precluded from absorbing the blows of racism. At the time of Lawrence Nixon's arrival in El Paso, the local newspaper had no qualms about printing derogatory words to describe African Americans. In characterizing Black participation in El Paso's annual Circus Day, city recorder Adrian Pool stated, "Circus day is one time the 'nigger' likes to celebrate and if his celebration includes a little over-indulgence without aggravated circumstances I wouldn't feel like fining." However, no session of the "corporation court" was held that afternoon, "owing to the absence of offenders."[65]

It is clear, as historian William Katz notes, that "the intrepid pioneers who crossed the western plains carried the virus of racism with them."[66] These pioneers of course included the white frontier people of El Paso, many of whom came from the racially divisive South, where social norms between Blacks and whites were rigid and strictly enforced. Racist sentiments in El Paso were not restricted to civilians. African American troops also felt the injustices of racial inequality. In 1900, soldiers of the Twenty-Fifth Infantry on assignment in El Paso fought townspeople. An officer sent to El Paso to investigate the episode observed that black troops were arrested for offenses that, when committed by whites, were overlooked, and he added that African Americans were abused even when they behaved "with perfect propriety." "There is unquestionably a very strong prejudice throughout all of the old slave states against colored troops, and this is quite a separate feeling from the ordinary race prejudice," the officer observed. Rather, he concluded, "a colored man in uniform represents authority, and this idea suggests superiority, which is bitterly resented. It is not because the colored soldier is disorderly—for as a rule, they behave better than white soldiers, and, even when drunk, are less troublesome to manage—but because they are soldiers." The War Department canceled the maneuvers and sent the Black troops to Fort Brown in Brownsville, Texas, instead.[67]

Anti-Black attitudes in El Paso were prevalent in all parts of society, including the courts. Upon sentencing Jasper Smith, an African American who was arrested for making an "insulting proposal" to a white woman, Judge Adrian Pool stated:

> Gentlemen, I am sorry that the maximum fine in this court is but $100; that, however, is the limit, and the court can go no further. Personally, however, I can warn Smith that if he can get out of the country by morning, he had better do it. There are many who would not hesitate to start a little bonfire in which Smith would be the chief actor. And I might also add that there are some that would resign office to participate in the affair.[68]

For Blacks, it was not uncommon that such an "insult" would merit not only the barbaric act of a lynching but the boastful suggestion that a city official would resign to participate in the lynching. The $100 fine already levied against Smith in the presence of a packed courtroom "buzzing with ill controlled anger" was not sufficient for such a minor offense; instead, the crowd thought that a Black man who violated the tenuous racial norms of this border city deserved death.[69] This seems odd considering that nearly two decades earlier Black men had been allowed to fraternize with white women on the border, permitting a more fluid, nuanced relationship when compared to other regions of the South. In 1893, Black men "engaged in militant protest" against enforcement of a Texas state law barring miscegenation, which would have "complicated the lives of all those who had married women of Mexican descent," who for legal purposes were deemed white.[70]

El Paso's NAACP Chapter

Although their numbers were modest, the members of El Paso's African American community were very active in their quest for racial equality and dignity. Part of that activism included creating a lyceum three years after Lawrence Nixon's arrival in the city.[71] Unbeknownst to them at the time, this lyceum would serve as the impetus for the founding of one of the first chapters of the NAACP in Texas. In the mid-nineteenth and early twentieth centuries lyceums flourished in the United States and were a forum for adult education. Prominent individuals such as Frederick Douglass, John B. Gough, Ralph Waldo Emerson, Henry David Thoreau, Abraham Lincoln, Susan B. Anthony, Elizabeth Cady Stanton, Victoria Woodhull, Anna Dickinson, Mark Twain, and William Lloyd Garrison all spoke at lyceums.[72]

Lyceums provided African Americans, who had a tremendous thirst for education after the Civil War, with the opportunity to explore ideas for racial uplift. Though led by community elites, lyceums were open to all classes. Many African American lyceums were literary and cultural clubs that sponsored lectures, public meetings, poetry and dramatic readings and performances, musical presentations, book discussions, and travel tours and that participated in charitable and civic activities. Participation in lyceums provided members with opportunities to practice public speaking and debating skills, to receive constructive feedback and group recognition, to build friendships, fellowship, and professional networks.[73] Activist, civil rights leader, and antilynching proponent Ida B. Wells Barnett described lyceum meetings in her diary entries of the late 1880s and early 1890s, noting that members listened to lectures on issues of race and racism and problems in Africa, along with her own presentations on a variety of topics, and heard readings from *Macbeth* and a speech by prominent former Louisiana Republican governor Pinckney Benton Stewart Pinchback.[74]

In 1913, various members of the African American community established the El Paso Lyceum and Civic Improvement Society (EPLCIS).[75] The EPLCIS met every Sunday afternoon at the Masonic Temple located at 409 S. Virginia Street.[76] After just a few meetings they decided to take the bold step of seeking membership in the NAACP, the premier civil rights organization.

The NAACP had been established in New York City in 1909—the centenary of Lincoln's birth, which was not wholly coincidental, as the founders, nearly all of whom were white, sought to bring attention to Lincoln's presidential accomplishments.[77] What was coincidental was that the impetus for founding the NAACP was the race riot that occurred six months earlier in Lincoln's adopted hometown, Springfield, Illinois.[78] The children of white abolitionists, along with white Jews and white liberals, came together out of genuine concern for the plight of Blacks in the United States. They were horrified by the attacks on African Americans in a northern city, having been accustomed for decades to seeing Black overt oppression restricted to southern states. The fear among liberal whites was that the barbarous way Blacks were treated in the South would now spread northward.

The NAACP invited some progressive African Americans to its initial meeting, including Ida B. Wells-Barnett, Mary Church-Terrell, Archibald Grimké, Kelly Miller, Bishop Alexander Walters, William Monroe Trotter, William Scarborough, and W. E. B. Du Bois. Du Bois would be the lone African American when appointments to the executive board were made and full-time paid positions were assigned.[79]

In its infancy the organization struck a delicate balance between the conservative strategies of the famous Booker T. Washington, Tuskegee Institute principal, author, and civil rights leader, and the lesser known but militant approach of civil rights activist, newspaper editor, and publisher William Monroe Trotter.[80] Trotter helped establish the Niagara Movement in 1905 and National Equal Rights League in 1908.[81] The Niagara Movement was instrumental to the subsequent formation of the NAACP. Along with George Forbes, Trotter cofounded the *Boston Guardian* in the same building that had once housed William Lloyd Garrison's *Liberator*. The *Boston Guardian* quickly became a nemesis for Booker T. Washington; according to Du Bois, "Opposition [against Washington] began to become vocal in 1901 when Trotter and Forbes began the publication of the *Boston Guardian*. The *Guardian* was bitter, satirical, and personal; but it was earnest, and it published facts. It attracted wide attention among colored people; it circulated among them all over the country; it was quoted and discussed. I did not wholly agree with the *Guardian*, and indeed only a few Negroes did, but nearly all read it and were influenced by it." Trotter famously chastised

Woodrow Wilson during a fall 1913 meeting at the White House after, despite promises to the contrary, Wilson allowed federal departments to segregate their workforces.[82]

Through public protests, demands for political participation, legal campaigns that focused on lynching and the redress of other racist assaults, the NAACP challenged institutional white racism in the United States. The official organ of the NAACP, *The Crisis: A Record of the Darker Races*, whose first issue appeared in November 1910, spread its message across the nation.[83] The first issue had a circulation of one thousand. A year later it reached nine thousand, and within five years the circulation increased to thirty-five thousand. Du Bois fought for the magazine's establishment and became its first editor. And though he believed that Booker T. Washington "had a tight hold of most" of the Black press, which resulted in the NAACP getting "a pretty raw deal from the colored press and none at all from the white papers," the *Crisis* nevertheless became a prominent voice.[84] Despite the South's insistent claims that the organization was too radical, or in later years allegedly dominated by communist sympathizers, the fact is the NAACP operated within the legal structure—primarily the court system—and as historian Manfred Berg reminds us, "remained firmly committed to the institutional and normative framework provided by the United States Constitution and the American political system."[85]

The members of the EPLCIS found themselves in a social and racial climate that pushed them to write to the New York national headquarters of the NAACP in September 1913 to request that an official branch be established in El Paso to fight against Jim Crow and racial oppression in the border city.[86] The NAACP responded to their request on December 5, stating "we are gratified to learn that you are interested in the work of this Association and that the El Paso Lyceum and Civic Improvement Society is contemplating becoming formally identified with us." In this initial letter to the EPLCIS, the NAACP was careful to stress that "you cannot announce yourselves as a branch until your constitution has been formally approved."[87] Months later, in May 1914, the national office mailed the constitution and bylaws that allowed the El Paso branch to officially become chartered. The local members planned their first meeting the following month, Sunday June 14, at which their officers were named. The El Paso NAACP executive committee consisted of Lawrence A. Nixon (chairman), Sylvester M. Collins, Le Roy W. Washington, John F. Kelley, John Slater, and Joseph H. Donnell.[88]

This initial step by El Paso Blacks was an important one. "Organization is sacrifice," emphasized W. E. B. Du Bois to his readers in the April 1915 *Crisis*: "It is sacrifice of opinions, of time, of work and of money, but it is, after all, the cheapest way of buying the most priceless of gifts—freedom and efficiency."[89]

Nixon would come to know that sacrifice. He lived it as a Black man, as a physician, and as a husband.

Booker T. Washington Visits El Paso

The establishment in El Paso of an NAACP branch—what was then considered one of the more aggressive or even radical civil rights organizations—produced a tremendous ideological shift among Blacks in the city. In September 1911, less than two years after Lawrence Nixon's arrival, the tiny Black border community of El Paso welcomed Booker T. Washington, one of the most celebrated African American leaders of his day. During the late nineteenth and early twentieth centuries, Washington had become the most influential African American in the United States, if not the world.[90] This was an extraordinary accomplishment considering Washington's humble origins. Born into the peculiar institution of slavery in 1856, Washington rose to prominence after becoming principal of Tuskegee Institute in Alabama and delivering his famous 1895 Atlanta Cotton States and International Exposition speech before a segregated audience. Washington used the occasion to exploit the white South's legend of the content African captive, which whites had transformed into a myth of Black loyalty during the Civil War and Reconstruction Era. In addition, Washington exhorted white-controlled business and industry to entrust its destiny to Blacks, saying, "Cast down your bucket ... among the eight millions of Negroes whose habits you know, whose fidelity and love you have tested in days when to have proved treacherous meant the ruin of your friends." Washington exploited the South's xenophobia with respect to European emigrants, promising a loyalty "that no foreigner can approach," and casting suspicion on those "of foreign birth and strange tongue and habits."[91]

Washington arrived in El Paso from Arizona on 24 September 1911.[92] It is not known whether Lawrence Nixon met Washington upon his arrival or heard him speak publicly while he was in El Paso—his first and only visit to the border city. One would think that owing to the prominent position Nixon held in the Black community—by being one of the few, if not the only, Black physicians in the city—that he not only would have been present to hear Washington speak but also would have played a role in the planning of the events or in carrying out the day's activities on Washington's arrival.[93] In all likelihood, Nixon heard Washington speak as a student during his last semester at Meharry when Washington visited the campus on 7 January 1906 and gave four addresses over the course of the day, the last of which was entitled "Young Men, Keep Yourselves Clean."[94] Nixon apparently thought highly of Washington, describing him in 1934 as the "greatest of all Negroes."[95] For Washington's El Paso visit, however,

Nixon was not mentioned in the press as having been present, acknowledged, or part of the formal events.

Although Nixon may not have been a visible or vocal community leader during his early years in El Paso, in some parts of the south Black doctors were accepted as spokespersons because few were what one would call "race men" (Black men who were committed to racial uplift through social, economic, and political means). Physicians instead tended to be "racial diplomats," those who did not accept Jim Crow as either right or just but who had learned to work within the South's racist caste system, developing successful institutions and businesses in a world governed by the "separate but equal" myth.[96] Historian Thomas Ward reminds us that many physicians actually depended on certain aspects of segregation for their livelihoods and were therefore not as interested as other Black leaders in trying to tear the Jim Crow system down at all costs. This conservative attitude not only made physicians more acceptable to whites as race leaders but also often allowed these racial diplomats to get more for their communities from the white society than aggressive race men.[97] Race men were usually viewed as agitators who were thorns in the side of the racial status quo, standing on firm principles and refusing to capitulate under the weight of white domination.[98]

Even if Lawrence Nixon did not attend Booker T. Washington's event in El Paso, he certainly must have been aware of it and learned what took place. The African Americans who did attend were conceivably his associates, friends, and perhaps patients. Prior to speaking publicly Washington visited the home of Charles W. Bradley, owner of two barbershops, and his wife, Geneva Bradley, who was a teacher at the segregated Douglass School. Washington then had dinner with a number of Black women at the home of Georgia Ann Perett.[99]

Washington was a staunch supporter of the temperance movement, and yet he dined at this home despite the fact that Arnold Perett, Georgia's husband, was a saloon keeper.[100] Local Blacks who were also on the platform at the Sunday night address of Booker T. Washington in the El Paso Theater included William Coleman, principal at Douglass School; Frederick D. Clopton, a teacher at Douglass School; Charles W. Bradley; Emory Douglass Williams, Las Cruces barbershop owner and farmer; LeRoy White, barber at Meroney's barbershop; Henry R. Wilson, Reverend at Second Baptist Church; Lemuel M. Sanders, Reverend at Visitors Chapel; Reverend E. L. Russell, Reverend L. J. Jacks, Amos Williams, janitor at City Hall; Jasper Williams, messenger with the Immigration Service; and William M. Sublett, mail carrier for the post office.[101]

Other "Bookerites" of El Paso who were in attendance included Exel T. Perrett, a railroad switchman; James G. Browne, Reverend at East El Paso Methodist Episcopal Church; Charles S. Long, pastor at Visitors Chapel; and George W.

Meroney, barbershop owner—all of whom had personal and professional relationships with Nixon.[102] Washington addressed the standing-room capacity crowd, more than 215 people. About one-third of the audience was Black; most were white, and it was whites who covered nearly all of the rental costs for the El Paso Theater, formerly named the Texas Grand.[103] Ironically, this would be the same theater that would screen the racist *The Birth of a Nation* for the first time in El Paso.[104] During his speech, the respectable Black working class and aspiring middle class of El Paso heard Washington assert that

> the outside world hears of the worst things that take place between the black man and the white man in the South. . . . In nine-tenths of the cases, the two races in Texas are living together in peace and harmony, but the world does not hear of this. It hears about the lynching, of the burnings, about the mob. In a large degree, as a race, we must learn to advertise our friends more and our enemies less.[105]

Washington elaborated:

> Is it possible for these two races unlike in color, unlike in tradition, to live together in peace and harmony for all time? . . . There is no greater enemy today to a state than the man, whether he be black or white, who will spend his time stirring up racial strife. . . . There is no greater friend today to a state than the man, whether he be black or white, who uses his talents and influence to promote the progress of both races and to see to it that peace and goodwill are maintained.[106]

As a clever and skillful tactician, Washington used psychology to manipulate whites in such a way as to benefit African Americans. Washington's El Paso address reflected advice no different from that of his previous speeches. He preached thrift, hard work, and the folly of racial antagonism, which at this unique juncture in United States history was unlikely to produce much in the way of gains for the masses of Blacks in the South. Just four years earlier, Washington even asked whites for their assistance in educating the infamous Black mammy so "that she shall be morally fit to come into contact with that pure and innocent [white] child!"[107]

After Washington finished his talk at the El Paso Theater, he gave addresses at the First Methodist Church and at the Second Baptist Church. The next morning Washington crossed into Ciudad Juárez and met with Mayor Guillermo Alvarez and the city council before moving onward to San Antonio.[108] Accompanying Washington to Ciudad Juárez were prolific writer and prominent sociologist Robert Ezra Park of Tuskegee, Coleman, Bradley, and Emory Douglass Williams. Gaston O. Sanders was an African American employed as a Spanish-language interpreter with the United States Immigration Service in El Paso who also was part of the Washington convoy into Ciudad Juárez.[109]

Jim Crow in El Paso

Notwithstanding Washington's claims, less than two years later Black El Pasoans would initiate the process to establish a chapter of the NAACP, making El Paso one of the first Texas cities to do so, if not the first.[110] What compelled them to take this step might have been the insidious level of racial intolerance and Jim Crow in El Paso.[111] Although race relations in El Paso were much better than in the rest of the state, prejudice was far-reaching enough to warrant Blacks to take action.

These racial affronts included barring Blacks from restaurants, hotels, swimming pools, and other public facilities. A lack of hotels and motels placed burdens on traveling Blacks. Lawrence Nixon was the beneficiary of this policy during the first half of 1933, when the famed lyric tenor Roland Hayes sent him a telegram from Los Angeles indicating that he would be stopping by El Paso on his way to Georgia. He hoped that since he wouldn't be able to find a hotel Nixon would open his doors to him. Hayes arrived at nearly midnight with his brother and niece in a new Chevrolet Sedan and departed three hours later, but not before he and Nixon talked at length while the others slept.[112] The celebrated Harlem Renaissance poet Langston Hughes found Jim Crow in the borderlands odd. Recalling an April 1932 trip to El Paso and Ciudad Juárez, he observed that

> it was strange to find that just by stepping across an invisible line into Mexico, a Negro could buy a beer in any bar, sit anywhere in the movies, or eat in any restaurant, so suddenly did Jim Crow disappear, and Americans visiting Juarez, who would not drink beside a Negro in Texas, did so in Mexico. Funny people, Southerners![113]

Jim Crow also required segregation in movie theaters. In many theaters throughout the nation Blacks were relegated to the side aisles or balconies, abhorrently called "buzzard roosts," "crows' nests," or "nigger heaven." Some Denver theaters were known to issue special red tickets to Black customers, which were only for upstairs seating and to sell tickets to Blacks that were stamped "Good only in the upper right balcony," as well as to ring a bell to beckon ushers to escort Black ticket holders to the balcony.[114] Theaters in El Paso such as the Crawford and Texas Grand adhered to this policy.[115] The Plaza Theater, the city's premier movie palace, followed the path of the Crawford and Texas Grand twenty years later when it opened in September 1930 by allowing Black patrons to only enter through a side entrance that led to a special balcony.[116]

Medical services in El Paso were also segregated owing to Jim Crow practices. In 1910, the year Lawrence Nixon arrived in El Paso, H. Arthur Magruder, a dentist who had worked in El Paso for ten years, advertised his dentistry services in the *El Paso Herald*, boldly proclaiming "I Don't Work for Negroes."[117] In the residential arena too, El Paso limited Blacks to certain areas, such as the second ward neighborhood near downtown. This could be done in subtle ways, but it was also often accomplished through overt tactics such as racially restrictive covenants that simply stated "said property shall not be sold to nor occupied by Negroes, nor for any immoral use."[118] By forcing Blacks to live in overcrowded areas, racially restrictive covenants "imposed social disintegration, social pathology, and personal ill health on them."[119]

Besides Jim Crow, Blacks in El Paso also had to contend with racist imagery. The 2 June 1914 edition of the *El Paso Herald* contained an advertisement featuring the Gold Dust Twins that not only belittled African Americans by way of crass caricatures but also offended both Mexicans and Mexican Americans, who were the majority of El Paso's inhabitants.[120] The advertisement shows a map of Mexico painted black to resemble the supposed dirt and filth of the country and a map of the United States painted white, presumably already clean and pure. The Gold Dust Twins are visibly cleaning Mexico with their product, broom, mop, and bucket.[121] In addition, Black El Pasoans had to contend with Aunt Jemima and her speaking in stereotypical Black-southern dialect ("I'se in town, Honey!") in local newspaper advertisements.[122]

6. "I'se in town, Honey!" Aunt Jemima Buckwheat Flour advertisement, *El Paso Herald*, 20 February 1919.

Segregation in El Paso also permeated the educational system. One visitor to the city noted of the all-Black Douglass School that "no white children can go to it," adding that "no negro can attend a white school; and yet I saw children in the negro school *whiter than you or I*."[123] Some southern states even went so far to prohibit Blacks in courtrooms from swearing on the same Bible as whites, from engaging in games of checkers with whites, and even from patronizing the same prostitutes as whites![124] Lawrence J. Nixon, Lawrence A. Nixon's son, recalled years later how as a young boy he and his father were removed from their seats at an El Paso circus by the circus manager at the insistence of two police officers. The younger Nixon remembered that the circus was held in "a large, oval tent, and the best seats were in the center, and we were moved to the very end."[125] Those who dared to cross racial barriers faced public verbal abuse and embarrassment, and at times violence and death, including lynchings. In an eighty-five-year period (1882–1968), approximately 4,742 Blacks were lynched and as many if not more were "victims of legal lynchings (speedy trials and executions), private white violence, and "*nigger hunts*," murdered by a variety of means in isolated rural sections and dumped into rivers and creeks."[126]

The level of activism by the Black community in El Paso—to minimize the effects of Jim Crow and address issues of racial inequities—can be seen in the number of members the local NAACP branch had. The NAACP annual report for 1917 states that under the leadership of Jasper B. Williams and Frederick D. Clopton the El Paso branch of the NAACP recruited "45 members and has been protesting against discrimination in certain stores and in street cars."[127] By 1921, the El Paso branch had increased its membership to 103 members, although the rest of the NAACP chapters in Texas were experiencing a decline in membership.[128] The total Black population in El Paso County during the early 1920s was approximately 1,548, of whom 1,096 were at least twenty-one years old.[129] Since there were 103 NAACP members, that means that over 9 percent of the Black community were dues-paying members at this time.

The Death of Esther J. Calvin Nixon

The second half of the decade also saw many dramatic events for Lawrence Nixon. His maternal grandmother, Lucy Patterson Engledow, died on 1 January 1917.[130] Months later, in April 1917, the United States would enter World War I, and by June 1917 conscription laws were passed for the compulsory enlistment of able-bodied male citizens between the ages of twenty-one and thirty. In September 1918 the age range was expanded to eighteen to forty-five years old, making the thirty-five-year-old Nixon eligible to fight.[131] Nixon quickly registered, submitting his draft card to the local El Paso draft board the same month

7. Nixon's first wife, Esther Josephine Calvin. Courtesy of the Beth Elnita Nixon family collection.

8. Lawrence Joseph Nixon, ca. 1919. Courtesy of the Beth Elnita Nixon family collection.

the new directive was issued.[132] He never was called for military duty, since the war ended in November 1918, but he did find himself fighting a different battle. Tragically, his childhood sweetheart and wife, Esther, died of influenza in the early morning hours of 21 February 1919, despite her having a husband who was a medical doctor.[133] Esther Nixon supported Lawrence through eleven years of marriage and had cared for their child since the time he was born. Jennie V. Nixon, Lawrence Nixon's mother, would move in from Marshall with Lawrence to assist with the rearing of her grandchild.[134] Charles B. Nixon, Lawrence Nixon's father, had died in Marshall, Texas, in 1910.[135]

The disease was so powerful that it would ultimately kill more people than any other outbreak the world has ever known, fifty million to one hundred million, or 8 to 10 percent of the then population. Typically influenza kills the elderly and infants, whose immune systems are weak or still developing. But the 1918–1919 influenza outbreak killed young women and men who were in their prime, in their twenties and thirties.[136] Another unusual characteristic of this disease was the speed in which it attacked. Most of the deaths occurred in a twenty-four-week period, and more than half of them from mid-September to December 1918. Some scholars have noted that this influenza strain killed more people in twenty-four weeks than the Bubonic plague killed in a century; it killed more people in twenty-four weeks than AIDS has killed in twenty-four years.[137]

In El Paso, the epidemic hit hardest in the fall of 1918 and in parts of the city that were "south of the tracks," which of course was a euphemism for the south side of El Paso where mostly poor, African Americans, Mexicans, and Mexican Americans resided. The *El Paso Herald* aptly observed that "the city has not only neglected the elementary welfare of half of its population, but it has tolerated conditions in that section that have constituted a terrible menace to all the rest of the city." This neglect resulted in the El Paso Board of Health reporting 131 deaths the week of 18 October, 102 of whom were Mexicans or Mexican Americans. The hospitals and clinics at both Fort Bliss and the city were filled and overtaxed, and city leaders called for more doctors and nurses to assist. A makeshift hospital was created at the twenty-eight-room Aoy school located on Seventh and Kansas to address the many south-side patients. It is likely that Lawrence Nixon was one of the many physicians attending the ill, particularly on the south side of El Paso, where he and his family lived and worked. Although by December 1918 the numbers of reported cases began to decline to twenty to forty per day, people continued to die, but at a much slower pace.[138] Esther Nixon would be among that group when she passed two months later. For Lawrence Nixon it would be a tremendous emotional loss. He would not marry again for sixteen years.

CHAPTER 3

Bullets and Ropes

Wading in Bloody Waters, 1919–1924

> Out of this war will rise, soon or late, an independent China;
> a self-governing India, an Egypt with representative institutions;
> an Africa for the Africans and not merely for business exploitation.
> Out of this war will rise, too, an American Negro, with a right to
> vote and a right to work and a right to live without insult.
>
> W. E. B. Du Bois, 1918

In the spring of 1918 in an editorial for the *Crisis*, Du Bois voiced his hope that Black Americans would soon be accorded the basic rights all Americans deserved.[1] It is likely that Lawrence Nixon, as a member of the El Paso NAACP, received and regularly read the monthly *Crisis*, which was delivered to the homes of thousands of African Americans throughout the country.[2] The words from its most famous editor would be prophetic.

Heeding Du Bois's call, Nixon helped dismantle the racial status quo in Texas. Nixon knew the political realities and implications of his affiliation with an organization that posed a threat to business as usual in the state. This did not deter him, however, from addressing issues relevant to the NAACP's purpose. Nixon's involvement, by way of the local NAACP, in the Henry Lowry tragedy and his attempts to secure an all-Black swimming pool in El Paso through his association with the local Negro Ministerial Alliance were deliberate steps he took to help make Du Bois's "American Negro" who would have a "right to vote and a right to work and a right to live without insult" a reality. Beyond Nixon, the whole Black El Pasoan arena was evolving. Movements such as the Texas's Juneteenth celebration provided a way for Black El Pasoans to join together in solidarity and strength and to exercise their political influence.

Unfortunately, violence continued unabated against African Americans after World War I. Bernice Love Wiggins eloquently wrote about the treatment of Black soldiers in her poem "Ethiopia Speaks":

Lynched!
Somewhere in the South, the "Land of the Free,"
To a very strong branch of a dogwood tree.
Lynched! One of my sons,—
When the flag was in danger they answered the call
I gave them black sons, ah! Yes, gave them all
When you came to me.

You called them the sons of a downtrodden race,
The Negro you said, in his place must stay,
To be seen in your midst is deemed a disgrace,
I remembered, oh yes, still I gave them that day
Your flag to defend.

And knew when I sent them to your fields of battle,
To suffer, to bleed, to be hewn down like cattle,
Not to them be the plaudit, should victory they win,
History scarcely records it,—too dark was their skin,
'Twas truth I spoke in.

    My sons:
How it grieves me for I taught them, 'tis true
That this was their country and for her to die,
Was none less than loyal, the right thing to do,
Brave and loyal they proved and now they ask why
Their country ill treats them, because they are black,
Must I take it back?
Until in the South, the "Land of the Free,"
They stop hanging my sons to the branch of a tree,
Take it back till they cease to burn them alive,
Take it back till the white man shall cease to deprive.

My sons, yes, my black sons, of rights justly won,
    'Til tortures are done?

Mary wept for tortured son, in days of yore
Ethiopia weeps for her sons, tortured more,
Mary forgave, 'twas her Savior son's will,
Ethiopia forgives, but remembers still,

And cries unto God with uplifted hands,
"Innocent bloods bathe the lands."

Lynched!
Somewhere in the South, the "Land of the Free,"
To a very high branch of a very strong tree,
Lynched! One of my sons,—
When the flag drooped so lowly they heeded the call,
I gave them, my black sons, Ah, yes, gave them all,
When you came to me.[3]

The "war to end all wars" demanded that African Americans participate un-critically and patriotically, to offer their manpower and moral support, as the country had asked them to do in previous wars. Nixon too supported the war and wasted no time completing and submitting his draft card to the local El Paso draft board.[4] Yet many African Americans, including those in El Paso, were frustrated by the irony and hypocrisy of the nation asking African Americans to fight for democracy overseas while they were being denied it in the United States. As Francis J. Grimké stated after the war, "That shameful record is going to be written up, and published, so that the whole world may read it, and learn how these black men, who went out from these shores to die at their country's call, were treated simply because of the color of their skin."[5] And it wasn't just the African Americans who stayed home who were frustrated but also the soldiers who had fought and who, upon returning from abroad, continued to feel the stings and blows of white supremacy.

The economic exploitation of and the physical violence against African Americans in the South was so severe that Blacks began to flee the South in record numbers to seek opportunities elsewhere. By 1918, more than one hundred thousand Afro-Texans had become part of the Great Migration by moving to western and northern states. The Great Migration commonly refers to the movement of millions of southern Blacks (and to a lesser extent Blacks from the Caribbean) to urban parts of the United States in the North, Midwest, and West from 1910 to 1930 and from 1940 to 1970.[6] The city of Austin, Texas, lost over one-third of its Black population within three years. The Texas border city of Laredo witnessed its Black population decline from 205 to 41 between 1900 and 1920.[7] Somewhere between 275,000 and 750,000 southern Blacks migrated from the South to the North between 1916 and 1918.[8]

El Paso also saw a decline, although a much less pronounced one than other Texas cities. The Black population in El Paso County decreased from 1,562 in 1910 to 1,548 in 1920.[9] There was a total population in the county of 101,877 at the time, which meant that Blacks were 1.5 percent of the overall population.[10] By 1930, the Black population in El Paso County totaled 1,970, of which 1,886 resided in the first precinct. The total population in the county was 131,597, which meant that Blacks were still nearly 1.5 percent of the overall population.[11] The African Americans who stayed in El Paso remained because they believed they would be afforded the same rights and opportunities as those who sought these liberties in the North.

The NAACP in Texas, 1918–1921

Whites who took on the cause of equality for African Americans, such as the NAACP national executive secretary John R. Shillady, were also the targets of threats from hostile whites. Shillady became executive director of the NAACP in 1918. He and James Weldon Johnson were credited with greatly increasing NAACP membership. Under Shillady's leadership, the NAACP decided to take a stance on lynching. He oversaw *Thirty Years of Lynching in the United States: 1889–1918*, the first NAACP book publication.[12]

Shillady's pummeling during his visit to Austin, Texas, in the summer of 1919 exposed the danger of being affiliated with the NAACP in Texas.[13] He was prompted to go to Texas after Governor William P. Hobby called for an investigation of all NAACP branches within the state and threatened to close them for allegedly operating without a state charter after Austin NAACP branch president Pinckney A. Williams had the temerity to protest the beating of a Black veteran, observing that veterans "have returned to old homes but are not going to submit to old conditions."[14] In other words, he suggested that Texas had better get used to a "New Negro," one who was no longer going to tolerate the racial status quo of the recent past. Williams was simply attempting to address the poor treatment and gross disrespect received by Black soldiers upon their return from overseas duty, but his remarks were enough to cause the governor to order the Texas Rangers to investigate "Bolshevik" activities within the Black community.[15] Texas officials secured a copy of the *Crisis* and concluded that it was subversive and that for that reason the NAACP could be forced to close all its branches in the state.[16]

Calvin M. Cureton, the Texas state attorney general, ordered local NAACP branches to submit their administrative and financial records for review. This order alarmed the national office, thus precipitating Shillady's attempt to meet with Hobby. Shillady wanted to make clear that the NAACP was not a threat to the state, that it was merely attempting to secure for Afro-Texans those basic rights that were guaranteed to all Americans by the U.S. and state constitutions.

Ultimately Shillady did not get a meeting with the governor or the attorney general; instead he received a severe beating at the hands of Judge David J. Pickle and Constable Charles Hamby outside the Driskill Hotel in plain view on the afternoon of 22 August 1919.[17] Soon after, these same officials boastfully told the tale of their involvement in the affair. "I whipped him and ordered him to leave because I thought it was for the best interests of Austin and the State," Pickle proclaimed. The governor concurred, asserting that "Shillady was the only offender in the connection with the matter," and then offered the following advice: "Your organization can contribute more to the advancement of both races by keeping your representatives and their propaganda out of this state than in any other way."[18] Governor Hobby already knew who John Shillady was, as Shillady had publicly printed a telegram protesting the 4 June 1918 lynching of Sarah and Tenola Cabaniss in Hunstville.[19]

When NAACP cofounder and board member Mary White Ovington wrote law enforcement officials in Austin, the deputy sheriff replied that Shillady was confronted by "red-blooded white men" who did not want "Negro-loving white men" in Texas.[20] Shillady was physically and emotionally demoralized and within a year resigned his post. In June 1920, African American James Weldon Johnson became the NAACP acting secretary, and subsequently the board formally approved his permanent appointment, making Johnson the first African American to hold this position within the organization. At this time, the board also appointed Walter White, "an African American from Atlanta, who had fair complexion, blond hair, and blue eyes, . . . the organization's chief investigator of lynching and mob violence."[21]

The NAACP of 1919 in this instance was less aggressive than the NAACP of 1913, which, as historian Gerald Horne notes, had called for the formation of a "vigilance committee." This was an avowed "call to arms . . . to protect the colored people in their several communities from aggression." The NAACP wanted to "federate local vigilance committees among colored people in every community in the United States."[22] However, the NAACP of 1919 was a bit wiser in its word choice and smarter in its political and social activism. The Texas branches proceeded gently, although their numbers dipped during the period after Shillady's assault. In 1918, the NAACP in Texas had eleven branches with a total of 2,562 members.[23] Yet by the end of 1921, due to the violence and intimidation NAACP branches and members faced in Texas, the organization saw most of its branches in the state become dormant, and membership dropped by more than half to 1,074.[24] This climate of fear and repression did not stop Nixon from taking on causes important to him and his community. His affiliation with an alleged subversive organization such as the NAACP could have placed him in an awkward position with his medical clients or put him at odds with more conservative local leaders, but the historical record does not suggest that he in any way muted his actions.

The Lynching of Henry Lowry

The trauma Nixon underwent as a result of his experiences with racial violence did not stop him from assisting others who found themselves at the hands of bloodthirsty racist mobs. The lynching of Henry Lowry is a case in point. Lowry fled to El Paso after having murdered two whites and injured two others in Arkansas on Christmas Day 1920. Knowing that a lynch mob would kill him if he stayed, Lowry quickly left Arkansas for Mexico in order to take advantage of the safety and anonymity that the borderland was thought to possess.[25] Henry Lowry was poor and Black at a time when this combination could be deadly. His barbaric lynching made national news, landing on the front page of the *New York Times*, which reported that the mob kindly honored Lowry's request for a last meal.[26] The incident began in Nodena, Arkansas, in December 1920, when the forty-something-year-old Lowry decided, after having worked for two years, to get an accounting of his balance and depart from the farm he was working on debt free.[27]

As a sharecropper, Lowry felt trapped economically and wanted to go elsewhere to carve out his niche. For decades this region of the South had been one of the poorest in the nation.[28] He visited the home of the sixty-nine-year-old white landowner, Osben T. Craig, who was known to exploit Blacks and treat them cruelly.[29] Lucy Oliver, a sharecropper on the Craig farm, recalled years later that Osben Craig was "mean to black people" and that he "beat black folks who would let him." Lowry stood over six feet in height and had a reputation that included standing up for himself as well as his people. He commanded the respect of his fellow sharecroppers as a thirty-third-degree Mason, which was "the highest level within the Masonic order, awarded only to men of outstanding character and leadership qualities." Mrs. Lucy Oliver recalled that "Mr. Henry," as Lowry was known to the local Black community, "didn't take nothing off of nobody," including the Craig family.[30]

After the Civil War, sharecropping became entrenched as a more decentralized system of agricultural production on previously large plantations that were now divided into small plots of land, mostly thirty to fifty acres each. Plots were leased year to year to individual families, and at the end of the season they received compensation that included a share of the crop, usually one-third to one-half. Generally, sharecroppers were responsible for feeding and clothing themselves, while the landlord supplied all the farming provisions.[31] However, Osben Craig owned everything, including the tools used and the clothes worn by sharecroppers, as well as the local commissary that sharecroppers were obligated to patronize. In addition, Craig rarely settled balances or reimbursed sharecroppers' expenses; instead he worked Blacks year to year without payment.[32] During Lowry's initial meeting with Craig, Craig physically assaulted him to make the point that a proper updated accounting would not be forthcoming.[33]

On 25 December 1920, Lowry returned to the Osben Craig home and this time he was armed. Soon after Craig answered the door an argument ensued. The elder Craig threw a stick at Lowry; Lowry attempted to flee, but then he was fired on by Craig's son Richard. Lowry returned fire to defend himself, instantly killing Osben Craig and one of his married daughters.[34] Two of Craig's sons were also wounded in the exchange.[35] Lowry quickly fled the Craig property and was protected by J. T. Williams and his family, who hid Lowry in their home for two days. Henry Lowry was fortunate that the white mob that arrived at the Williamses' home did not find him. When it came time to make his escape, Lowry covered his footwear with turpentine to mask his smell from scent hounds—a common practice among southern Blacks running for their lives.[36] A mob of nearly six hundred anxiously looked for Lowry but to no avail.[37] Morris Jenkins and, his wife, Jennie Jenkins, along with Mott Orr, John Radditt, and Walter Johnson—all members of the Turrell Odd Fellows Lodge—made Lowry's escape to El Paso possible by providing logistical and financial assistance.[38]

While in El Paso, Lowry rented a room at 1201 East Third Street, which was located in the Segundo Barrio district just east of downtown. Until the mid-1960s this neighborhood was home to many of El Paso's African Americans.[39] Lowry would have been successful in making a discreet escape into Mexico had it not been for his limited funds. In the short time he spent in the city, Lowry was able to secure employment that would pay him "$40 a month and board," and he intended to send for his wife, Callie Lowry, and his daughter as soon as he could save up enough money. Soon after settling into El Paso, Lowry wrote his Masonic comrade Morris Jenkins asking him to let his family know where he was and to tell them to plan on making the journey to the Southwest in the coming months.[40] Unfortunately, Osben Craig's son Richard was the local postmaster and clerk of court, which put him in a position to intercept Lowry's letter and inform local authorities of Lowry's whereabouts. They in turn contacted El Paso officials.[41] On 19 January 1921 Lowry was arrested by Captain Claude T. Smith of the El Paso Police Department at a local downtown bank, as Lowry worked the furnace. Lowry explained to the detectives that the shooting was initiated by the Craig family and that he acted solely in self defense. Lowry of course knew his fate was sealed and stated the obvious to the arresting officer: "If they take me back to Arkansas, they'll burn me sure."[42] The same day of his arrest the landlady at his rooming house heard about Lowry's troubles and immediately contacted the local branch of the NAACP, then led by Le Roy W. Washington.[43] Washington quickly contacted Frederick C. Knollenberg, an Anglo attorney who was also a member of the El Paso NAACP, to see if he would represent Henry Lowry.[44]

Lawrence Nixon, Le Roy Washington, Fred Knollenberg, and an unnamed local minister visited Henry Lowry in jail.[45] LeRoy White, Nixon's good friend who had moved with him to El Paso in 1910, could have been the unnamed local minister. White was a founding member (1913–1914) and former president (1918) of the local NAACP and assistant pastor of Shiloh Baptist Church, which Le Roy Washington also belonged to. Nixon must have had on his mind the lynching that he had witnessed in Cameron, Texas, over a decade earlier as he stood by powerless and immobilized in his medical office in downtown Cameron. Now he found himself in the midst of a power struggle between the institutional law enforcement apparatus and a man from the working class who sorely needed assistance.

It was decided that the best course of action was for Lowry to not fight extradition efforts if Arkansas governor Thomas C. McRae would guarantee his safety in Little Rock.[46] On 20 January, Knollenberg negotiated directly with the Arkansas governor by telegraph, and McCrae gave assurances that Lowry would be protected.[47] Two days later, on 22 January, Arkansas deputies D. H. Dickson and J. J. Greer arrived in El Paso and departed the next morning with Lowry in hand.[48] Ironically, McRae "proclaimed 23 January 1921 as Law and Order Day" in Arkansas, which was the same day he communicated with Knollenberg and just days prior to Lowry's vicious lynching.[49] McRae gave orders to Arkansas deputies to bring Lowry straight to Little Rock so as to avoid the emotional atmosphere of the local community in Nodena.[50] The governor also unsuccessfully attempted to communicate with Dwight H. Blackwood, the sheriff of Mississippi County in Arkansas, to inform him of his orders that Lowry not be harmed and be fully protected from mobsters.[51] Deputies Dickson and Greer had different plans for Lowry that included taking him to Sardis, Mississippi, and tipping off mob leaders well in advance of their arrival. Sardis is 166 miles east of Little Rock, Arkansas, and 103 miles south of Nodena. Since they were arriving from the west they were grossly off course and clearly intended to deliver Lowry to hoodlums and vagabonds. This obvious detail did not escape Governor McRae's notice. He was troubled by the officers' return train route:

"The round-about way through New Orleans, Mississippi and Tennessee instead of direct to Texarkana and thence to Little Rock and the state penitentiary" was simply not logical.[52] A mob of unmasked men took Lowry "with lamb-like docility" from Dickson and Greer and publicly announced their intentions to lynch him.[53]

Lawrence Nixon would read about Lowry's fate in the *El Paso Herald*, which did not condemn the obstruction and actions of the lynchers.[54] Instead, the *Herald* indicated that Blacks should feel fortunate because the United States spends a "mere 40 minutes burning a negro," as compared to China, where the punishment of criminals for certain crimes is extended over five or six days.[55] Governor McRae, however, was outraged and stated that the lynching was "the most disreputable act ever committed in Arkansas."[56] The gory details of Lowry's public lynching would make anyone ill. In the late afternoon of 26 January 1921 nearly six hundred people descended on Osben Craig's farm to watch Henry Lowry's body slowly roast for nearly an hour while mob leaders threw dry leaves and poured gasoline on the embers. Lowry's wife and young daughter were forced to watch.[57] Lowry met the same fate as fifty-nine other African Americans that year: lynched in a nation that was "on its way to Hell and Destruction."[58]

Native Arkansan and Yale-educated William Pickens, NAACP field secretary, immediately traveled to the Delta to investigate the murder. He found that the "rural districts of Arkansas are more unsafe for colored people to-day than they were thirty-odd years ago; perhaps more than they have ever before been." The Mississippi River Valley—which encompassed Mississippi County—Pickens concluded, was the "Congo of America," where "labor is forced, and the laborer is a slave," though the form of slavery "is a cunningly contrived debt-slavery, to give the appearance of civilization and the sanction of law."[59]

In the end, Pickens blamed the sharecropping system for the lynchings that had occurred after the war. Historian Nan Elizabeth Woodruff tells us that "Pickens correctly saw the persistence of sharecropping as the root cause of much of the postwar violence that swept the Delta, yet he failed to see the other side of the issue—the growing postwar militancy of rural Delta peoples that had grown out of wartime changes."[60] The number of lynchings was indicative of the number of men and women no longer willing to remain docile. Henry Lowry's death was the result of a change in the mindset of a people. Blacks in the early twentieth century were no longer willing to stand idly by in the face of danger, violence, and injustice; they became more militant, and this militancy entailed Blacks becoming, like Lowry, more assertive in their demands for protection and constitutional rights. Many others would meet Lowry's fate in their fight for fairness, but time proved that for each man and woman who was met with aggression, dozens of others were willing to keep fighting.

Lawrence Nixon, Race, and Public Pools in El Paso

Lawrence Nixon not only took on civil and human rights issues but also became involved in local civic matters through a community organization known as the Negro Ministerial Alliance.[61] He headed this committee, and as their spokesperson he petitioned the city of El Paso in the spring of 1924 on behalf of the Black community with respect to a swimming pool that the city had agreed to build. Nixon had been given the impression the previous year that the proposed pool would be in Washington Park, the city's largest playground. Located between Alameda and Franklin canal, the popular park hosted a "bathing beach, baseball grounds, children's grounds, zoological collection," and a "free automobile camp," all of which were off limits to Blacks.[62] Having a public pool for the African American community in Washington Park, the premier recreational area in El Paso, would have confirmed the conventional wisdom that El Paso was more racially tolerant than other Texas locales. However, although the city had agreed to finance the construction of a pool for the Black community the year before, its location was the subject of dispute. Further, past and future promises notwithstanding, a public pool for Black El Pasoans would never get built, even though the El Paso City Council went so far as to approve the allocation of $17,038 for a "negro swimming pool and recreational center" south of Dudley field—an area, the council stressed, that was "not a part of Washington park, and is separated from the park and Dudley field by a canal."[63]

Members of the Negro Ministerial Alliance consisted of Lawrence A. Nixon, Jerry B. Baldwin, William B. Gray, and Le Roy W. Washington, all members of the local NAACP.[64] Baldwin was either the manager or the owner of the Elite Barber Shop and Cigar Store and at the time secretary of the El Paso NAACP.[65] William Bristow Gray was a forty-eight-year-old Black barber from Tennessee.[66] The Negro Ministerial Alliance made its formal petition for the public pool on 18 April 1924. Speaking for the organization, Nixon expressed reservations over the city's proposal to build the pool at the all-Black Douglass School. In 1923, councilmen Andrew B. Poe, a forty-seven-year-old shoe merchant, and Harvey P. Jackson, forty-four-year-old vice-president of Texas Mortgage Company, accompanied by the city engineer and Lawrence Nixon, had looked over potential sites throughout the city for a segregated pool.[67] "It seemed that a location at Washington park would be the most convenient," Nixon asserted. The Negro Ministerial Alliance was "under the impression that the matter had been decided in this way"—that the all-Black pool would be built in Washington Park and not at the Douglass School location—until, to their surprise, they read "in *The Herald* that the council had chosen a site at Douglass school" instead.[68] In 1920, Douglass School had moved one and a half miles northeast from its old location in the Mexican and Mexican American enclave of Chihuahuita.[69] At 200 Washington Street, Washington Park was two miles east of the new Douglass School location, which was at 101 South Eucalyptus Street. Many Blacks in El Paso "felt the proposed pool at the Douglass school would be inconvenient" because, as Nixon stated, the Black community "would not have the advantage of car service. If it were placed at the Douglass school it would be off the car line."[70] Presumably Nixon was referring to public transportation, which many Blacks would have relied on to get to Washington Park, since most probably did not live within walking distance or have their own vehicles.[71]

Prior to the 1920s some large northern cities had municipal pools, but few could be found elsewhere. The municipal pools that did exist in the South and the West were typically indoors, which is perplexing considering the regular heat waves this region of the country experiences. Yet during the 1920s and 1930s over a thousand communities nationwide constructed swimming pools.[72] The building occurred in two phases, the first of which lasted from 1920 to 1929. The nation's relative prosperity during this period permitted cities such as El Paso to address the increasing demand for outdoor leisure activities by building public pools.[73] Owing to generally improved working conditions, Americans now had more leisure time. Strikes, worker agitation, and reforms had forced employers to lower the number of hours they required their employees to work per week.[74] By 1920, the average time spent on the job had dropped to forty-eight hours weekly, compared to fifty-five hours in 1910 and sixty hours in the 1890s. The reduced amount of hours required at work created disposable time, resulting in a demand for recreation and leisure facilities, including public pools.[75]

The federal government initiated the second building phase in 1934, during the Great Depression, which lasted until the end of the decade. Historian Jeff Wiltse notes that the New Deal swimming pools were as "phenomenal a public works endeavor as the much-touted Grand Coulee Dam and the Tennessee Valley Authority." These public pools provided leisure and recreation for millions of Americans, "who desperately needed relief from the heat and hard times."[76] This was particularly true for the Southwest, where temperatures easily reached triple digits during the peak summer months.[77]

Many whites during this time, according to historian Wiltse, objected to swimming with African Americans for three reasons. First they feared coming into contact with the same water that Blacks had touched or swum in. The only way many whites would swim in a pool after Blacks was "if the water was drained and the tank scrubbed."[78] Many whites of the 1920s thought Blacks to be unclean, uncouth, and unhealthy—prone to carrying transmissible maladies such as smallpox, venereal diseases, and tuberculosis.[79]

Second, Wiltse asserts, many whites objected to the idea of Black men viewing the scantily clad bodies of white women and interacting with them in such "intimate and erotic public spaces." The irrational fear that Black men would act on their "supposedly untamed sexual desire for white women" by accidentally or purposely touching them perpetuated sexism and racism, restricting white women's social and sexual choices by limiting their opportunities to meet and form relationships with Black men.[80]

Third, whites worried that exposed Black male bodies at public pools could pose a threat to white masculinity. "Turn of the century manhood," writes Gail Bederman, "constructed bodily strength and social authority as identical." The integration of public pools during the interwar years would have resulted in a number of Black men displaying "powerful and muscular physiques and thereby conspicuously" challenging whites and their racist notions of Blacks being physically and biologically inferior.[81]

Richard Dudley, the mayor of El Paso from 1923 to 1925, told Lawrence Nixon and the alliance that he was "in favor of a pool for negroes, and if the bond issue carries, a pool will be built. We will consult with your people and a site will be chosen which will be satisfactory to all concerned."[82] "To all concerned" was coded language for "Anglos," who would have the last word on where the all-Black pool should be located. No mention is made in newspaper accounts as to where Mexican Americans went to swim, sunbathe, and wade.

As mayor, Dudley undertook the construction of numerous public buildings and recreational facilities, but he staunchly opposed the idea of building the pool for Black El Pasoans in close proximity to the popular whites-only pool in Washington Park, stating, "I have never been, and am not now, in favor of a pool for negroes in the park." If an all-Black pool were built adjacent to the all-white pool in heavily used Washington Park, it would bring many El Pasoans in close proximity to each other, socially and sexually, thus raising the specter of violating the racial etiquette of the city. It was no doubt for this reason that Dudley stated that he was "against having the two pools in the park. The council voted in favor of building a pool for you, and I am strongly in favor of carrying it out," but he told Nixon patronizingly that he wanted "to see it put in a place that would be to your best interests. I would advocate the arrest of a white man for interfering with your liberties just as quickly as I would that of a negro."[83]

Furthermore, Dudley stressed that El Paso has "always had perfect harmony between the two races" and that he thought "it would be unwise to create a situation that might lead to trouble."[84] The son of a Baptist preacher and a child of the segregated South who was born and raised during the Civil War and Reconstruction era, Dudley was a moderate Democrat who was not about to challenge the racial norms that El Paso wanted to preserve.[85] Clearly, the mayor was thinking about his political standing, expediency, and reelection when he declared,

> there has always existed in El Paso the best possible feeling between the negroes and whites and I do not think it would be the part of wisdom to promote anything that would tend to disturb that feeling. *We are not going to start any war.* I am opposed to putting the swimming pool in Washington Park because I think we could find a more appropriate place. You are entitled to a pool and we are going to build one, but I am not going to do anything I think would create *trouble for myself* or anyone else.[86]

Dudley's suggestion of a possible race "war" implied that Anglos in El Paso could easily erupt in anger and become violent if forced to share the same park with Blacks.

Conceivably still fresh on the minds of many, including Dudley and others in El Paso, were the racially charged disturbances of the previous five years, including the riots that occurred in twenty-five cities across the nation during the 1919 "red summer," a phrase coined by James Weldon Johnson and meant to underscore the amount of blood that was shed by African Americans in these riots. Violence erupted in Longview, Texas, just twenty-three miles west of Marshall—Lawrence Nixon's town of birth and upbringing—in July 1919. Chicago likewise witnessed racial mayhem in July, while Elaine, Arkansas, saw a riot in October 1919 and Greenwood, Oklahoma, saw one in June 1921.[87] In May 1922 a month-long reign of terror was carried out against Blacks in Kirvin, Texas, during which time there were multiple lynchings.[88] The Rosewood massacre in Florida in January 1923 made national news, dozens of African Americans having been killed, including Sam Carter, Lexie Gordon, Mingo Williams, Sarah Carrier, James Carrier, and Sylvester Carrier.[89]

Lawrence Nixon departed from the city chambers after the mayor issued his paternalistically racist statements, but not without leaving the formal written swimming pool petition with the city council asking for the Washington Park location.[90] Blacks in El Paso would never secure their own pool as promised by the Dudley administration.[91] However, nearly thirty years later, in 1953, it would become a moot point, since most public pools throughout the nation were required to integrate after a variety of successful legal challenges. The *El Paso Herald-Post* reported that by refusing to review the case of *Williams vs. Swope Swimming Pool*, "the Supreme Court ruled in effect" that Blacks "must be admitted to the Swope Park Municipal Swimming and Wading Pool in Kansas City, Mo.," upholding the court of appeals injunction "requiring the admission" of Blacks "to the half million dollar pool."[92]

African Americans in El Paso continued to fight for respect and the allocation of resources to meet the needs of their community, resulting in a minor victory nine years later in 1933, when the city, under park commissioner Hugo Myer, did allow Blacks to use the Seventh Street swimming pool on "alternative four day periods."[93] Two months later, in October 1933, Anglo attorney Frederick Knollenberg pressed forward with Nixon's pool request when he himself presented a petition signed by 123 people (one of whom was perhaps Nixon, since he knew Knollenberg through the NAACP) to the city council asking that a swimming pool for Blacks be built in the new addition the city had proposed for Washington Park. The petition experienced a similar fate as Nixon's: it too was ignored and immediately "tabled."[94]

El Paso's 1923 Juneteenth Celebration

Although African Americans in El Paso never did secure their own pool, they nevertheless appeared to have some influence over local Anglo political elites when these elites sought votes. In June 1923, Dudley County attorney Will H. Pelphrey and Sheriff Seth Orndorff would place themselves directly before the Black community in an effort to sway voters by attending the Juneteenth celebration program at Pastime Park in east El Paso.

Juneteenth is a holiday that celebrates the emancipation of the African captives in Texas after Union forces arrived in the state and on 19 June 1865 declared the institution of slavery illegal, thus enforcing Lincoln's previously ignored 1 January 1863 Emancipation Proclamation. Since then Blacks in Texas have annually observed their Freedom Day, and beginning in the 1990s this observance spread to other parts of the country, becoming an official holiday in a number of other states.[95] In 1918 the NAACP chapter in El Paso attempted to initiate a movement "to concentrate on the observance of the real emancipation day, according to history, the anniversary" of which was 1 January.[96] The unsuccessful campaign was viewed as an elitist attempt to neglect the folk traditions of the masses, and most of El Paso's Black community continued to support the 19 June date.[97]

At El Paso's 1923 Juneteenth celebration, Mayor Dudley denounced lynchings and affirmed "a square deal" for all races.[98] The phrase "square deal" was coined by President Theodore Roosevelt "in the 1904 election to convey the essence of his domestic policies for the economy and antitrust actions: a 'square deal' for laborers and consumers as well as big business." In the years following Roosevelt's initial use of the phrase, "square deal" became synonymous with "fair treatment" or "an equitable arrangement."[99]

Sheriff Orndorff further stated that African Americans in El Paso County had made "remarkable progress" and referenced the large number of Black employees in his lower valley ranch, who were "giving excellent service and rearing their families to be good citizens."[100] In addition, Black leader Jasper Williams, first president of the El Paso NAACP, was on hand to give a speech:

> I have a profound respect for the M.E. [Methodist Episcopal] church, for Abraham Lincoln, the great emancipator, for the Republican party of Lincoln, and for all other agencies that have contributed towards the uplift of the negro in America. The negro is an American to all intents and purposes. Of all the races which have contributed to the peopling of this nation none has shown more enthusiastic loyalty then [*sic*] the negro. His war record is excellent, covering a period from 1788 to the present. America's march toward . . . wealth and world power has been stimulated by the product of negro labor, by genius of negro intellect and by his unfaltering citizenship. The negro has tried to answer Lincoln's call to the higher life by buying homes, building churches, schools, banks and powerful insurance companies. He has answered the civilization around him by copying its virtue and vices. He has answered the teachings of the church by forgiving more than any other race on earth has been called upon to forgive.[101]

It is interesting that Williams would be so complimentary toward Republicans while in the presence of at least one Democrat, Mayor Dudley, and perhaps more (the county attorney and sheriff may also have been Democrats). It shows Williams's political courage and refusal to mute his words regardless of his audience and demonstrates his confidence in his virtue.

It is unknown whether Lawrence Nixon attended either Juneteenth celebration on this day, though he scarcely could have been unaware of the attention Blacks were receiving from the political class of El Paso. This attention may have given Nixon hope that with continued pressure from Black community activists such as himself and members of the local NAACP, which included Afro-Latinos such as Rudolph W. López, Jews such as Louis Laskin, and Protestant Anglos such as Fred Knollenberg, the racial climate in El Paso might become more nuanced.[102]

Unfortunately, Nixon was not triumphant in his quest to integrate public pools in El Paso, nor in his attempt to protect Lowry from the terrorism of furious whites. His next foray into leadership and activism would test his persistence and perseverance—even more so than his previous experiences in El Paso. As we shall see in the next chapter, his efforts to secure the vote for Blacks in Texas during the Democratic primaries would become a twenty-year protracted struggle, but one that resulted in victory for African Americans.

CHAPTER 4

Nixon, the NAACP, and the Courts, 1924–1934

We are looking for someone who is not afraid.
William Pickens, 1923

Lawrence Nixon once said that the Black man just "wants true democracy as laid down in the constitution, and feels he will be satisfied if he gets that."[1] Was the ballot, then, the ticket to freedom for Black America? Joseph Madison, former NAACP voter registration director, argued that "it has been the ticket to the train but the train has not arrived at the final destination which would be the sharing of wealth and power. The great problem is that in many black communities there is not even a stop to board the train."[2] In the decades following Nixon's involvement in the struggle for political participation, the right to vote remained an important component of the NAACP's strategic approach. The logic was that unrestricted access to the polls and the "intelligent" use of the ballot would provide the Black community with the tools necessary "to win inclusion into the democratic and egalitarian promise of America."[3]

Nixon helped lay the foundation for Black voting rights in the South as the central plaintiff in two landmark U.S. Supreme Court cases: *Nixon v. Herndon* (1927) and *Nixon v. Condon* (1932), and the little-discussed case of *Nixon v. McCann* (1934), Nixon's third attempt to dismantle the all-white Democratic primary.[4] Nixon, along with the NAACP, helped set legal precedent that ultimately led, in *Smith v. Allwright* (1944), to the dismantling of all-white primaries throughout the entire South.[5] The political and social climate at the local, state, and national levels during the 1920s, as well as the 1923 Texas law that barred African Americans from voting in the Democratic primaries, compelled Nixon and the

NAACP to take action. Change was brewing for the South, and though for many the change brought hope, there were others who saw this change as a threat.

El Paso and the Ku Klux Klan

Nearly six decades had passed since the end of the Civil War and the passing of the Thirteenth Amendment, but the war still burned in many southern communities. In December 1865, soon after the Civil War ended, six former Confederates met in a law office in Pulaski, Tennessee, and cofounded a secret society that became known as the Ku Klux Klan. The organization grew and eventually began to engage in violence and terror. The group's membership flourished during the Reconstruction era but eventually began to decline by the late 1870s.[6]

The Klan that regained strength in 1915 vehemently hated not only African Americans but also Japanese and other Asians, Roman Catholics, Jews, and all foreign-born individuals.[7] Many people tend to associate the revival of the twentieth-century Klan with the infamous film *The Birth of a Nation*. This controversial movie glorified the Klan and represented Blacks as inept and corrupt, suggesting at the same time that they had dominated southern politics during the Reconstruction period. The film played an important role in increasing the Klan's membership. The film actually preceded the start of the Klan's revival, which originated in Atlanta, Georgia. *The Clansman*—the film's original name— first premiered in Riverside, California, on 1 January 1915. It then made its way to Los Angeles on 8 February 1915 and eventually to the White House on 18 February 1915, where it received a warm reception from President Woodrow Wilson. It was on this occasion that Supreme Court chief justice Edward D. White, a former Confederate soldier, confided to Thomas Dixon—the film's writer—that he had once been a member of the KKK. Since he felt the nation was making a new start after the Civil War, Dixon encouraged the filmmaker to change the title to *The Birth of a Nation* for its premier in New York City on 3 March 1915.[8]

The Klan's revival is attributed to the unjust lynching of Jewish businessman Leo Frank in 1915 for his alleged involvement in the killing of Mary Phagan, a young white woman.[9] On 16 August 1915, after outgoing Georgia governor John Slayton commuted Frank's death sentence to life in prison, a lynch mob from Marietta killed Frank. Three months after this tragedy, Thomas Watson, a former congressman and leader in the Populist Party, encouraged the revival of the Klan as a means of restoring local rule.[10] On 26 October 1915, a formal application was submitted to the state of Georgia for the Klan's charter, and a month later initial members climbed up Stone Mountain, where they engaged in their first ritual and ceremonial cross burning.[11]

The Birth of a Nation premiered in Atlanta on 6 December 1915 with much anticipation and buzz, resulting in a recruitment bonanza for the terrorist organization. By 1921, the organization had spread, with the film's assistance, throughout the West and North and had a membership of about one hundred thousand. Four years later, membership in the Klan had risen to nearly five million across four thousand local chapters.[12] Although the Klan may have originated in the South, the organization of the 1920s had more support and members in the North, including the states of Indiana, Ohio, and Illinois.[13] The Klan had more members than other well-known and large groups such as the American Federation of Labor.[14]

The main driver of the Klan's spectacular rise in 1920s was that it provided "individuals with an effective vehicle for preserving status-based political and economic interests."[15] The Klan also appealed to many during this era because of the tremendous changes the nation was undergoing. According to a leading historian of the Klan, the typical recruit

> is tossed about in the hurly-burly of our industrial and so called democratic society. Under the stress of social competition he is made to realize his essential mediocrity. Yet according to traditional democratic doctrine he is born free and the equal of the fellow who is out-distancing him in the race. Here is a large and powerful organization offering to solace his sense of defeat by dubbing him a knight of the Invisible Empire for the small sum of ten dollars. Surely knighthood was never offered at such a bargain![16]

In Texas, Klan membership increased sharply in the early 1920s when imperial wizard William Simmons personally helped bring the organization to Houston. Its rapid spread to cities and towns throughout the state, including El Paso, resulted in tens of thousands of new members joining the ranks of the organization. In El Paso particularly, a perception of a general breakdown of law, order, and social morality drove the rapid rise in the Klan's popularity.[17] A dramatic increase in violent attacks against Texan Blacks ensued. According to John Hope Franklin and Alfred Moss,

> In Texas the Klan became the instrument of a new enslavement, forcing blacks to work and pick cotton at wages they would not have accepted if the decision had been left to them. Throughout the South and Southwest African Americans lived in constant fear of the hooded bands of night riders who burned crosses to terrify those whom they considered undesirables. In the West the Klan was also active, especially against the Japanese. There were floggings, brandings with acid, episodes of tarring and feathering, hangings, and burnings. The victims were largely, though not entirely, African Americans.[18]

In March 1921, Klansmen castrated Black Houston dentist John Lafayette Cockrell, killed nine African Americans throughout the state in May 1922, and tarred and feathered Black Houston dentist R. H. Ward in 1925.[19]

To place El Paso's Klan activities in local and national perspective, it is important to keep in mind that in the early 1920s only four other cities—outside of Texas—in the entire country had more Klan rallies during those years than El Paso, which had a total of 7. These cities included Terre Haute, Indiana (12 rallies), Indianapolis (16), Altoona, Pennsylvania (17), and Pittsburgh, Pennsylvania (15). Texas led the nation with the most Klan rallies during this era—216 scattered throughout 112 cities. Of Texas cities, El Paso ranked third. Only Fort Worth and Dallas had more, with 12 and 23 respectively. Houston had 4 and San Antonio had 6.[20] These Klan activities were indicative of Texas's dangerous racist attitudes toward Blacks and other minority groups.

By 1920, El Paso had the second largest Mexican/Mexican American population of any U.S. city (San Antonio had the most) and was the only major southwestern city with more Mexicans and Mexican Americans than Anglos.[21] Their large numbers in the city attracted the ire of the local Klan because most Mexicans and Mexican Americans were nonwhite, Roman Catholic, and perceived to be un-American. The Klan continued to hate Blacks, but it also extended its disdain to Catholics, Jews, immigrants, labor unions, communists, and socialists. Klan leaders such as Hiram Wesley Evans, a Dallas dentist who became the Klan's imperial wizard from 1922 to 1939, summed up the group's sentiments about Blacks: "The Negro is not a menace to Americanism in the sense that the Jew or Roman Catholic is a menace. He is not actually hostile to it. He is simply racially incapable of understanding, sharing in or contributing to Americanism."[22] The Klan also targeted for attack Anglo "moral transgressors and bootleggers" in its "crusade for conformity."[23] El Paso's geographic location was ripe for Klan rhetoric. In the first half of the 1920s, the Mexican Revolution and the conflict that ensued on the U.S./Mexico border was still fresh in the minds of many, bringing a sense of insecurity that caused many Anglos to become convinced that Mexicans on both sides of the border "were cruel mercurial people inherently prone toward social disorganization."[24]

Maintaining law and order in El Paso required upholding the prohibition of liquor, causing a rise in crime due to its lucrative illegal distribution. For many middle-class Protestants of the time—including those aspiring to the middle class—abstinence from alcohol was thought to differentiate them from working-class people. Protecting children from exposure to alcohol and other addictive drugs was important to Klansmen in El Paso.[25] In February 1923, John W. Dye, U.S. consul in Ciudad Juárez, reported that a grand jury investigation "revealed that drugs are being peddled to school children in El Paso," and in at least one instance a seventeen-year-old "prominent and popular society girl of El Paso" died following a "dope party" in Juárez.[26] Incidents such as these helped the Klan's recruitment efforts by demonstrating that its services were needed to protect the community and especially children from the threat of alcohol and other drugs.

During the first half of the 1920s, El Paso had between fifteen hundred and thirty-five hundred Klan members, a small number of whom were police officers.[27] Klan activism rooted deeply in southern politics was directed toward ensuring that "100 percent Americans" were elected to political office. The Klan's success in Texas was enough to see to it that Earle B. Mayfield became the first member of the Ku Klux Klan to join the U.S. Senate in 1922. Nearly seventy-five other congressmen were elected to the U.S. House of Representatives as a result of Klan politicking.[28] After defeating ex-governor and anti-Klan candidate James E. Ferguson in the Democratic primary, Mayfield went on to defeat Republican challenger George E. B. Peddy in the general election. The defeated Ferguson charged that in Dallas "the Ku Klux Klan is in the saddle. It has elected nearly all the county officials, and the law, therefore, can be violated with impunity."[29] Simply put, the Klan derived its prestige and support from political and civic leaders, and "without them the organization would have had no real base of power from which to expand."[30]

In the process of advocating efficient government at the local level, Klan leaders attacked Catholics for their alleged political fraud. Combining the themes of immigration and corruption, the Klan claimed that "in certain Texas towns like El Paso, and Corpus Christi, and in many towns in Arizona and New Mexico where the Roman Catholic influence is a power in politics, these Mexicans are voted at the polls like sheep in order to thwart government by loyal Americans."[31] Charles V. Porras, a Mexican American from El Paso who was born in 1901 and one of the election judges that would deny Nixon the ballot in the 1924 Democratic primary, recalled the physical intimidation and fear that many Mexican and Mexican Americans had in regard to voting or political activism. "They feared for physical hurt from the majority of the so-called Anglos. Because in those days, shooting down a Mexican was not looked upon as any serious crime," Porras stated.[32]

It was in this climate—the Klan deeply entrenched in the minds of many in El Paso—that Nixon began to challenge the revised 1923 Terrell Election Law that barred African Americans from voting in the Democratic primary. This law dated back to Alexander Watkins Terrell, father of the Terrell Election Law of 1905, which mandated the poll tax requirement. In regard to Blacks, chapter 32 of the *General Laws of the State of Texas*, titled "Qualifications of Voters in Democratic Primaries," explicitly states that under the 1923 Terrell Law,

> all qualified voters under the laws and Constitution of the State of Texas who are bona fide members of the Democratic party, shall be eligible to participate in any Democratic party primary election, provided such voter complies with all laws and rules governing party primary elections; however, in no event shall a negro be eligible to participate in a democratic party primary election held in the state of Texas, and should a negro vote in a Democratic primary election, such ballot shall be void and election officials are herein directed to throw out such ballot and not count the same.[33]

This amendment, SB 44, was proposed in early 1923 by Texas state representative Douglas Davenport of Bexar County. State senator Richard M. Dudley, who later would become El Paso's mayor, prevented the bill from coming to the floor during the first regular session. Yet Texas governor Pat M. Neff resurrected the bill during the second session of the legislature, saying, "It's a demand of the Democratic platform, isn't it?" Dudley was not able to defeat the bill during this second attempt, and the house passed the bill by a vote of ninety-three to eleven. The bill was presented to Governor Neff on 10 May 1923, and inexplicably it became law ninety days after adjournment without his signature.[34]

Prelude to the Revised 1923 Law

The roots of the Terrell Law of 1923 can be traced back to Texas's Reconstruction era. After the Civil War, southern whites developed strategies to suppress and eventually eliminate Black political participation and in particular voting. One strategy that southern states in the 1870s and 1880s employed to minimize the Black vote was to pass laws granting the legislature or the governor the power to appoint local government officials who had previously been selected by popular vote. Black politicians were not often appointed, and so the interests of Blacks were frequently ignored. Another tactic was to divide Black majorities into multiple voting districts so they could always be outvoted by unified white voters. In other southern states the opposite approach was taken by gathering the Black voting bloc into a single district so that the Black vote could swing only a single election out of multiple contests.[35]

Yet another gambit was the poll tax. In 1902 the Texas constitution was amended, as in many southern states, to require the payment of a poll tax as a qualification for voting.[36] By this time, most southern states had already adopted the poll tax as a prerequisite for voting, including Georgia (1877), Virginia

(1876–1882; 1901–1902), Mississippi (1890), South Carolina (1895), Louisiana (1898), and North Carolina (1900). Regrettably, in *Williams v. Mississippi* (1898), the U.S. Supreme Court ruled that the poll tax prerequisite was not discriminatory.[37] Before the tax's 1902 adoption in Texas, white voting rates stood well above 60 percent: 88 percent in 1900 and 62 percent in 1902. However, in 1904 only 46 percent of whites voted. The dramatic reduction was followed by a voting rate of just 27 percent of eligible voters in the next election.[38] The poll tax, in conjunction with disenfranchising techniques such as literacy tests and understanding clauses, allowed the South to evade the reach of the federal government.

A brief history of the repeated attempts to impose the poll tax is vital to the understanding of its final adoption. Terrell, a Civil War Confederate veteran, carried weight in Democratic circles, having served as a judge in the state courts, as a member of the Texas legislature, and as American diplomat to Turkey.[39] During his tenure as a member of the legislature in 1878, he repeatedly introduced poll tax legislation. Some may view the poll tax as having been targeted at poor whites who supported the Populist movement during the 1890s.[40] But the evidence suggests that it was Blacks who were the main targets of the poll tax. Five of the eight attempts to impose a poll tax occurred before the rise of Populism in Texas, and two others before the fusion movement of 1896 posed any real threat to the political hegemony of the Democrats in the state. No doubt it was also intended to serve as a voter registration system to prevent repeat voting among cowboys and labor gangs in West Texas and other mobile portions of the population. But the fear of African Americans voting, particularly within the Black Belt of Texas, was the overriding issue.[41]

The poll tax amendment was approved by a substantial majority during the election held on 4 November 1902.[42] In February 1903, the Texas legislature passed the first Terrell Election Law, which provided for the regulation of party primary elections and conventions. One of the provisions of this law was that all qualified voters should be eligible to vote in any party primary, so long as they took and passed the prescribed party test. Up to the time that this law was enacted, party committees controlled nominations and conventions.[43] This primary law became particularly important, since Texas was essentially a one-party state, and primaries of the Democratic Party determined election to statewide, district, and county offices. African Americans continued to vote, albeit in lesser numbers.[44] The practice of paying poll taxes for Blacks and Mexicans in exchange for their votes became common among politicians. It was so common, in fact, that the Terrell Election Law of 1905 declared such a practice to be a misdemeanor.[45]

The question of admitting or barring African Americans in Democratic primary elections was a pressing one for the 1903 and 1905 laws. The 1903 Terrell Election Law declared that "the county executive committee of the party holding any primary election may prescribe additional qualifications necessary to participate therein."[46] Since there were no other statewide qualifications for voting in primary elections, the Democratic Party in the state could, if it wished, bar Blacks from voting in a primary by having county executive committees outline additional rules targeted at African American voters. But even these provisions were not good enough for the political elites of the Lone Star State. Many Texas whites were opposed to Blacks casting any vote in the Democratic primary no matter how few their numbers.[47]

Between 29 August and 5 September 1923, just months after Governor Neff supported and approved the amendment to the Terrell election law, the NAACP held its Fourteenth Annual Conference in Kansas City, Missouri. The NAACP selected Kansas City to lend moral support to the fifty-four former military men of the Third Battalion of the all-Black Twenty-Fourth Infantry at Leavenworth Federal Prison. These soldiers were wrongfully convicted for engaging in a 1917 uprising against whites in Houston, Texas. Led by James Weldon Johnson, over 558 delegates, including LeRoy W. Washington of El Paso's NAACP, proclaimed 11 November 1923 as "Houston Martyrs' Day."[48] Representative Leonidas C. Dyer, a white Republican from Missouri, addressed the conference and spoke about new plans to reintroduce the Dyer Antilynching Bill during the next session of Congress, a bill he had first introduced in 1919.[49] The bill, HR 13, had passed the House chamber by a vote of 231 to 119 on 16 January 1922 but saw its defeat in December 1922 by a Democratic filibuster in the Senate.[50]

During this 1923 meeting, NAACP field secretary William Pickens instructed LeRoy Washington to return to El Paso and find a Black Democrat to "present himself at the polls at the time of the election."[51] Pickens stressed, "We are looking for someone who is not afraid."[52] Given the history of violence and terrorism against African Americans in the state and in particular the activities of the Ku Klux Klan, locating a Black person who was not afraid in Texas was by no means an easy task. LeRoy Washington thought immediately of his longtime friend Lawrence Nixon.[53]

Four months after this meeting between Pickens and Washington, Lawrence Nixon paid his poll tax, just as he had done the previous thirteen years. The amount was $1.75, and Robert D. Richey, El Paso County tax collector, issued the poll tax receipt on 15 January 1924. The receipt indicates that the forty-one-year-old Nixon had been a resident of both the city and the county for fourteen years, his occupation was listed as "MD," his address as 2029 Myrtle, and his precinct number as nine. Nixon's poll tax qualified him to vote in elections, and the records state that he did indeed vote in a local election on 7 May 1924.[54]

It also made him a good candidate to challenge the revised 1923 Texas Terrell Election Law, because the NAACP needed someone who had regularly paid his poll tax. The NAACP looked for several other qualifications as well, which Nixon likewise possessed. The person had to be an African American registered as a Democrat. Soon after arriving in El Paso in 1910, Lawrence Nixon paid his poll tax and registered to vote as a Democrat, notwithstanding the political philosophy of his father. During much of Charles B. Nixon's lifetime most Black people throughout the country were either registered members of or sympathetic to the Republican Party because of the party's role in abolishing slavery and its attempts to secure some civil rights for African Americans. This history of party loyalty made it difficult for many Blacks to break away from the Republican Party, even in Texas, where Republicans were by the 1920s politically irrelevant.[55] Charles B. Nixon was among those Blacks who had this mindset; he claimed he "had no respect for a Negro Democrat" and felt that a Black man "would not want to vote with the Democrats."[56]

The prominent political scientist Ronald Walters reminds us that

one of the first questions Black leaders faced was the character of their position toward the Republican party in the post-1877 period. The natural inclination of most Blacks was to continue to vote Republican and hope to weather the storm of neglect. Others, however, felt that a discipline inherent in providing political support to a party is that when it betrays the interests of the group, that support should be withdrawn and the party, thereby, punished. Accordingly, by the early 1900s there had developed among some Black leaders (notably among what would become the Niagara Movement group of 1905), an anti-Republican sentiment. However, Black leaders with this tendency were effectively cancelled out by the more moderate leadership of Booker T. Washington and his associates, who still counseled Blacks to vote for Republican candidates.[57]

The Democratic Party was viewed as the white man's party, and those few Blacks who did join risked being called a "house negro" or an "Uncle Tom." Prominent Black nationalist and intellectual Hubert H. Harrison explains that as recently as the turn of the twentieth century, Blacks "who joined the Democratic Party were regarded by their fellows much as white Americans [came to] regard pacifists and pro-Germans in War time—and they were treated accordingly."[58]

Ironically, it appears that William Pickens also had reservations about African American Democrats. Throughout the 1920s and 1930s, Pickens believed

Democratic presidential candidates should be a third choice for Blacks, after Socialists or Progressives and Republicans.[59] Nixon's decision to become a registered Democrat in Texas is a bold example of his independent thinking on the issue of party affiliation. Undoubtedly, most of his clients, friends, and neighbors in El Paso, as well as his own attorney, were Republicans, but he nevertheless affiliated with the Democrats at least at the local level.

It was not so much that Nixon believed in the ideals and philosophy of the traditional Democratic Party; rather, he understood that during this time in Texas the Democratic Party was the only party Blacks could turn to if they wanted to engage in the political process.[60] Like James Monroe Trotter, father of civil rights activist William Monroe Trotter, Nixon was "characteristically independent." When Republican president Rutherford B. Hayes withdrew the last federal troops from the South in 1877, James Trotter considered it an affront to Black people. By 1883, the elder Trotter had become even more disillusioned: "Although it cannot be fairly claimed that the colored 'break' from the so-called Republican party has been general, yet it has been of proportions so large as to occasion surprise and delight." He also proudly asserted, "we did not go over to the Democrats, the Democrats came to us."[61]

The person the NAACP backed also had to derive personal income independently of the white community. Whoever would rise to the challenge needed to not depend on whites for a livelihood and financial survival. This almost required that the person be of the professional, educated class. Nixon certainly had a middle-class educational background, and his medical practice allowed him to sustain his family, since most of his Mexican, Mexican American, and African American patients could not receive medical services from other physicians. Even so, Nixon may have felt the financial pinch for his political assertiveness and actions. Drusilla Nixon commented that she felt "in some of his business dealings he was sort of rebuffed" because of his involvement in the NAACP cases.[62]

Finally, the person had to be courageous, particularly during this time when racial violence against African Americans was increasingly tolerated at the highest levels of government. Years later, Drusilla Nixon aptly stated that "any place that there was anyone trying to change things, there was always trouble." She also recalled that "my husband's lawyer [Frederick C. Knollenberg], the same lawyer who took this case, said to him, 'Get rid of all your property but what you're living in because this thing [challenging the Texas all-white Democratic primary] is going to be like a snowball, and you might have to leave suddenly.'" Drusilla also said that Lawrence told her that "some of the people who had been very good friends quit speaking to him" because they were not pleased by his challenging the status quo. These Black detractors felt that Nixon was "going to stir up trouble" for them—and they proved to be correct.[63]

The stage was thus set: on a fateful summer day—26 July 1924—Nixon tried to vote in El Paso. He was stopped by two men, election judges Champ C. Herndon and Charles V. Porras, who refused Nixon's request to vote in the Democratic primary despite his being a longtime Democrat who had his poll tax paid and had a receipt to prove it. Nixon's Anglo attorney, Fred Knollenberg, filed a $5,000 damage suit against Herndon and Porras in the federal district court. Knollenberg charged that the 1923 Texas law violated the Fifteenth Amendment that provided that all qualified voters were permitted to vote. Attorney William H. Fryer and attorney Robert E. Cunningham, who was also the chairman of the El Paso City Democratic Executive Committee, represented the defendants, Herndon and Porras. Fryer and Cunningham presented three arguments. First, they maintained that the election judges acted properly because the rules were established by the Democratic Party, a private entity. Second, they asserted that Nixon's Fifteenth Amendment rights were not violated. And lastly, they claimed that the issues being raised by the plaintiff were more political in nature and thus beyond the scope of the court's jurisdiction. The case lingered in the courts for six months before Fryer and Cunningham asked Judge Du Val West of the U.S. district court in San Antonio for a dismissal, which he gladly provided on 4 December 1924.[64]

In 1925, the Supreme Court of the United States agreed to hear *Nixon v. Herndon* on writ of error. The NAACP then sent Knollenberg and his law partner Robert J. Channell much-needed assistance, which arrived via the organization's National Legal Committee.[65] The attorneys who joined Knollenberg and Channell included some of the best legal minds the nation had to offer at that time—African American James A. Cobb, progressive Arthur B. Spingarn, Jewish advocate Louis Marshall, and former abolitionist Moorfield Storey. After several years of numerous delays, the case was finally argued on 4 January 1927.[66] Two months later, a reversal was issued; a unanimous decision was rendered on 7 March 1927 in favor of Lawrence Nixon. Based on the premise of "the denial of equal rights of the law," the court ruled "that the Texas law prohibiting negroes from voting in the Democratic Primary was unconstitutional."[67] The justices on the bench were chief justice and former U.S. president William H. Taft and associate justices Oliver W. Holmes Jr., Willis Van Devanter, James C. McReynolds, Louis Brandeis, George Sutherland, Pierce Butler, Edward T. Sanford, and Harlan F. Stone. The *Beaumont Journal* extolled Holmes's opinion as "a masterpiece of lucid reasoning" and discredited the 1923 law barring Black Democrats as "the high-water mark of legislative folly that attempts to cure all evils by statute." The *Houston Post-Dispatch* countered sarcastically, observing that "some day as many as seventeen negroes might attempt to enter our primaries and swamp our one million or so patriots."[68]

The ruling was an important victory for the NAACP, whose defense fund received significant monies from the Garland Fund, making the case possible.[69] Dean J. R. Reynolds of Haven Teachers College in Meridian, Mississippi, wrote Nixon two days after the decision comparing the verdict to the famous *Dred Scott v. Sandford* (1857) ruling; he made a donation to help "swell the coffers" of the NAACP, hoping that "every Negro in America would send at least $1 so that more than a million dollars would pile up in this defense fund."[70] James Weldon Johnson, NAACP secretary, regarded the decision "as one of the most far-reaching since the Civil War."[71]

This view of the high court's edict was not, however, shared by Arkansas senator Thaddeus H. Caraway, who "expressed astonishment at the decision of the United States Supreme Court in the Texas primary case, denying the right of a state to deprive Negroes of the vote."[72] Texas governor Dan Moody concurred, saying ominously that "some legislation will be necessary to protect the ballot. . . . Certainly the Legislature can give the Party Executive Committee power to fix qualifications of primary voters."[73] In the summer of 1927, Nixon, evidently concerned by these gestures, took the time from his busy medical practice to write fellow Texan Charles I. Francis of Wichita Falls, who was the vice chairman of the state Democratic executive committee. In his letter, Nixon stressed how important it was for the Texas Democratic Party to embrace the Supreme Court's decision and no longer try to prevent Blacks from voting. Francis responded by advising Nixon that "the Republican Party in its platform and through its presidential nominee has made a bid for Negro support, and it may be that the Republican policies are more in line with your ideas of government than those of the Democratic Party of Texas."[74]

Back in El Paso, the reaction on the part of the political elite was equally negative. "Negroes will never vote in Texas Democratic Primaries," stressed Robert Cunningham, chairman of the El Paso City Democratic Executive Committee. County judge Edward B. McClintock agreed, commenting, "Supreme Court or no Supreme Court, here is one executive chairman who will see that they [Black people] do not vote."[75] McClintock further asserted that "the Supreme Court has held the Texas Democratic primary law prohibiting Negroes from voting unconstitutional, but they can't keep the various local executive committees from passing rules prohibiting the Negro vote."[76]

Since, as one white newspaper observed, "the [Texas] Democratic primary in ninety-nine cases out of a hundred, determines in this state what men shall rule over the Negro citizen," it was only logical that Black people wanted to vote in the primaries.[77] The Texas Democratic primary was tantamount to the general election, and Black people naturally wanted to have a say in that outcome, given that the Republican Party was ineffectual, if not nonexistent.[78] The Texas white primary statute was the only one of its kind in the country. In other southern states, African Americans were excluded from Democratic primaries by party rule, not by state statute. *Nixon v. Herndon* had little, if any, impact on the constitutionality of white primaries in other states.[79]

Two months after *Nixon v. Herndon*, on 9 May 1927 newly elected Texas governor Daniel J. Moody, a conservative Democrat, asked the legislature to repeal article 3107, which the Supreme Court had declared unconstitutional, and recommended a new law that would give state political parties, including the Democratic executive committees, the authority to determine eligibility to vote in their primaries.[80] Although objections were raised, the law passed. At least one House of Representatives member, Alexander Royce Stout, recognized how misguided the statute was: "In my humble judgment, it is far more dangerous to entrust our whole political destiny to a few men than the scare of the Negro question can ever be. I believe the whole affair makes a mountain out of nothingness, and it is un-American and un-democratic." Stout's concerns about the implications of such a law were coupled with an assertion that in any case the governor's new law would not be necessary since the South "has always handled the 'nigger' in a satisfactory manner and will continue to do so."[81]

As expected, the executive committee of the Texas state Democratic Party quickly passed a resolution excluding Blacks from party membership.[82] Nixon obviously objected to this and said as much in a letter he wrote in July 1928 to W. L. Thornton, a Democratic committeeman in Dallas: "I demand that you and the members of the Democratic Executive Committee of the State of Texas, amend your instructions so as to allow me, and all other qualified Negro Democratic voters to participate in the Primary, or we will be compelled to enforce our rights in the Federal Court."[83] Under the authority of Texas law, the executive committee of the Texas Democratic Party created a rule that indicated "all white Democrats who are qualified under the constitution and laws of Texas" would be allowed to vote. Predictably, when Lawrence Nixon attempted to vote in the Democratic primary in July 1928, election officials in El Paso, Charles H. Kolle and James C. Condon, refused him the ballot, citing the amendment to the voting law that the Texas legislature had passed the previous year.[84] This refusal would force Nixon and his legal team to petition the U.S. Supreme Court to hear the case.[85]

James Marshall, Nathan R. Margold, and Arthur B. Spingarn, along with El Paso attorney Fred Knollenberg, represented Nixon before the high court.[86]

Nixon contended that the hastily approved law that granted the Democratic executive committee the authority to determine its own voter criteria was passed to circumvent *Nixon v. Herndon*, which held unconstitutional an act barring Blacks from the primaries.[87] The issue in *Nixon v. Condon* (1932), which was argued on 7 January 1932 and reargued on 15 March 1932, was whether the state properly could be held responsible for the racially discriminatory actions of the party. The Supreme Court rendered a five to four decision on 2 May 1932 favoring Nixon, finding discriminatory state action on the ground that the Texas legislature, rather than the state Democratic Party, "had reposed authority in the party executive committee to prescribe membership qualifications."[88] Although he won the suit, Nixon did not collect the initial $5,000 he sought. Instead he was forced to settle for $1 plus costs. At the time Nixon told the press that he was satisfied because he was "fighting only for a principle."

The justices, all of the liberal wing of the court, who ruled on Nixon's behalf included Chief Justice Charles E. Hughes and associate justices Louis Brandeis, Harlan F. Stone, Owen J. Roberts, and Benjamin N. Cardozo. Justices James C. McReynolds, Willis Van Devanter, George Sutherland, and Pierce Butler dissented. However, the language in the ruling allowed Texas officials to again evade the spirit of the decision: "Whether a political party in Texas has inherent power today without restraint by any law to determine its own membership," Cardozo wrote, "we are not required at this time either to affirm or deny."[89] In other words, the high court failed to rule on whether the Democratic Party had the authority to empower the state committee.[90] While declaring that the Texas Democratic executive committee did not have the power to ban Blacks, regrettably the high court did not decide whether it was permissible for the Texas Democratic Party to bar Blacks at their convention.[91] Despite this loophole in the ruling, white supremacist H. L. Hunnicutt was still displeased with the decision and wrote to the high court to inquire how each justice voted "on the nigger case," which he asserted was a "grave question to us in Texas" and struck "at the very foundation of what little civilization we have left." Hunnicutt further lamented that no state can survive "a large nigger vote which is corrupted."[92]

According to legal scholar Michael Klarman, the unresolved question was whether the Constitution prevented a political party from excluding Blacks from membership when the state had not altered the party's "natural" decision-making apparatus. On 24 May 1932, just weeks after the *Nixon v. Condon* ruling, the delegates at the annual convention of the Texas state Democratic Party passed a resolution barring Blacks from membership, thereby nullifying *Nixon v. Condon*'s rationale for the unconstitutionality of the white primary.[93] The Democratic Party had acted on its own, free from state influence over its own voting and membership criteria. The court now had to confront directly the question of whether the state was constitutionally responsible for a political party's independent decision to bar Blacks from membership.[94] At least one writer of the time opined that although Cardozo's decision appeared to help Blacks, it nevertheless would ultimately benefit the Texas Democratic Party, since by ceding its power, the state was thus allowing the party "to prescribe its own qualifications for membership."[95]

By restricting the vote to whites during its 1932 state convention, the Texas Democratic Party not only set the stage for another Nixon challenge but also precluded Mexican Americans from voting. Mexican Americans who lived in Austin and in Travis County were prevented from casting their votes in the Democratic primaries on 4 August 1934 for the nomination of U.S. senator, governor, and district, county, and precinct officers. The primary election committee took the position that Mexican Americans did not "belong[] to the 'white' race."[96]

When Nixon attempted to vote in the 1932 Democratic primary on 23 July and 27 August, he was thwarted again by El Paso election judges George L. McCann and Frank Brenk.[97] And once again, Nixon, represented by attorney Fred Knollenberg, sued for his right to vote in the Democratic primary. In his February 1934 decision of the case of *Nixon vs. McCann*, Judge Charles A. Boynton, of the U.S. District Court in the Western District of Texas, El Paso division, awarded Nixon $5 while ruling that the newly adopted Democratic state convention rule attempting to ban African Americans from voting in their primaries did "not in itself exclude negroes from voting in primaries" but rather simply stated that whites could vote. Thus, when the Democratic executive committee instructed the Democratic El Paso County chairman to exclude Blacks, it was an action by the executive committee and not the convention.[98] Five months later on 12 July 1934, James Burr V. Allred, the Texas attorney general and soon to be governor, declared that Black Texans were not "entitled to vote in coming Democratic primaries." Although surprised by Allred's ruling, Nixon resiliently asserted on behalf of Afro-Texan Democrats that "we certainly are not giving up the fight." Allred resolutely committed the power of his office when he said "the Democratic party has always been a white man's party in Texas, and the attorney general's department will do everything in its power to keep it such." El Paso County Democratic chairman Ernest Guinn, in consultation with county attorney David E. Mulcahy, agreed with the attorney general but still wondered whether a formal order excluding the nearly four hundred Black El Paso Democrats from voting in the upcoming 28 July primary was necessary. He quickly determined, however, that Allred's ruling was sufficient.[99]

The African American editor of the *Houston Defender*, Clinton F. Richardson, rhetorically asked, "Is 'white supremacy' endangered by a few thousand black men and women casting their votes for Democratic candidates in a state that is overwhelmingly white and democratic?" Regrettably, the answer was yes. The fact is that many whites in Texas felt that "this is a white man's government way down here in Texas. This is a white man's country. The Texas Negro is popular in his place—that of hewer of wood and drawer of water."[100] The statement confirms that many white people still viewed Blacks in Texas as subservient. On 13 July, Richardson sued the Harris County clerk Albert Townsend for $10,000 for his refusal to grant Richardson an absentee ballot.[101] In El Paso, Nixon was surprisingly permitted to vote in the primary, but election officials marked "colored" on the face of his ballot, and ultimately his ballot would be rejected and would not count.[102]

El Paso's NAACP and Its Many Colored Faces

Without question, the NAACP was essential in the success of both Nixon cases, and Nixon readily acknowledged the organization's supportive role. As a representative of the NAACP, Nixon took the time to write to the editor of the *Houston Defender* in 1935 to ask for the paper's assistance in convincing its east Texas readership to give credit to the efforts of the civil rights association. Nixon wrote, "We had received two favorable Supreme Court decisions against the Texas Democratic primary practices not because of any individual effort, but because a great national organization—the N.A.A.C.P.—had prosecuted those cases." Regarding other failed challenges to the all-white Democratic primary in Texas, Nixon wrote that they "had succeeded only in wasting, in the aggregate, a considerable sum of money." Somewhat frustrated by the lack of progress in general and by the lack of support from this newspaper in particular, Nixon paternalistically, if not sarcastically, ended his letter by remarking that "you East Texans have succeeded most admirably in tearing down everything that had been built for you."[103] Nixon obviously admired the NAACP for its courageous stance, principles, and outreach, so much that he became a life member of the organization in June 1928.[104]

As an official delegate representing the El Paso branch, Nixon attended the national organization's Sixteenth Annual Conference, which was held from 24 to 30 June 1925 in Denver, Colorado.[105] While at this NAACP conference, Lawrence Nixon met Edna Tandy, the person who four years later, in 1929, would introduce him to his future second wife, Drusilla E. (Tandy) Attwell. It was at this conference that the NAACP proclaimed five key principles as its aim: "The

9. *Left to right*: Drusilla E. (Tandy) Nixon, Drusilla Ann Nixon, Lawrence A. Nixon, Edna Angela Nixon, and Edna Tandy, Drusilla's sister. Courtesy of the Beth Elnita Nixon family collection.

10. Drusilla Elizabeth Tandy, ca. 1920. Courtesy of the Edna A. (Nixon) McIver family collection.

complete abolition of lynching and mob law; full political freedom; industrial democracy; better education; and the absolute ending of segregation on race and color." The organization believed that the values that the United States professed to hold were not only worthy enough to fight for but also necessary to fight for if the nation was to be redeemed from its evil past and present. As the Fifteenth NAACP Annual Conference in 1924 had made clear, "It is not to obtain mere benefits and privileges for the Negro that the National Association for the Advancement of Colored People is striving; it is striving to vindicate the American idea. That idea is: that every man shall have opportunity for the highest self development and that his achievements shall not be denied recognition on their merits."[106]

The local branch was diverse in its ethnic representation: its members included individuals who were African Americans, Afro-Latinas/os, and ethnic whites of German, Jewish, and Russian ancestry. For example, in the 1929 El Paso NAACP membership roll, African American Mary López and her Afro-Latino husband Rudolph W. López were listed as members.[107] When and why Rudolph López arrived into El Paso is not clear, but he, like Lawrence Nixon, was very active within the relatively small Black enclave in the city. He not only was a member of the local NAACP but also was involved in musical groups at Douglass School and various churches in the city. For a brief time López was heard on the local AM radio station KTSM, and he was a member of the Prince Hall Masonic House, achieving the rank of thirty-third-degree Mason. In addition, he was active in the American Legion and the St. James Myrtle United Methodist Church.[108] Nixon must have served as a mentor to the younger López, who was named an honorary pallbearer at Nixon's funeral on 8 March 1966.[109]

Another individual who made El Paso's NAACP multiracial, multiethnic, and multicultural was Louis Laskin, a white Jewish storeowner who was listed as an NAACP member in 1924 and thus must have known Lawrence Nixon.[110] Laskin was one of the proprietors—his older brother Israel Laskin being the other—of the Globe Department Store located in downtown El Paso.[111] Jewish involvement in the NAACP is not surprising; a number of Jews, particularly those who arrived from Europe after 1880, sympathized with the plight of African Americans in light of their own historical oppression.[112] Besides being directly involved with the NAACP in El Paso as members, some were also actively engaged in social justice causes, such as endorsing the passage of the Costigan-Wagner antilynching bill. Edward P. Costigan was a Democratic U.S. senator from Colorado who cosponsored the bill with New York Democratic senator Robert F. Wagner. The bill proposed punishing sheriffs who did not adequately protect prisoners within their custody from mob rule. Although First Lady Eleanor Roosevelt supported the bill, her husband President Franklin D. Roosevelt did not, and it did not pass.[113]

In a show of solidarity among the various constituencies of El Paso, on Sunday 3 February 1935, progressive whites and many Jews met at the predominately African American Second Baptist Church in El Paso's Second Ward neighborhood to read the letters that had been sent to various politicians in support of stopping the barbarity of lynchings in the nation.[114] The groups included the Women's City Government Club and individuals such as Rabbi Joseph M. Roth and Rabbi Martin Zielonka.[115] Next to them all stood attorney Frederick C. Knollenberg, another white member of the El Paso NAACP throughout the 1920s.[116] Knollenberg was a self-described "country boy" and a "green country lawyer" with a mouth full of "gold teeth and a jovial personality."[117] As one of the few Anglos in El Paso's NAACP, Knollenberg served as Lawrence Nixon's legal counsel during his court battles with the judicial system to secure the right to vote during the Texas Democratic primaries. El Paso lawyer Julian Bernat described Elisha F. Cameron and Fred C. Knollenberg as "two fine old gentlemen of the old school. They were good lawyers and good people." Bernat, who practiced in Cameron's firm, said that his partner spoke often and proudly of his involvement in the case. "It was a challenge to them, but they went ahead and did it."[118] In describing Knollenberg to Walter White, national secretary of the NAACP, in 1932 LeRoy Washington wrote:

> He is very interested in our welfare here and throughout the country. There has never been a time when we have called on him for legal advice or aid but that we got it without question as to the fee. In fact, he is the only lawyer whom we have found here, as yet, who will go to the bat with and for the NAACP, locally and nationally. As we understand it, he is thoroughly conversant with southern tactics in evading the law.[119]

Fred Knollenberg's friendship with Nixon and his association with groups like the NAACP speak to a long and storied tradition of white progressives who actively participated in endeavors that led to the forward progression of African people in this nation. His life and professional work is an example of the legacy of liberal whites and their commitment to demanding and defending social justice for all oppressed groups.

Conclusion

Dr. Lawrence Nixon precipitated two landmark U.S. Supreme Court cases that laid the foundation for Black voting rights in the South. Clearly, the *Nixon v. Herndon* (1927) and *Nixon v. Condon* (1932) cases helped set the legal precedent that led to the monumental *Smith v. Allwright* (1944) U.S. Supreme Court case that dismantled all white-only primaries throughout the South.[120] Coke Stevenson, governor of Texas at the time, commented that the *Smith v. Allwright* decision was a "monstrous threat to our peace and security."[121]

The end of legal disfranchisement against African Americans not only modified the politics of the Democratic primary but also altered the democratic process as a whole. Throughout the South, thousands of Blacks began to register in larger numbers; about 3 percent registered in 1940, but by 1952, 20 percent had registered, an increase due mostly to *Smith v. Allwright*.[122] Although Nixon pointed out in 1952 that voters "do not have a secret ballot in Texas, the poll tax still stands and there are various means of intimidation that might keep voters generally from using their own judgement when casting their ballots," by the mid-1960s, Black participation in politics had succeeded in "inject[ing] a new liberal element" into the Democratic Party.[123]

Racially progressive and pro–federal government, African Americans held political beliefs that stood in contrast to the traditional political values of historically conservative Democrats. By the 1970s, Black voters, as part of a bloc of voters made up of white moderates, progressives, and liberals, were able to sway elections. In addition, conservative candidates began to lose to strong moderate candidates, who made conservatives look like relics seeking to defend an undemocratic, racist political system. As the new racial reality secured a foothold, conservative Democrats fled the party en masse and became Republicans. They began to couch their politics in more coded language and subtly used race-baiting to persuade constituents to vote for them.[124]

Nixon's political activism in Texas was steadfast and helped usher in many social changes. From the perspective of today his actions might seem nonthreatening, but the threat of violence against Nixon from the El Paso Klan was real. Despite Nixon's past experience with racial violence, he still became politically engaged. When one considers the violence inflicted on African Americans throughout the South during this era, one has to conclude that Nixon must have been courageous.

CHAPTER 5

Optimism and Rejection, 1925–1962

You have no idea how many people are dying
from the lack of sympathy.

unnamed undertaker, 1897

El Paso's Frederick Douglass National Tubercular Hospital

In the mid-1920s, while in the midst of battling in the courts for the right to vote in the Texas Democratic primary, Lawrence Nixon continued to address the health care needs of African Americans.[1] From 1926 to 1934, Nixon invested a large amount of time and resources into establishing a hospital in El Paso for Black patients with tuberculosis. His efforts reveal a great deal about access to the health care system for African Americans in El Paso during this period. Nixon's work also highlight his ideas, politics, and persistance. Clearly, he was committed to his patients as well as to community and racial uplift.

For all groups "throughout the nineteenth-century, tuberculosis (or consumption as it was then called) was the most common cause of death in the United States, as in much of western Europe."[2] The disease attacks the lungs and is usually fatal if left untreated. Historically, tuberculosis (or TB as it is commonly known) has been linked to "poverty and environmental factors" and "has always had a socioeconomic and political profile."[3] During the antebellum period, enslaved Blacks suffered respiratory infections such as TB disproportionately more than whites, due in large measure to scantly constructed quarters or cabins that did not protect them from the elements. The immune systems of New World Africans were not accustomed to "microbes that caused various pneumonias and tuberculosis," which impacted their "immunological rigor."[4]

In 1933, New Mexico had the second highest TB death rate. Texas also had a high rate, ranking fourteenth among all states. Arizona, New Mexico, Nevada, Colorado, and California were referred to as "sun care" states because mortality rates were skewed by the high number of TB patients who went there to be cured, ease their pain, or die in comfort.[5] Nationally, TB was especially deadly for African Americans. Between 1900 and 1940, Black mortality due to pulmonary TB ranged from 8.4 percent to 15 percent; white mortality for the same period, in contrast, ranged from 3.2 percent to 9.8 percent.[6]

The statistics reflect the pervasive impoverishment of African American communities and thus the impact and severity of institutional racism and Jim Crow throughout the nation. Booker T. Washington recognized this when in 1915 he attacked segregation by saying that "wherever the Negro is segregated it means that he will have poor sewerage, poor sanitary conditions generally, and this reflects itself in many ways in the life of my race to the disadvantage of the white race."[7] One scholar suggests that "any African American alive in or before 1940 may well have either known or been closely related to someone who had suffered with or died from tuberculosis." No doubt many Blacks were concerned about this insidious disease. Many who were aware of these dismal statistics agreed that Black activism, especially on the part of Black doctors and other health care professionals, was key to reducing Black tuberculosis mortality.[8]

During this period, whites often perceived African Americans as "vectors of disease," with the potential to infect whites.[9] To combat this pervasive idea and raise awareness about TB prevention and other health issues, in January 1915 Booker T. Washington launched Negro Health Week.[10] Lawrence Nixon and other Black doctors in El Paso, including Vernon Collins (who would become the El Paso NAACP president in the 1950s), Eugene R. Gravelly (who moved to El Paso from Dewitt County, Texas), and dentist Emerson M. Williams, conducted health clinics on various topics during El Paso's observance of National Negro Health Week.[11]

Additionally, in support of better health care for African Americans, in 1923, the National Medical Association (NMA) formally launched the Black hospital movement with the creation of the National Hospital Association (NHA). Founded in 1895, the NMA was established to help organize and promote the interest of the African American medical profession, whose members included physicians, dentists, surgeons, and pharmacists. The NMA created the NHA in an effort to improve the standards among the Black hospitals already in existence. The NMA worried that tougher guidelines from accrediting bodies could make Black hospitals obsolete. These fears were well founded, given the closure of most Black medical schools in the previous two decades. Between 1900 and 1923, the Carnegie Foundation for the Advancement of Teaching invited the influential Dr. Abraham Flexner to evaluate the nation's 147 medical schools. As a result of Flexner's critique, eight of the ten Black medical schools in the country were forced to close. Howard University and Meharry, Nixon's alma mater, were the only two Black medical schools to survive this stinging and damning report.[12] The NMA thus encouraged Black doctors to become active in the hospital reform movement, not only in the name of self-interest and self-preservation but also, and more importantly, for the betterment of the overall Black community.[13] Nixon became part of this reform movement and attempted to open a hospital in El Paso to address the needs of Black TB patients.

The earliest documented evidence of Nixon's initiative to establish a hospital for TB patients dates to 1926. On 15 May 1926, Nixon wrote a letter addressed to Dr. Edward Starr Judd, one of the founding partners of the Mayo Clinic in Rochester, Minnesota, requesting literature that might be of assistance to his hospital efforts and also to ask Dr. Judd to serve on the board of directors for the "Fred Douglass National Tubercular Hospital for Negroes." Dr. Henry S. Plummer, in the absence of Dr. Judd (who was away from the city at the time), replied to Dr. Nixon indicating that such literature did not exist and that Dr. Judd would reply directly regarding the request that he become a part of the board of directors.[14] Judd eventually wrote Nixon a supportive letter indicating that "this is very commendable and I shall be glad to do anything I can to help you."[15] Judd, however, left unaddressed Nixon's request that he join the nascent hospital board. This must have been a disappointment for Nixon, since a connection to Judd, with his affiliation with the Mayo Clinic, could have provided a crucial boost to the TB hospital project. Judd's board membership could have potentially established a network of friends and professional contacts, some of whom may have been able to secure financing for the hospital in the form of low-interest loans from the government or grants from foundations. Having visible white support for such a project was regarded as vital, since in the eyes of many it would bestow credibility and prestige on Nixon's cause.

During this time, TB ranked among the top three causes of mortality among Blacks in urban communities.[16] Lawrence Nixon's vision was to treat African Americans not just in El Paso or the Southwest but nationwide, including in the inner cities. In a December 1933 letter to Dr. Kendall Emerson, president of the National Tuberculosis Association, Nixon expected "an institution for the tuberculars" geared toward the "twelve or fourteen millions of Negroes." Nixon further elaborated that "we felt we were not projecting our plan on too great a scale when we thought of the hundreds of thousands of Negro sufferers from

Tuberculosis and respiratory ailments."[17] His grand plan included 1,157 beds, with room to expand for an additional 600 beds, which were more beds dedicated to Black tuberculosis patients than in the entire country combined.[18] And he wanted a hospital that was "so attractive, so cheerful and so well equipped, that there would be no question" that those Black patients "needing treatment" would be able to "avail themselves of an opportunity they have *never* had before."[19]

Part of Nixon's impetus for establishing a Black hospital specifically for TB patients may have been the fact that neither New Mexico nor Texas had such a facility. In 1921 Texas governor Pat Neff rejected attempts for the state to formally establish an all-Black TB hospital. House of Representative member Orlando B. Black of San Antonio (who later became mayor of that city) introduced HB 36, which called for the allocation of $300,000 for a Black sanatorium. The bill was initiated by the all-white Texas Public Health Association and endorsed by the all-white Texas State Medical Association. State senator William H. Bledsoe of Lubbock sponsored the senate version of the bill, SB 38, and ensured its passage in that chamber.

However, Governor Neff vetoed the proposed appropriation of $300,000 on 20 February 1921. Neff argued that the state already operated one such sanatorium and that if a hospital were to be built for Negroes, it should be located adjacent to the existing facility so as to use the existing central plant and equipment.[20] The backers of the bill stressed that the state "loses $14,600,000 annually from loss of services" and "$200,000 for medical care and treatment" because of Black laborers' illnesses. Legislators who wanted the bill to pass hoped that Neff would see having a Black TB facility as a type of "health insurance," since so many Blacks in Texas worked in close proximity to whites.[21] Sadly, white support of this important legislation "was predicated on concerns that the black domestics who cared for their children, cleaned their homes, drove their cars, and prepared their meals might import tuberculosis into white households."[22] Nixon may have been dispirited by the governor's actions since that meant a further delay in addressing the pressing needs of saving Black TB sufferers in Texas, or Nixon could also have been encouraged by Neff's veto by seeing it as an opportunity to start his own facility.

Nixon solicited the advice of experts, consultants, and other professionals on a variety of issues related to the establishment of the hospital, including the practicality of certain locations. In considering placement, Nixon contracted Lieutenant Colonel Albert A. King, an army officer stationed at Fort Bliss, to prepare a formal report on Evergreen Ranch in Socorro, New Mexico. In his letter, Nixon does not explain why he was interested in this location. Evergreen

Ranch, which was owned by the Salvation Army, was located 190 miles north of El Paso and 76 miles south of Albuquerque, New Mexico. Nixon would have been required to move to Socorro to run the day-to-day operations of the facility. Dr. John A. Kenney, the former personal physician to Booker T. Washington and editor in chief of the *Journal of the National Medical Association*, voiced his concerns to Nixon about this prospective location; Nixon "must take into consideration" that the Evergreen Ranch "is far removed from the center of civilization, and that our people as a whole have not a great deal of money with which to travel such distances, and that many who could be helped, could they reach the location, will die where they are because of lack of funds." However, this concern notwithstanding, the central New Mexico location offered healthful benefits and seemed ideal in many other regards. Finding the climate to be "excellent," the water supply "abundant," the quality of the ranch "excellent," the surroundings "good," and recreational opportunities "fair," King "recommended [the site] for a tubercular sanitarium."[23]

The Salvation Army was prepared to sell the ranch to Nixon, but this deal never took place.[24] By 1933, Nixon no longer had a New Mexico location in mind for the hospital. By then, presumably persuaded by arguments like Kenney's, Nixon had decided to focus on building a hospital in El Paso. Nixon wrote Kendall Emerson on 12 December, stating, "we have selected for our location a section of land some eight or ten miles north of El Paso, on the eastern side of the Franklin Mountains, where the elevation is 4,200 feet. This land is costing us ten dollars an acre, making the whole section cost us but $6,400."[25] In fact, Nixon had secured an option to purchase 960 acres at this site outside the city's limits.[26] The attorney handling these legal transactions and property negotiations for Nixon was none other than Fred Knollenberg. To express his commitment to Nixon's efforts and improved health care for Blacks, Knollenberg wrote Nixon and the Federal Emergency Administration, alerting them that he would donate his own private land to this worthy cause—seventy-seven acres in Vado, New Mexico—if that would help support the application and so ensure the desperately needed financing from the federal government.[27]

Nixon ultimately persuaded six prominent individuals to serve on the hospital board: William Pickens, field secretary of the NAACP; George S. Schuyler, a well-known conservative commentator, *Pittsburgh Courier* columnist, and New York City resident; Emory D. Williams, a longtime friend of Nixon's and Las Cruces, New Mexico, NAACP branch president; Arthur Q. Shirley, a physician from San Angelo, Texas; Henry J. Mason, a friend of Nixon's from Marshall, Texas, and a Wiley College classmate; and LeRoy W. Washington, longtime Nixon friend and NAACP El Paso chapter president.[28] All of the board members were African Americans. Although no proof exists, Nixon must have attempted to get at least one local prominent white person to serve; El Paso certainly had numerous white bank presidents, mining and railroad executives, military officers, political elites, attorneys, accountants, and medical professionals who could have served on the board of directors and made important contributions with their skill sets and contacts. Documentation does show that he attempted to get the endorsements of powerful white leaders, such as El Paso mayor Ray E. Sherman, the city's county judge, the county medical society, and the chamber of commerce.[29] It is possible to argue, however, that by having an all-Black board, Nixon was breaking away from traditional practices of having rich all-white boards chairing Black institutions.[30]

Nixon did not seek to establish a hospital as a means of self-aggrandizement or for his personal enrichment. Nixon was not overtly outspoken, and he was not the kind of person who craved attention. He also did not practice medicine to increase his income or status or to obtain material possessions. Drusilla Nixon, whom Lawrence married in 1935, recalled her husband saying that "we have all the things we need and some of the things we want."[31] He applied this philosophy in a practical way by charging his patients very little. Some white doctors would tell him, "you ought to go up on your prices. If you'd go up on your prices you would make just as much money as you do now but you'd work less." True to his nature, Nixon replied, "Now if everybody gouges these people, they'll never have anything." In his fifty-three years of practicing medicine in El Paso, "the most he ever charged was $2 for an office call and $4 for a house call."[32] It was this level of commitment to his patients that pushed Nixon to seek an all-Black hospital.

Nixon also sought to establish an all-Black hospital so that he would be able to have hospital privileges. Hospitals in El Paso, such as the City-County Hospital, Masonic Hospital, Hotel Dieu, and William Beaumont General Hospital, allowed doctors who were members of the local medical society to have hospital privileges. The El Paso County Medical Society did not allow Blacks to become members, however. This racist policy agitated Nixon, who used it as another reason to not raise his prices: "Why should I go up on my prices when they don't allow me to belong to the [El Paso] County Medical Society?"[33] Since he was not allowed to join the local medical society, he decided he would not raise his prices, which was a small way of not giving in to the pressure of other local doctors who wanted Nixon to increase the price of his services. Nixon's low prices undoubtedly attracted more clients for him over his white counterparts. He clearly must have seen his defiance as a way to protest their segregated policy.

11. Lawrence and Drusilla Nixon in the desert of El Paso, Texas, or nearby New Mexico, ca. 1930s. Courtesy of the Edna A. (Nixon) McIver family collection.

The local hospitals such as William Beaumont General Hospital strictly and proudly enforced Jim Crow.[34] When Nixon had a patient that needed to be hospitalized, he had to seek the assistance of white doctors such as Branwell Fanning Stevens, who would admit Nixon's patients into Hotel Dieu under their own names and allow Nixon to continue treating them.[35] Nixon's patients included African Americans, but his practice was "almost entirely Mexican." Nixon also had some Anglo patients, along with other ethnicities; his wife remembered that "it was the United Nations in his office. He had quite a few Philippinos."[36]

Nixon was so committed to the hospital project that he resorted to directly writing the U.S. president, Franklin D. Roosevelt. In the two-page letter, Nixon referred to the $2.4 million loan request on file with the Public Works Administration's deputy administrator, Colonel Henry M. Waite. Nixon asserted that "the Negro is not only relatively but absolutely, because of his economic status, the greatest host for the tubercle bacillus in Texas" and asked that "some special provision should be made whereby the loan and grant might be recommended."[37] It is not known if President Roosevelt ever responded to Nixon's letter directly, yet because of the scale of his project, the National Tuberculosis Association did not agree to endorse Nixon's effort. The association of Black physicians, the National Medical Association, also did not support Nixon's plans, citing what was regarded as an unfavorable location—ten miles outside of the city—for most Blacks. Still other organizations did not contribute the start-up money necessary to launch his project. Thus, without national or major institutional backing, it was not a surprise that on 11 June 1935 Nixon received the disappointing news from Horatio B. Hackett, assistant administrator of the Federal Emergency Administration of Public Works, that his application for that agency's funds had been denied. Hackett wrote:

> After a careful review our examiners have concluded that approval of the above-entitled application for a loan with which to finance the construction of a tubercular hospital could not be recommended. It is the opinion of our Legal Division that the applicant is not a public body and since this project is not a hospital which is partially financed from public funds, this application cannot be included in the comprehensive plan as required under Section 202(e) of the National Industrial Act. In these circumstances, I regret to inform you that this application has been finally disapproved.[38]

Traditional or classical "progressives" of the 1880s to the 1920s wanted to create a better America; however, that America did not seem to want to include healthy, longer-living Black people. As the Progressive Era came to an end, Nixon was left wondering why there were no backers, no supporters, and no financiers for the Douglass Tuberculosis Hospital. Evidently, he was a progressive in an unprogressive era. In spite of this rejection, however, Nixon remained committed to the proposition of bringing improved medical facilities to African Americans in El Paso, the Southwest, and throughout the nation. Nixon continued to serve the medical needs of all within the community, without any bitterness, anger, or malice. Although this particular effort ended in failure, his commitment to the project, the arguments he brought to bear to support it, and his vision of it tell us a great deal about his racial politics. He was not static or dogmatic in his thinking on the issue of race. At the national level, the debate within the African American community on the issue of integration versus separation raged on throughout the 1920s and 1930s. Nixon may have believed philosophically in the goal of integrated health care facilities, but at this point he made clear that he wanted a Black hospital to serve Black patients, which suggests he recognized that although integrating already established white hospitals would probably be preferable, the fact was that integration was a slow process. The health improvement and advancement of Black people "could not afford to wait for integration's eventual development" because the cost would be literally the deaths of Blacks.[39] Nixon was acutely aware that Black people needed immediate medical attention from Black physicians and nurses, who could care for them with dignity and respect and in a culturally sensitive manner.

Nixon's position was in direct opposition to the NAACP's official position on the vital issue of integration versus separatism. Civil rights activists were increasingly leery of continuing to support the establishment of all-Black institutions and were now much more focused on forcing white America to integrate mainstream institutions. The NAACP considered the mere existence of all-Black hospitals to be a tacit acknowledgment of the legitimacy of Jim Crow, segregation, and the entire edifice of racial oppression. The premier national civil rights organization argued that Black hospitals "hindered efforts at integration because they provided white hospitals with excuses to continue their discriminatory practices."[40] Nixon's political positions and activism make it clear that he did not believe in segregation. He challenged the segregation and exclusion of Black Texans in the Democratic primary. He did, however, believe in Black people having access to services, rights, and privileges. He had attended segregated private schools and witnessed the power of Black institutions and the value of Black-run organizations. He knew Black institutions were transformational; they gave Black people pride in themselves and hope for the future of the race. Nixon's determination in his nine-year hospital campaign demonstrates his commitment to Black people, Black institutions, and Black organizational building. NMA members were "fully cognizant of the danger inherent in any segregated proposition" but believed it had more to offer "than loud mouthed preachment against segregation in the abstract." This was in fact precisely the position that the NMA took relative to the NAACP.[41] One group, the Southern Conference for Human Welfare (SCHW), seemed to share Drusilla and Lawrence Nixon's political views and beliefs and was committed to multiracial coalition building as a means of addressing the South's many-faceted problems with respect to race, economic disparity, and political exclusion. The SCHW would, for a brief while, give Drusilla and Lawrence the support they needed to achieve progress in the Black community.

Southern Conference for Human Welfare

The SCHW had its formal beginnings in 1938 when a group of white southern liberals convened a meeting in Birmingham, Alabama, to discuss the wretched state of affairs in the region. The group mostly concerned itself with civil liberties, civil rights, and equal protection under the law for all citizens.

Drusilla and Lawrence Nixon joined the SCHW as charter members of the El Paso chapter in 1945. They also served on the organization's executive committee. The Nixon name was well known locally due to Drusilla's extensive community outreach and Lawrence's status as a prominent physician, along with their political activism in trying to gain the right for Blacks to vote in the Texas Democratic primary, attempts to secure a pool for Blacks at Washington Park, and numerous other initiatives. By lending their name to the El Paso SCHW, the Nixons helped legitimize the group's local efforts and promote its progressive agenda. However, the rest of the nation was not ready for this political worldview, and three years later in 1948, the Nixons appeared on the front pages of El Paso's newspapers connected to an organization defined as having Communist ties.[42] This in turn led people to question the Nixons' patriotism, their loyalty to the United States, and even their belief in democracy. However, Drusilla and Lawrence Nixon were not Communists. In fact, years earlier, Lawrence Nixon was quoted as saying that although there were some Black Communists, "the race is not a fertile field for radical doctrines" and that African Americans simply wanted "true democracy as laid down in the constitution."[43]

Nonetheless, the professed views of the Nixons and others within the SCHW did not stop the Federal Bureau of Investigation (FBI) from launching a formal inquiry that included covertly examining nearly every action of the El Paso SCHW. Almost from the inception of the El Paso chapter, the FBI had a surveillance program that included a number of informants within it.[44] The FBI began monitoring the El Paso SCHW in November 1945 and documented that Beach Langston, an English professor at "the College of Mines," was the chapter's chairman and that Dorothy Mapp was its secretary.[45] Twenty El Pasoans paid their dues at this initial meeting of the El Paso SCHW. Although they were not identified by name in the FBI report, presumably Drusilla and Lawrence Nixon were among this group.[46] By October 1946, the FBI had three confidential informants, two of whom were Martha McCall and George Webber, who began to furnish the bureau with names of members, dates of meetings and events, and information about what the El Paso SCHW hoped to accomplish.[47] Oddly, no mention is made of either Drusilla or Lawrence Nixon in any of the FBI Internal Security C reports that were generated by these informants.[48]

As members of the El Paso SCHW, the Nixons were part of a national organization whose supporters included well-known liberals such as Mary McLeod Bethune, Virginia Durr, Aubrey Williams, Walter White, Frank P. Graham, Lillian Smith, Lucy Randolph Mason, and James A. Dombrowski. The Nixons' involvement in the El Paso chapter makes it clear that by the mid-1940s, they both held political beliefs that were at least left of center if not progressive. Although the FBI stated that the El Paso SCHW "reaches far to the left of center," the national SCHW, like many white southern organizations committed to social justice, was conflicted over the race issue.[49] It inherited the ambiguous racial attitudes common to most southerners. The group expressed sympathy for the oppression that African Americans experienced as a consequence of Jim Crow and racial violence, yet it still supported separate and equally funded schools and playgrounds and accepted segregation in housing and public accommodations and in hiring practices. The organization did break with regional practices by advocating integrated meetings and admitting Blacks to its executive councils and by working for the abolition of the poll tax. At best, these gestures signified a symbolic, indirect, and partial integration of Blacks into southern political life. However, as one scholar noted, "here its integrationist tendencies ended." The contradictions were obvious but unsurprising. Before World War II, the SCHW "did not attack segregation where it was strong—and it was strong nearly everywhere."[50] Nonetheless, the organization was one of the few in the South that offered any serious resistance to the racist status quo, and so the Nixons joined it for the "betterment of the [El Paso] community." Lawrence Nixon recalled that many of the El Paso SCHW charter members were young people who were attracted to Frank P. Graham, the southern liberal who was known as an advocate for Black rights and who was the honorary president of SCHW.[51] Graham would also be branded a Communist, yet he refused to renounce his SCHW association.[52]

The El Paso SCHW sponsored activities that tried to create dialogue between the city's two largest groups, Mexican Americans and Anglos, and also sponsored speakers who addressed issues that the organization deemed important.

For example, it sponsored the November 1947 visit of U.S. senator Glen H. Taylor of Idaho, who spoke on the "vital issues of the day."[53] According to the FBI's surveillance, about 110 people were in attendance, of which "approximately 25 were negroes, about 25 Mexicans, and the rest a mixture of a cross section of the white population."[54] In his talk, Taylor asserted that the United States was "dangerously close" to becoming a military dictatorship and that the military was in charge of the nation's foreign policy agenda. Taylor also denounced the post–World War II Marshall Plan (which advocated U.S. assistance in rebuilding Europe's infrastructure) as an attempt to buy allies for a war with Russia. "If we want peace, our foreign policy should be to make friends with Russia," Taylor told his El Paso audience, which likely included both Drusilla and Lawrence Nixon.[55]

The El Paso SCHW also fought on behalf of Mexican Americans. For example, it opposed and successfully prevented the deportation of Humberto Silex, a Nicaraguan-born labor organizer for the International Union of Mine, Mill, and Smelter Workers.[56] Silex was one of the first people in El Paso to realize the need for starting the El Paso SCHW, whose bulletin asserted that it was an organization "seeking to combine all liberals dedicated to abolish discrimination on account of race, creed, or color." From the outset, Silex and the El Paso SCHW were aware that one of the major issues in the El Paso/border region was "the unfair treatment of the Mexican-Americans."[57] Silex was instrumental as a labor union leader for the American Federation of Labor and Congress of Industrial Organizations and helped establish the International Union of Mine, Mill, and Smelter Workers at El Paso's American Smelting and Refining Company.[58] In the 1940s, Silex worked tirelessly across "citizenship lines" to organize Mexican and Mexican American workers at El Paso's Phelps Dodge copper refinery, Southwestern Portland Cement Plant, and Ciudad Juárez's Confederación de Trabajadores Mexicanos.[59] Due to these union activities, El Paso business and political elites attempted to unjustly expel Silex from the United States in July 1946 for his involvement in an assault against Victoriano Tapia that occurred on 5 October 1945, while the two were employed at the American Smelting and Refining Company. Silex pleaded guilty to aggravated assault, posted a $200 peace bond, and paid a $35 fine in the El Paso County Court at Law.[60] However, Silex's pleading guilty gave his detractors an opportunity to deny his citizenship request and thus force his deportation on the grounds of the conviction. Since most union members in El Paso were, like Silex, documented noncitizen residents, the El Paso SCHW believed the Silex deportation proceedings sent a chilling message that unionizing would be punished.[61] The El Paso SCHW believed that the attack against Humberto Silex was "in effect anti-union" and "anti-foreign born," that it was "an attack against our civil rights and shows discrimination against a minority."[62] Luckily for Silex, in 1946 Texas governor Coke R. Stevenson issued an unconditional pardon in the assault case, which allowed for his citizenship request to proceed.[63] In spite of this, federal judge Robert Ewing Thomason held that Silex was "not a person of good moral character" and denied Silex his citizenship request in 1949.[64]

The organization's agenda included a myriad of national, state, and local issues. A glance at one of the El Paso SCHW bulletins reveals that it participated in the Fair Employment Practices Commission (FEPC) mass rally and petitioned Texas legislators (led by African American Dr. Vernon Collins, Rabbi Klein, Jesus Sesa, Robert Gafford, and Cleofas Calleros) about a variety of local and state issues that were important to it. The El Paso SCHW sent letters to then-Congressman Robert Ewing Thomason expressing disapproval of his "anti-labor votes in the 79th congress" and "asking him to sign discharge petition on F.E.P.C. Bill and Unemployment Compensation Bill" and to support the Wagner-Murray-Dingell bill; to *Herald-Post* editor Ed Pooley commending his support of El Paso police chief Lawrence T. Robey for his selection of four Black police officers; to a member of the Hotel Workers Union "commending his stand in the case of Wm. Horren," a Black delegate of the United Steel Workers Union, "when the Hotel Ambassador in Washington attempted discrimination"; and to President Harry S. Truman asking him to repeal "the fact finding order for F.E.P." and to support New Mexico senator Dionisio "Dennis" Chavez for "his stand on F.E.P.C."[65]

The El Paso SCHW also raised funds and petitions in protest of the racially motivated February 1946 Columbia, Tennessee, killings, and member Ida Rosenwasser donated seventy books to the Smeltertown library on behalf of the organization. Additionally, El Paso SCHW members Mollie Shapiro, Mrs. Lucio Flores, and Regina Boyd helped make Office of Price Administration price surveys, assisted by Ana Valasquez "of the LULACS," the League of United Latin American Citizens, a Hispanic civil rights organization founded in Corpus Christi, Texas, in 1930. The El Paso SCHW also sponsored a citizens committee to aid smelter strikers and "put on series of fund raising activities and distributed educational material enlightening El Pasoans" about the Hicks-Hayward Strike of November 1946. The group also passed resolutions supporting El Paso County attorney Ernest Guinn's investigation of local milk industry monopoly and actively supported Homer Price Rainey for governor in 1946.

The El Paso SCHW often published bilingual newsletters and referred to itself as "Conferencia del sur por el bienestar humano." The chapter was also "instrumental in enlisting the aid of the American Committee for the Protection of Foreign Born," who offered the services of their counsel, Carol King, and gave much support to the Texas Civil Rights Congress, the national Civil Rights Congress, and the Congress of Industrial Organizations.[66] And El Paso SCHW was very active in encouraging undocumented individuals to become U.S. citizens through the promotion of citizenship classes in both Spanish and English in their newsletters and meeting agendas.

Both Lawrence and Drusilla Nixon gave speeches at El Paso SCHW meetings. Lawrence directed a poll tax meeting in 1946, during which he gave a talk titled "Pay Poll Tax to Abolish Poll Tax."[67] Drusilla Nixon was the guest speaker for the 9 January 1947 meeting. The title of her talk was "'Building a Better South' and Its Relations to the Southern Conference Program for 1947"; according to the summary in the El Paso SCHW newsletter, the talk addressed "the problems and possibilities for El Paso schools."[68]

Despite the good deeds and work of the El Paso SCHW, the *El Paso Herald-Post* published a fourteen-hundred-word front-page article on 22 January 1948 that smeared the El Paso chapter with the "red" label for its ties to the SCHW national leadership, ties the officers of the El Paso SCHW challenged, denying that the national organization was "Communist dominated or subversive."[69] Earl R. Browder, former leader of the Communist Party USA, in testimony before the House Committee on Un-American Activities (HUAC), stated that the SCHW was a Communist Party "transmission belt," and in a 12 June 1947 report, the HUAC, chaired by New Jersey Republican John Parnell Thomas, claimed that the national SCHW was a "deviously camouflaged Communists-front organization" and that "communists themselves claim SCHW as their own."[70] Unfortunately, the *El Paso Herald-Post* did not do the due diligence required in its 22 January 1948 El Paso SCHW reporting. Almost exactly a year earlier, on 20 January 1947, the board of directors of the American Civil Liberties Union (ACLU) had determined that the HUAC had "greatly abused" its powers, exposing "red plots that either did not exist, or were manufactured." The HUAC fear of Communists, the ACLU board observed, "arose largely from imagination," and it was indeed "genuine American liberalism" that was being assailed with "'smear' methods, innuendo, distortion and other propagandistic devices reminiscent of fascist techniques." No mention is made in the *Herald-Post* article of the ACLU's report.[71] In October 1947, months before the January 1948 *Herald-Post* article, noted Columbia law professor Walter Gellhorn concluded that HUAC's report was "empty of merit" and that the allegations against the national SCHW were based on "semi-truths" rather than "credible evidence," which proved that HUAC had been "either intolerably incompetent or designedly intent upon publicizing misinformation."[72]

The *Herald-Post* was a conservative newspaper, while the rival *El Paso Times* was liberal. The two newspapers served as "rallying points for the community."[73]

Edward M. Pooley, the editor of the *Herald-Post* during this period, had not only a political agenda in discrediting the El Paso SCHW but a racist one. According to a January 1947 FBI report, Pooley "has been very much opposed" to the El Paso SCHW, remarking that "one of the main reasons for his antipathy has been the inclusion of Negroes in the [SCHW] membership." The report goes on to document that between 7 and 13 January 1947 there was a flurry of negative El Paso SCHW articles, editorials, and letters to the editor published in the *Herald-Post*, whose publication, the bureau asserted, Pooley "was very definitely the driving force behind."[74]

After the El Paso SCHW "red" allegations were made public, the El Paso YWCA quickly disavowed its association with the El Paso SCHW. Oddly, the YWCA itself had been spurned for alleged radicalism by the Daughters of the American Revolution nearly twenty years earlier.[75] The El Paso YWCA board of directors met on 1 November 1947 and directed President Mrs. C. M. Ainsworth to formally declare that the El Paso SCHW was no longer welcome at its East Franklin Street facility, which it had been using for regular twice-monthly meetings.[76] It appears that the issue of race was also a point of contention. The FBI reported that the officials of the El Paso YWCA "received various complaints from the general public . . . regarding the use of the YWCA building by the SCHW. . . . This feeling of disapproval, as evidenced by the numerous complaints, was also caused by the 'mixed' attendance at the meetings, that is, the presence of Negroes and Whites together, which is definitely contrary to the prevailing customs in El Paso, Texas."[77]

The El Paso SCHW responded with a public rebuttal, arguing that the decision of the YWCA's board was "undemocratic." Regina Boyd, the executive secretary of the El Paso SCHW, emphasized that the claims of the HUAC were baseless and that there was "no proof" of Communist ties. Molly Shapiro, a well-known El Paso Jewish activist, treasurer of the El Paso SCHW, and a close family friend of the Nixons, was certain that the organization neither was a Communist front nor had been involved in so-called subversive activities. Shapiro stated that the El Paso "YWCA has been nice to us, they are lovely women. I'm sure they're very much ashamed of the [YWCA] Board's action." The SCHW, according to Shapiro, was "organized to help the underdog, to fight discrimination against minority races. My husband and I were charter members when the El Paso Chapter was formed three years ago. If the organization were Communistic we never would have joined."[78]

Drusilla Nixon also rejected the idea that the El Paso SCHW was "Communist-dominated"; rather, she viewed the politics of the organization as being "liberal." Drusilla had been a member of the YWCA ever since she was fourteen years old, and she recalled how much she valued the long-standing EP-YWCA relationship, a relationship she certainly would not have jeopardized by joining an organization linked to Communists.[79] However, in the political climate of the 1940s and '50s, organizations that critiqued institutional racism were often deemed Communist, particularly if they challenged the racial etiquette and status quo of the day.

Referring to a list of names of SCHW officials and members in the HUAC report, the El Paso SCHW further stated that "even if the 62 names" of those who HUAC claimed were "Communist" were in fact so, it was difficult "to see how the small number from a total group of well over 25,000 could warrant the labeling of the organization as communist dominated." Only one of the 62 people on the list claimed "to be a member of the Communist Party," and even though he was identified as a member of SCHW, according to the El Paso SCHW, in fact he was "not a member of the Southern Conference for Human Welfare."

Political pressure, internal squabbles, and funding shortages derailed this uniquely southern organization, forcing the national officers to vote for its demise in November 1948.[80] By January 1949 the El Paso SCHW became dormant, although a number of its 250 members paid dues to the national organization in hopes of reviving the El Paso SCHW in the fall of 1949.[81]

For those brief three years, from 1945 to 1948, Drusilla and Lawrence Nixon were active members of the El Paso SCHW, keeping issues of equality and the promise of the American ideal before the city and its international surrounding region years before the major legislative breakthroughs for civil rights of the 1960s.[82]

Desegregation in Texas

As he aged, naturally Lawrence Nixon became less active in the community; however, Drusilla Nixon, who was sixteen years younger than Lawrence, remained engaged in local affairs, playing a role in the city's formal integration that was effected with the 1962 El Paso city ordinance.[83] In the Southwest, there were other cities that addressed the issue of race prior to El Paso. The election of Henry B. Gonzalez to San Antonio's city council was instrumental in the "successful passage of an ordinance desegregating all city owned public facilities" between 1953 and 1956.[84] The city of Houston had, in 1960, silently integrated seventy lunch counters in department stores, drugstores, and supermarkets during the last week of August. This occurred nearly two years before El Paso would allow African Americans to eat at downtown lunch counters, cafés, and restaurants. One of the unique things about Houston's integration was that it transpired under the assurances from the local press that there would be no coverage of the event. Houston's political and financial power cadre was anxious to avoid embarrassment and bloodshed and thereby maintain the city's image as a prospering, progressive southern city "ripe for investment and international trade." John T. Jones, publisher of the *Houston Chronicle*, "felt that it was necessary to suppress the news to accomplish integration without violence," giving credence to an old banker's adage: "When peace reigns, interest runs."[85]

Additionally, unlike in El Paso, integration in Houston interestingly came to pass without local or state legislation. Moreover, months prior to August 1960, another Jim Crow barrier had fallen. On 21 May, Houston's public library, city buses, and Jespersen Stadium had calmly integrated without fanfare.[86] William P. Steven, editor in chief of the *Houston Chronicle*, spoke truly when he stated that "integration is an essential fact in the demonstration of democracy. . . . It is necessary for the full development of the economy . . . and it is the only way to make our foreign policy mean anything in a world of mostly dark skins."[87] On 1 April 1962, without much fanfare or local press coverage, convention hotels in downtown Houston dropped their policy of segregation.[88] Nine days later, Colt Stadium followed suit. At this time Colt Stadium became a ballpark free of official racial discrimination on the playing field, in seating arrangements, restrooms, press facilities, and employment, as well at the exclusive Fast Draw Club. Many in Houston were proud to have integrated this particular public facility without external pressure or white backlash.[89] However, although Houston's downtown lunch counters and convention hotels had opened their facilities to Blacks, their restaurants and movie theaters remained segregated.[90]

Austin, the state capital, held on to segregation practices until it was forced to acquiesce to desegregation by the national civil rights legislation of 1964. In the aftermath, Austin activists helped "draft a fair housing ordinance in 1968, which was passed by the City Council, but overturned in a referendum. It was not until 1977 that the city adopted the ordinance for good."[91] In the early 1960s, civil rights advocates in Austin had attempted to get the city council to establish a human relations commission. The council eventually did approve the establishment of the Austin Human Relations Commission, but not before five NAACP members had protested in around-the-clock sessions at city hall. During the regular weekly council session on 2 April 1964 (exactly three months prior to President Lyndon B. Johnson's signing of the Civil Rights Act of 1964 into law), NAACP members gave speeches and read passages from various books continuously for nearly two weeks, filibustering the council's regular agenda. On 13 May, the city council finally established the Austin Human Relations Commission.[92]

In Albuquerque, New Mexico (a state where Latinas/os and Native Americans outnumber all other groups, including whites and African Americans), integration came sooner than in any city in Texas.[93] Modeled on a Portland, Oregon, antidiscrimination ordinance, the Albuquerque civil rights ordinance was passed on 15 February 1952—over ten years before El Paso's.[94] Soon afterward in 1955, the New Mexico state legislature implemented a state statute resembling Albuquerque's city ordinance—nine years before the national 1964 Civil Rights Act was passed by the U.S. Congress.[95]

When compared to other western cities such as Albuquerque, El Paso lagged far behind in antidiscrimination policies. To many, especially those African Americans who worked in the homes of white employers, the reluctance to integrate was mind-boggling.

> You let me work in your homes. I stay with your children weeks at a time, sometimes they know me better than their own mother. I even sleep in your house. You know that my color doesn't rub off on your sheets. And I can't eat in your restaurants. Why? What are you afraid of? What are you afraid of?[96]

El Paso City Council alderman Bert Williams initially proposed the antidiscrimination ordinance on 7 June 1962, but it was not the first desegregation regulation the city had seen.[97] In 1957, El Paso elected Raymond L. Telles Jr., "the first American of Mexican descent to be elected mayor of a major southwestern city this century." Under the Telles administration, Mexican Americans joined the ranks of the police and fire departments in larger numbers than in previous years.[98] When asked to speculate as to the reason for such dismal figures in a city whose majority populace was Mexican American, the white fire chief responded that his men slept all in one room, and "how could we expect white boys to sleep with Mexicans?"[99] According to historian Mario Garcia,

> lawyer Albert Armendáriz remembers Telles' concern about discrimination in city jobs when he took office. The new mayor believed he could not openly attack this process without jeopardizing his administration. Instead, he appointed men such as Alfonso Kennard and Armendáriz to the civil service commission and asked them to investigate the matter and institute changes. Armendáriz quickly discovered that both the police and fire departments refused to accept qualified Mexican Americans and that the commission sanctioned such discrimination. Only a handful of them in either department had been approved and only under exceptional circumstances. Armendáriz's investigation and revelations forced the commission to adopt new hiring procedures that led to the appointment of Mexican American policemen and firemen. Armendáriz notes that Telles never claimed credit for this breakthrough. It was not in his nature to boast of such

things. Nevertheless, his quiet leadership integrated city departments.... "That's the reason that we have a Mexican American Chief of Police today," Armendáriz concluded in 1982, "this is a product of Raymond Telles."[100]

During the 1950s and 1960s—during which time Telles rose to power—Mexican Americans in El Paso made up 50 percent or more of the city's population.[101]

Telles also confronted discrimination in public facilities that impacted African Americans. El Paso's premier cinema, the Plaza Theater, sold tickets to African Americans but relegated them to the back rows of the balcony area. Telles met with the Plaza's management, informing them that such a practice would no longer be tolerated and that if the theater persisted the city was prepared to take legal action against it. Telles noted that "the procedure of discrimination against blacks" at the Plaza Theatre "was immediately stopped."[102] These two acts by Telles set desegregation in motion, but it would be several more years before a city ordinance mandating integration would be enacted.

During the 1960s the Black population of El Paso grew from 5,891 (2.1 percent of the overall population) in 1960 to 7,441 (2.3 percent) in 1970—a nearly 21 percent increase in ten years.[103] At the time of the ordinance, El Paso had over 126,000 Chicanas/os, whose numbers increased to nearly 185,000 by 1970. The total city population stood at 276,687 in 1960 and 322,269 by 1970.[104] The Asian and Native American population was not as high as that of African Americans in El Paso.[105]

The 1962 antidiscrimination ordinance had its origins in late 1961 or early 1962, when a group of UTEP African American undergraduate students approached the Anti-Defamation League (ADL) of El Paso during one of its regular meetings. According to Albert Schwartz, who had been chairman of the local group since the end of World War II, "a couple of black students had approached ADL and had made their concerns known to the organization, during one of our meetings."[106] Soon after, Schwartz and the ADL decided to get involved and take action on behalf of these students. In a videotaped interview, Schwartz recalled,

we listened to the young people and decided they were right. That we should dig into this and find out a little bit more about what could be done to change things. And so eventually we did, but it didn't happen overnight. It took a lot of work, and a lot of good people. And eventually, long before the U.S. government decided that there would be integration, we were able to successfully integrate El Paso.[107]

Schwartz and others soon formed an ad hoc council, of which Drusilla Nixon was a member, that later became called the Citizens' Committee on Human Relations. According to Obra Lee Malone, a longtime African American resident of El Paso, Blacks were "concerned about the racial situation in our city."

Malone added, "You would see the signs around that say 'we reserve the right to refuse service to anyone'; we really knew what that meant was 'No Blacks allowed!'" According to Malone, the antidiscrimination ordinance "touched upon three matters," namely, access to restaurants, movie theaters, and motels/ hotels. The Citizens' Committee on Human Relations, of which Malone too was a member, "concluded that the best way to get this ordinance done" was in a manner that would be "as quietly and with as little publicity as possible." This was the same tactic employed in Houston. "I think our approach, that is, 'don't widely advertise it,' turned out to be justified because it got passed without a whole lot of pre-passage publicity."[108] Other Blacks involved in this endeavor included Robin E. L. Washington, who in 1961 helped create the El Paso Community Association, a group of African Americans who fought for integration in El Paso schools and other public facilities.[109]

Ordinance 2698 applied to restaurants, hotels and motels, and places of public entertainment. It excluded bars, boarding houses, and private clubs and other areas of entertainment.[110] The council passed the ordinance 14 June 1962 by unanimous vote. Days later, Joe Newman, member of the Northeast Democratic Club, prepared a petition to put the antidiscrimination ordinance to a public referendum. Newman's motive was "to let the people have a voice," and he "welcomed any help."[111] R. A. Ramey had joined Joe Newman to create a formal committee to officially take a position against the ordinance and prevent its passage.[112]

On 19 June 1962, Mayor Ralph E. Seitsinger vetoed the antidiscrimination ordinance.[113] It was the first time in more than a decade that an El Paso mayor had used his veto power.[114] Seitsinger said he had received an equal number of letters and phone calls supporting and opposing adoption of the ordinance.[115] The forty-six-year-old mayor from Iowa explained that he was a "believer in integration 100 per cent, but that it should come voluntarily from the fullness of the heart and not from legislation."[116]

The council meeting to vote on the mayor's veto took place on 21 June at Liberty Hall instead of the regular city chambers because of the many people in attendance, nearly two hundred in all. Speaking in favor of the ordinance was Alfonso Kennard, vice president of the El Paso Chapter of the Political Association of Spanish-Speaking Organizations. After Richard Cuellar Sr. requested those in favor to stand up, the vast majority gladly stood to show their support for the passage of the ordinance. There were about fifty African Americans present at the meeting. Ed Given clearly was not pleased by this show of support. Representing the Hotel, Motel, Tourist Court Association, he angrily said, "some of these people are of my own faith and I'm ashamed of them." "We're ashamed of you!" said attorney Dick Marshall in response. Marshall, who was representing the Jewish community and the Citizens Committee on Human Relations, stated, "El Paso is 80 to 100 years behind Eastern cities in integration and 10 years behind Albuquerque and Santa Fe which are getting more conventions than we are." John Dennis, a retired police officer, wanted the issue to be placed on the ballot during the next local general election so the voters could make the decision instead of the city council members. Irving Klister argued that Catholics were against segregation and cited Pope John XXIII's recent canonization of Martín De Porres, an Afro-Peruvian. The Reverend Charles Burges of the Presbyterian Church of the Divine Savior read a resolution from the El Paso Council of the Churches commending the city council's initial vote of approval for this much-needed ordinance.[117]

A three-fourths majority of the four aldermen was required to override the mayor's veto. After two hours of deliberation, aldermen R. R. "Buck" Rogers, Ray S. Watt, Bert Williams, the original author of the ordinance, and Ted R. Bender voted unanimously for the ordinance once again, overriding the mayor's veto.[118] Led by an unnamed Black woman in the Liberty Hall audience, nearly everyone began to sing "America." Historically this song has been sung by many reform groups—members of the temperance movement, participants in the women's rights movement, abolitionists, and those engaged in civil and human rights—to express their patriotism and love for the nation despite their critique of oppression and injustice by the status quo.[119] Attorney James Hammond, representing the Texas Restaurant Association, and attorney Abner Lipscomb, representing the Motel Owners' Association, were opposed to the ordinance because it was not broad enough and suggested instead that the ordinance should include all businesses, including barber shops, beauty parlors, and apartment houses.[120] Supporters of the ordinance gave the city council a standing ovation. Many of them wept openly when again it passed unanimously, including Drusilla E. Nixon, who "wept into her white-gloved hands."[121] Years later, Drusilla recalled fondly,

And, oh, it was a big to-do! They had to have meetings in Liberty Hall because so many people came. Everyone talked pro and con. So finally, whoever the mayor was said that if it passed, he would veto it. Ted Bender was going off on his vacation and he said, "Mr. Mayor, if you veto this I will fly back from my vacation to vote on it again." They were to vote on it that next week. And sure enough, he vetoed it; and sure enough, Ted Bender came back! And it passed. Of course, everybody thought there was going to be a terrible rush of the people in the restaurants. We had been without restaurants for so long that it just didn't interest us, not like *that*. But it was so good and it has been so wonderful to walk in a restaurant and know that you can order a meal just like anybody else.[122]

Also in attendance at this historic city council meeting was Lawrence A. Nixon's firstborn, Lawrence J. Nixon. He happened to be in town vacationing from Pittsburgh, visiting various family members, including Lawrence and Drusilla Nixon. The younger Nixon felt that the city had "taken a step in the right direction."[123]

With the aldermen's overriding of the mayor's veto, El Paso became the first city in Texas to pass such a resolution. The event made national news, *Newsweek* claiming that El Paso "became the first entirely integrated city in Texas, the first in all the South and Southwest to come to terms with the most divisive issue of the republic."[124] In addition to the 1962 ordinance, El Paso would eventually pass an ordinance "providing for open access in the purchase and renting of housing."[125] The "integration ordinance," as it was dubbed in the local media, went into effect on 22 June 1962. According to the ordinance, a fine of up to $200 could be levied against those persons or establishments who refused service in a hotel, motel, restaurant, or movie to any person solely on the basis of their race, color, or religion.[126]

Coda

Dr. Nixon will become an institution as he
represents all the Negroes in Texas.

Anonymous

By 1948, when Nixon was sixty-five years old, his vibrant career as a civic leader and activist had slowed drastically. After the SCHW folded, he no longer engaged himself with any organization or activity dealing with social justice causes. Between 1948 and his death in 1966, he lived a relatively quiet life, devoting himself primarily to his medical practice and his family. Perhaps this was because his lifelong advocacy work had drained him; perhaps, too, he was stung by the indignity of being labeled a radical for his membership in the SCHW. The public, however, and especially African Americans, had not forgotten his political and professional contributions.

In 1954, the year of the *Brown v. Board of Education of Topeka* case and nine years prior to his formal retirement from medicine in July 1963, Nixon was honored as a longtime member of the Lone Star State Medical, Dental, and Pharmaceutical Association (LSSMDPA), an organization of African American health professionals. Sol White, an LSSMDPA member from Beaumont, Texas, helped host the organization's annual statewide convention in Beaumont. On 9–10 June the association honored a number of Black doctors who had practiced for more than forty years, including Nixon.[1] Certainly, for Black medical professionals in Texas during this period, given the pervasive racism and economic hardship they faced, the mere fact of having been active for more than forty years was an achievement. Nixon's contributions, however, went substantially beyond his important work as a physician. Locally, in the state, and nationally, he was a pioneering civil rights activist and a health care innovator. After the public announcement of his retirement, the El Paso National Bank's Dick Landsheft wrote Nixon, thanking him for his many years of service to the community and congratulating him on his retirement.[2]

Less than three years after his retirement, a tragedy occurred. Nixon's car was sideswiped on Interstate 10 in El Paso by a speeding vehicle as Nixon was attempting to merge into traffic from an entry ramp. Upon impact, his vehicle overturned, and he suffered severe injuries to his neck. Other passengers in the car with Nixon included his wife, Drusilla, whose right shoulder was broken, and their oldest daughter, Drusilla Ann Nixon, who suffered minor injuries. Lawrence Nixon was rushed to the hospital but never recovered from his injuries. In his last days he found himself in terrible agony and begged his younger daughter, Edna, and her husband, physician William James McIver, to help end his life. According to Edna, her father was in so much head and neck pain after the accident that he begged family members to "get a gun and shoot me!" His family never considered granting this request. Fortunately, Nixon did meet with a kinder ending. Five days after the accident, on 6 March 1966, he passed away in the hospital, surrounded by his family and friends.[3] Drusilla lived another twenty-four years, dying on 10 May 1990 in Albuquerque, New Mexico.[4]

Letters of condolence to the Nixon family came in from many, including long-time El Pasoan and freshman Democratic congressman Richard White, then Democratic Texas governor John Connally, and the Office of Alumni Affairs at Meharry Medical College in Nashville, Tennessee.[5] The people who gathered to mourn his death and celebrate his life attested to Nixon's unifying power and widespread influence among El Paso citizens. Antonio Arredondo's role as one of Nixon's honorary pallbearers is a telling example of Nixon's relationship with the Mexican American community.[6] Arredondo rented Nixon's Myrtle Avenue property, where he owned and managed the Prescription Depot Drug Store. Originally from Indé, Durango, México, Arredondo arrived in El Paso in November 1909, prior to the Mexican Revolution, and by the late 1930s he had opened his own pharmacy, which served the community for over thirty years.[7]

It is apparent that he and Nixon had become close friends. Lawrence Nixon's medical practice was "almost entirely" Mexican and Mexican American; regrettably, there is scant documentation of this fact because his patient medical records have been lost.[8] Unsurprisingly, in a 1934 letter to Drusilla, Nixon encouraged African Americans to "master the Spanish language," as he himself had, recognizing that "there is more for us to gain—taking thought for the future—by acquiring a knowledge of the countries to the south of us and by

12. Lawrence A. Nixon in his home office, ca. 1950s. Courtesy of the Edna A. (Nixon) McIver family collection.

cultivating the friendship of our southern neighbors then [*sic*] there ever can be from the knowledge of the other European languages."[9]

Locally, the name Lawrence A. Nixon is revered by many in the El Paso community, who remember him personally or know of him through the press and local lore. El Paso has celebrated Nixon's memory by naming a street, Nixon Way, in his honor, and in 1991 Nixon Elementary School opened at 11141 Loma Roja Drive.[10] He is one of the few prominent African Americans people can point to who left an indelible mark on the borderlands city of El Paso. Elsewhere in Texas, however, he is scarcely remembered. In his hometown of Marshall and at his alma mater, Wiley College, there is no presence or memory of Nixon whatsoever. Wiley has an area in the center of campus specifically dedicated to honoring prominent graduates and faculty. The four-foot-high granite blocks memorialize professors such as Melvin B. Tolson Sr. and graduates Heman M. Sweatt and James L. Farmer Jr., and there is also a historical marker on the grounds of the school honoring James L. Farmer Sr. But there is no recognition of Nixon, one of the institution's most famous graduates. This is an example of the historical neglect of Nixon's remarkable life of advocacy and public service.

State and national literature lacks information documenting Nixon's pioneering role in medicine, politics, and the civil rights movement. Without question, Dr. Lawrence Nixon's contribution to the United States, Texas, and El Paso testifies to the importance of being an activist in the confrontation of complex, long-standing issues that directly affect the well being of all of this nation's citizenry.

The particular, if not unique, racial climate in El Paso, and by extension the borderlands, permitted Nixon to take a proactive stance and engage in a heightened level of activism. Nixon understood that the borderlands or the Southwest's "more fluid race relations created a vacuum for a more confrontational" Black leadership style. His "ability to be more audacious in his activism, without the threat of mass acts of violent retribution" against El Paso's Black community, allowed him to be comfortable resisting in ways that were perhaps "uniquely western."[11] In 1934 Nixon believed that most African Americans lived in areas of the country "where the white element occupies the lowest intellectual status" and thus was prone to being reactionary and violent toward Blacks. However, Nixon held that the southwest borderlands had a "white population more intelligent and with less of that unreasoning prejudice." Nixon hoped that Blacks would do as he had done twenty-four years earlier and move to the borderlands, because in the deep South, the Negro

> is not really wanted by the bulk of the white population where he lives in eternal fear of his white neighbor; here he is needed to reclaim this vast, unused territory and may breathe with a comparative sense of freedom. There he can never hope to improve his status and his presence will always retard the progress of his section. Here he will not only improve his own condition but may become an asset to his section.[12]

Perhaps Nixon's journey into the Southwest contributes to the "concept of western openness and freedom" that helped Blacks advance.[13] But it is also conceivable that the "frontier, with its attractive land and its spirit of ruthless freedom, may have at the same time encouraged the westward march" of various systems of oppression such as the institution of slavery, Jim Crow, discrimination, and racial violence.[14] Acutely aware of this, Nixon stressed that

> since all of this southwestern territory was acquired as a direct result of the desire to extend and perpetuate Negro slavery—all the other considerations being secondary—it is highly fitting that this ill-gotten territory should be used to improve the status of the American Negro. Not the least of the advantages to be derived from this locality are the possible future opportunities *and protection* arising as the result of our proximity to Mexico.[15]

Realistically, Lawrence Nixon knew that white rage could erupt against African Americans at any moment despite the borderlands' promise of racial tolerance. Thus, he acknowledged not "knowing what kind of hell the future will hatch out for us in this country" and saw Mexico as a possible alternative and "strategic location [that] may prove to be the greatest element contributing to our survival."[16]

Upon close examination of the life of Lawrence Nixon, one finds how perseverance, strong character, and courage, coupled with a desire to succeed and engage in community activism, made a significant difference in the lives of countless people within and beyond the borderlands. His public life from the early to mid-1900s had a positive impact on the physical health of African and Mexican Americans, as well as the state of Black politics for an entire region.

Notes

Notes on Usage

1. Jeffrey B. Perry, *A Hubert Harrison Reader* (Middletown, CT: Wesleyan University Press, 2001), xxxi. On capitalizing "Negro," see Donald L. Grant and Mildred Bricker Grant, "Some Notes on the Capital 'N'" *Phylon* 36.4 (1975): 435–43, and Joyce Moore Turner and W. Burghardt Turner, eds., *Richard B. Moore, Caribbean Militant in Harlem: Collected Writings, 1920–1972* (Bloomington: Indiana University Press, 1992), 223–38. Booker T. Washington also embraced this idea; see Louis R. Harlan and Raymond W. Smock, eds., *The Booker T. Washington Papers: 1904–1906*, 14 vols. (Urbana: University of Illinois Press, 1972–89), 1:188, 207; 9:6–7; 10:383, 572, 614–15, 620; 12:10–11; 13:469.

2. See Paul Allatson, *Key Terms in Latino/a Cultural and Literary Studies* (Oxford, UK: Blackwell, 2007), 11, George Reid Andrews, *Afro-Latin America, 1800–2000* (New York: Oxford University Press, 2004), 7, and Suzanna Oboler and Anani Dzidzienyo, "Flows and Counterflows: Latinas/os, Blackness, and Racialization in Hemispheric Perspective," in *Neither Enemies nor Friends: Latinos, Blacks, Afro-Latinos*, ed. Anani Dzidzienyo and Suzanna Oboler (New York: Palgrave MacMillan, 2005), 29.

3. Catherine Pratt and Joseph P. Pickett, eds., *The American Heritage Guide to Contemporary Usage and Style* (Boston: Houghton Mifflin Harcourt, 2005), 90.

4. George J. Sánchez, *Becoming Mexican American: Ethnicity, Culture, and Identity in Chicano Los Angeles, 1900–1945* (New York: Oxford University Press, 1993), 277n1.

5. Pratt and Pickett, eds., *The American Heritage Guide to Contemporary Usage and Style*, 32.

6. Ibid., 225.

Introduction: Tale of a Doctor, History of a Land

1. The epigraph to this chapter is quoted in John C. McCall, *Dancing Histories: Heuristic Ethnography with the Ohafia Igbo* (Ann Arbor: University of Michigan Press, 2000), 51.

2. James L. Hicks, "This Man Mason," *Amsterdam News*, 30 April 1960, 1; Gilbert R. Mason and James P. Smith, *Beaches, Blood, and Ballots: A Black Doctor's Civil Rights Struggle* (Jackson: University Press of Mississippi, 2000), ix. On Lula B. White, see Merline Pitre, *In Struggle against Jim Crow: Lulu B. White and the NAACP, 1900–1957* (College Station: Texas A&M University Press, 1999). On Juanita Craft, see Juanita J. Craft and Chandler Vaughan, *A Child, the Earth, and a Tree of Many Seasons: The Voice of Juanita Craft, an Oral Biography* (Dallas, TX: Halifax Publishing, 1981), Michael Phillips, *White Metropolis: Race, Ethnicity, and Religion in Dallas, 1841–2001* (Austin: University of Texas Press, 2006), and Harvey J. Graff, *The Dallas Myth: The Making and Unmaking of an American City* (Minneapolis: University of Minnesota Press, 2008). On Claude W. Black Jr., see Yvonne M. Armstrong, *Black Trailblazers of San Antonio, Texas: Their Businesses, Communities, Institutions and Organizations* (San Antonio, TX: Inkbiyvonne, 2006). On Warneta and Volma Overton, see Carolyn L. Jones, *Volma—My Journey: One Man's Impact on the Civil Rights Movement in Austin, Texas* (Austin, TX: Eakin Press, 1998).

3. "Racial uplift" is a laden phrase invoking unbridled assimilation of Africans in the Western hemisphere into European culture; see Lee D. Baker, "Saggin' and Braggin'" in *Anthropology off the Shelf: Anthropologists on Writing*, ed. Alisse Waterston and Maria D. Vesperi (Malden, MA: Blackwell, 2009), 53, and Lawrence Schenbeck, *Racial Uplift and American Music, 1878–1943* (Jackson: University Press of Mississippi, 2012), 6.

4. Héctor Calderón and José David Saldívar, eds., *Criticism in the Borderlands: Studies in Chicano Literature, Culture, and Ideology* (Durham, NC: Duke University Press, 1991), 5. On Américo Paredes's life, see Ramón Saldívar, *The Borderlands of Culture: Américo Paredes and the Transnational Imaginary* (Durham, NC: Duke University Press, 2006), and José R. Lopez Morín, *The Legacy of Américo Paredes* (College Station: Texas A&M University Press, 2006).

5. David J. Weber and Jane M. Rausch, eds., *Where Cultures Meet: Frontiers in Latin American History* (Wilmington, DE: SR Books, 1994), xiv.

6. Patricia Nelson Limerick, *The Legacy of Conquest: The Unbroken Past of the American West* (New York: Norton, 1987), 258.

7. Jeffrey P. Shepherd to Will Guzmán, October 15, 2008. Shepherd is an associate professor of history at the University of Texas–El Paso.

8. On Louisiana in general, and New Orleans in particular, which is a borderlands both geographically and culturally, see Gwendolyn Midlo Hall, *Africans in Colonial Louisiana: The Development of Afro-Creole Culture in the Eighteenth Century* (Baton Rouge: Louisiana State University Press, 1995), and Kimberly S. Hanger, *Bounded Lives, Bounded Places: Free Black Society in Colonial New Orleans, 1769–1803* (Durham, NC: Duke University Press, 1997). On Tennessee, see Cynthia Cumfer, *Separate Peoples, One Land: The Minds*

of Cherokees, Blacks, and Whites on the Tennessee Frontier (Chapel Hill: University of North Carolina Press, 2007), 14.

9. Samira Kawash, *Dislocating the Color Line: Identity, Hybridity, and Singularity in African American Literature* (Stanford, CA: Stanford University Press, 1997), 8; Blake Allmendinger, *Imagining the African American West* (Lincoln: University of Nebraska Press, 2005), xii–xiii, 131–32.

10. Touré F. Reed, *Not Alms but Opportunity: The Urban League and the Politics of Racial Uplift, 1910–1950* (Chapel Hill: University of North Carolina Press, 2008), 3, 11, 27–28, 30, 45, 37, 61, 169–70. With respect to educational attainment, Nixon was one of 1,613 Black college graduates in the nation among a Black population of 8.8 million (1900) to 9.8 million (1910) between 1900 and 1909; see "The American Negro in College, 1945–1946," *Crisis* 53.8 (1946): 237, and Nell Irvin Painter, *Creating Black Americans: African-American History and Its Meanings, 1619 to the Present* (New York: Oxford University Press, 2006), 156. On the size of the Black population between 1900 and 1910, see Monroe N. Work, ed., *Negro Year Book and Annual Encyclopedia of the Negro* (Tuskegee, AL: Negro Year Book Publishing Company, 1916), 364.

11. In February 1916, six years after Nixon's arrival, El Paso had a city civilian population of 61,902, of which 32,737 (52.8 percent) were of Mexican descent, 27,359 (44.2 percent) were Anglos, 1,514 (2.5 percent) were Blacks, 243 (.04 percent) were Chinese, 44 were Japanese, and 5 were Native Americans. If one adds the 7,047 Mexican "refugees," then the Mexican/Mexican American population of El Paso was 39,784, or 64 percent of the total population; see "El Paso's Population," *Fort Worth Star-Telegram,* 14 February 1916, 4.

12. I borrow the phrase "unapologetically Black" from Jeremiah A. Wright, formerly of Trinity United Church of Christ in Chicago, who was a disciple of James H. Cone, one of the major intellectual icons of Black liberation theology; see Robert M. Franklin, *Another Day's Journey: Black Churches Confronting the American Crisis* (Minneapolis, MN: Fortress Press, 1997), 36, and Roy L. Brooks, *Racial Justice in the Age of Obama* (Princeton, NJ: Princeton University Press, 2009), 65.

13. George Lipsitz, "Facing the Music in a Land of a Thousand Dances," *Sunburst* 9.2 (1993): 7.

14. On Blacks viewed as intellectually and biologically inferior, see Harriet A. Washington, *Medical Apartheid: The Dark History of Medical Experimentation on Black Americans from Colonial Times to the Present* (New York: Doubleday, 2006), 33–34, 38, 62, 90, 93.

15. Lawrence A. Nixon to Drusilla E. (Tandy) Attwell, 14 August 1932, N/MFP.

16. Quintard Taylor, *In Search of the Racial Frontier: African Americans in the American West, 1528–1990* (New York: Norton, 1998), 18–19.

17. Ibid., 17.

18. Richard White, *"It's Your Misfortune and None of My Own": A History of the American West* (Norman: University of Oklahoma Press, 1991), 577, 589.

19. Taylor, *In Search of the Racial Frontier,* 313.

20. Larry Tye, *Rising from the Rails: Pullman Porters and the Making of the Black Middle Class* (New York: Henry Holt, 2004), 95. National Public Radio (NPR) affiliate WHYY's "Fresh Air" host Terry Gross interviewed Tye on 30 June 2004 about his book, where he expands further on this phenomenon; see www.npr.org/templates/story/story .php?storyId=3049156 (accessed 8 January 2014).

21. Douglas Flamming, *Bound for Freedom: Black Los Angeles in Jim Crow America* (Berkeley: University of California Press, 2005), 11.

22. Ibid.

23. Ibid., 12.

24. Hazel V. Carby, *Reconstructing Womanhood: The Emergence of the Afro-American Woman Novelist* (New York: Oxford University Press, 1987), 22.

25. Darlene Clark Hine, "Black Professionals and Race Consciousness: Origins of the Civil Rights Movement, 1890–1950," *Journal of American History* 89.4 (2003): 1279–81. Specific parallel organizations that Hine mentions include the National Medical Association in 1895, the National Association of Colored Graduate Nurses in 1908, and the National Bar Association in 1925. For a brief history of each organization see Nina Mjagkij, ed., *Organizing Black America: An Encyclopedia of African American Associations* (Oxford, UK: Taylor and Francis, 2001), 389, 468, 408, 467, and David H. Jackson Jr., "The Growth of African American Cultural and Social Institutions," in *A Companion to African American History*, ed. Alton Hornsby (Oxford, UK: Blackwell, 2005), 312–24.

26. Joseph Alvin Chatman, *The Lone Star State Medical, Dental, and Pharmaceutical Association History* (Lubbock, TX: Chatman, 1959), 36 and 173.

27. Darlene Clark Hine, "The Corporeal and Ocular Veil: Dr. Matilda A. Evans (1872–1935) and the Complexity of Southern History," *Journal of Southern History* 70.1 (2004): 5.

28. Edward H. Beardsley, "William D. Chappelle, Jr., M.D.: A Physician and Churchman in South Carolina," *A.M.E. Church Review* 117.382 (2001): 54; Hine, "The Corporeal and Ocular Veil," 7n11.

29. Carter G. Woodson, *The Negro Professional Man and the Community: With Special Emphasis on the Physician and the Lawyer* (New York: Negro University, 1970), 126. See also Hine, "The Corporeal and Ocular Veil," 3, 4n1.

30. Flamming, *Bound for Freedom*, 12.

31. Ibid., 3, 9.

32. Hine, "Black Professionals and Race Consciousness," 1280.

33. Linda Royster Beito and David T. Beito, *Black Maverick: T. R. M. Howard's Fight for Civil Rights and Economic Power* (Urbana: University of Illinois Press, 2009); Florence Ridlon, *A Black Physician's Struggle for Civil Rights: Edward C. Mazique, M.D.* (Albuquerque: University of New Mexico Press, 2005); Gilbert R. Mason and James P. Smith, *Beaches, Blood, and Ballots: A Black Doctor's Civil Rights Struggle* (Jackson: University Press of Mississippi, 2000); Barbara R. Cotton, *Non Verba Opera = Not Words but Works: The Biography of Joseph Howard Griffin, M.D.* (Tallahassee, FL: B. R. Cotton, 1980); Sonnie Wellington Hereford III and Jack D. Ellis, *Beside the Troubled Waters: A Black Doctor Remembers Life,*

Medicine, and the Civil Rights in an Alabama Town (Tuscaloosa: University of Alabama Press, 2011); Hugh Pearson, *Under the Knife: How a Wealthy Negro Surgeon Wielded Power in the Jim Crow South* (New York: Free Press, 2000).

34. Rayford W. Logan, *The Negro in American Life and Thought: The Nadir, 1877–1901* (New York: Dial Press, 1954), iii, 52, 79; Kenneth Robert Janken, *Rayford W. Logan and the Dilemma of the African American Intellectual* (Amherst: University of Massachusetts Press, 1997), 219–21; August Meier, "The Negro and the Democratic Party, 1875–1915," *Phylon* 17.2 (1956): 175.

35. Thomas J. Ward, *Black Physicians in the Jim Crow South* (Fayetteville: University of Arkansas Press, 2003); James Summerville, *Educating Black Doctors: A History of Meharry Medical College* (Tuscaloosa: University of Alabama Press, 1983).

Chapter 1. Marshall, Texas, 1883–1909

1. The epigraph to this chapter is quoted in Sheldon Avery, *Up from Washington: William Pickens and the Negro Struggle for Equality, 1900–1954* (Wilmington: University of Delaware Press, 1989), 36.

2. Some sources incorrectly state that Nixon was born on 7 February 1884. In the 1900 census he is described as a seventeen-year-old Black male student who was born in February 1883. Also, Nixon indicates his birthday in four different accounts as 9 February 1883; see *Twelfth Census of the United States*, population schedule, Marshall, ward 2, Harrison County, TX, series T623, roll 1643, page 186B, line 83; "El Pasoan Ends Medical Career," *El Paso Herald-Post*, 24 July 1963, 6; Conrey Bryson, "Progress Report: A Letter from Dr. L. A. Nixon to the NAACP, 1952," *Password* 32.4 (1987): 186; registration card 3153, draft 1827, Local Board 1, El Paso, El Paso County, TX, 12 September 1918, www.ancestrylibrary.com (accessed 9 June 2009).

3. N/MFP. The middle names of Alfaretta, Annie, and Charles were obtained from Edna Angela (Nixon) McIver, Lawrence A. Nixon's daughter. In March 2009, I visited Mrs. McIver at her Albuquerque, NM, home.

4. On deaths, see family tree documents in Lawrence A. Walker Family Papers, Graham, North Carolina. For names and birthdates of Lawrence A. Nixon's siblings, see *Twelfth Census of the United States*, population schedule, Marshall, ward 2, Harrison County, TX, series T623, roll 1643, page 186B, lines 82–86. Oddly, Jennie Valerie Nixon (born March 1865), Lawrence Nixon's mom, is listed as the head of household, and there is no mention of Charles B. Nixon, Lawrence A. Nixon's father. Charles B. Nixon could have been away on one of the many trips he took as a porter when the census was conducted.

5. Alfaretta S. Walker, LAWFP.

6. Ibid.

7. Ibid.; Howard Dodson, "The Transatlantic Slave Trade and the Making of the Modern World," in *African Roots/American Cultures: Africa in the Creation of the Americas*, ed. Sheila S. Walker (Lanham, MD: Rowman and Littlefield, 2001), 119. On the

Bushongo and the Kuba Kingdom, see Rebecca Leuchak, *Kuba* (New York: Rosen, 1997), and Robert B. Edgerton, *The Troubled Heart of Africa: A History of the Congo* (New York: Macmillan, 2002). Kwe, Nharon, Hai, !Khu, and !Xo are several of the names that various groups in southern Africa used to refer to themselves. Bushmen and San are considered racist and sexist by some since they derive from "bandit" or "outlaw," yet at times Africans themselves used these terms; see Robert J. Gordon and Stuart Sholto-Douglas, *The Bushman Myth: The Making of a Namibian Underclass* (Boulder, CO: Westview Press, 2000), 5–7, and Elizabeth Marshall Thomas, *The Old Way: A Story of the First People* (New York: Macmillan, 2007), xiii–xv.

8. The political arguments for prohibiting the importation of African captives and the bill's progression through Congress are discussed in Donald L. Robinson, *Slavery in the Structure of American Politics, 1765–1820* (New York: Harcourt Brace Jovanovich, 1971), 324–38.

9. Edward Countryman, *Americans: A Collision of Histories* (New York: Macmillan, 1997), 102–3.

10. *Tenth Census of the United States*, population schedule, Marshall, ward 2, Harrison County, TX, series T9, roll 1309, page 339A, line 29.

11. Sylviane A. Diouf, *Dreams of Africa in Alabama: The Slave Ship* Clotilda *and the Story of the Last Africans Brought to America* (New York: Oxford University Press, 2009). The federal government's Works Progress Administration interviewed former African captives in the 1930s who "remembered the landing of Africans" as late as the 1850s. In 1935, for example, Wallace Quarterman, a Geechee, or Gullah, speaker, recalled African captives landing near his Darien, Georgia, home in 1844. In the late 1850s, a Georgia agricultural society offered a $25 prize "for the most physically perfect African imported that year," indicating that the illegal importation of African captives was not just tolerated but common knowledge and that the laws of the federal government were being flagrantly and arrogantly violated. The last known ship to smuggle African captives into Georgia was the New York–based *Wanderer*, which arrived at Jekyll Island (near Brunswick, Georgia) on 28 November 1858 with a cargo of 409 "salt backs," or African captives (Erik Calonius, *The Wanderer: The Last American Slave Ship and the Conspiracy that Set Its Sails* [New York: St. Martin's Press, 2006], 110; Donald L. Grant, *The Way It Was in The South: The Black Experience in Georgia* [Athens: University of Georgia Press, 2001], 29).

12. Alfaretta S. Walker, Nixon family story, LAWFP.

13. Ibid.

14. Wilma A. Dunaway, *The African-American Family in Slavery and Emancipation* (Cambridge: Cambridge University Press, 2003), 1–16, 52–59.

15. Alfaretta S. Walker, Nixon family story, LAWFP.

16. Michael Fellman, *The Making of Robert E. Lee* (Baltimore, MD: John Hopkins University Press, 2003), 54–75.

17. Charles L. Blockson and Ron Fry, *Black Genealogy* (Baltimore, MD: Black Classic Press, 1997), 108.

18. Alfaretta S. Walker, Nixon family story, LAWFP.

19. *Tenth Census of the United States*, population schedule, Marshall, ward 2, Harrison County, TX, series T9, roll 1309, page 339A, lines 29–38. The term "mulatto" was first used as an official category in the 1850 U.S. census and continued to be used until 1930 (Dominique Arel and David I. Kertzer, *Census and Identity: The Politics of Race, Ethnicity, and Language in National Census* [Cambridge: Cambridge University Press, 2002], 51–52). Today "mulatto" is rarely used in public or in popular culture; instead, "biracial" or "multiracial" is the preferred word among many.

20. Alfaretta S. Walker, Nixon family history, LAWFP.

21. *Tenth Census of the United States*, population schedule 1, Marshall, ward 2, Harrison County, TX, series T9, roll 1309, page 339A, lines 29–38.

22. Alfaretta S. Walker, Nixon family history, LAWFP.

23. Bryson, "Progress Report," 186; *Tenth Census of the United States*, population schedule, Marshall, ward 2, Harrison County, TX, series T9, roll 1309, page 339A, line 31. For Jennie Valerie Engledow's stated birth year in the census, see *Twelfth Census of the United States*, population schedule 1, Marshall, ward 2, Harrison County, TX, series T623, roll 1643, page 186B, line 82.

24. *Tenth Census of the United States*, population schedule, Marshall, ward 2, Harrison County, TX, series T9, roll 1309, page 339A, line 31. On the early history of the Texas and Pacific Railroad, see Richard N. Griffith Means, "Empire, Progress, and the American Southwest: The Texas and Pacific Railroad, 1850–1882" (PhD diss., University of Southern Mississippi, 2001). See also Augustus J. Veenendaal, *American Railroads in the Nineteenth Century* (Westport, CT: Greenwood Press, 2003), 67–68.

25. Bryson, "Progress Report," 186.

26. Eric Arnesen, *Brotherhoods of Color: Black Railroad Workers and the Struggle for Equality* (Cambridge, MA: Harvard University Press, 2001), 1.

27. Liston E. Leyendecker, *Palace Car Prince: A Biography of George Mortimer Pullman* (Boulder: University Press of Colorado, 1992).

28. Jack Santino, *Miles of Smiles, Years of Struggle: Stories of Black Pullman Porters* (Urbana: University of Illinois Press, 1989), 13–14.

29. Arnesen, *Brotherhoods of Color*, 17–18.

30. The "Sambo" image of African American men as happy, content servants was an invention of hopeful plantation owners "who wanted to believe that black men were less capable of exercising freedom than themselves" (Bret Carroll, *American Masculinities: A Historical Encyclopedia* [Thousand Oaks, CA: SAGE, 2003], 424). See Joseph Boskin, *Sambo: The Rise and Demise of an American Jester* (New York: Oxford University Press, 1988).

31. Santino, *Miles of Smiles, Years of Struggle*, 99.

32. Bertram Wyatt-Brown, "The Mask of Obedience: Male Slave Psychology in the Old South," in *Society and Culture in the Slave South*, ed. J. William Harris (New York: Routledge, 1992), 128–61. "We Wear the Mask" is the title of a poem by Paul Laurence Dunbar; see *The Collected Poetry of Paul Laurence Dunbar* (Charlottesville: University of

Virginia Press, 1993), 71. See also Marcyliena Morgan, *Language, Discourse and Power in African American Culture* (New York: Cambridge University Press, 2002), 16–17. "Ms. Ann" and "Mr. Charlie" are generic phrases used to describe white women and men; see James Baldwin, *Blues for Mister Charlie: A Drama in Three Acts* (New York: Samuel French, 1964), and William Safire, *Safire's Political Dictionary* (New York: Oxford University Press, 2008), 111.

33. Amy G. Richter, *Home on the Rails: Women, the Railroad, and the Rise of Public Domesticity* (Chapel Hill: University of North Carolina Press, 2005), 115.

34. Douglas Flamming, *Bound for Freedom: Black Los Angeles in Jim Crow America* (Berkeley: University of California Press, 2005), 8. Nixon purchased, rented, and sold land a number of times during his life in El Paso. For example, he sold 3.4 acres of property in the Boothville subdivision to John L. Winn for $36,500 in 1956; see "Three Property Sales Recorded," *El Paso Herald-Post*, 16 May 1956, 24.

35. Arnesen, *Brotherhoods of Color*, 1. Black women were also active with the Brotherhood of Sleeping Car Porters; see Melinda Chateauvert, *Marching Together: Women of the Brotherhood of Sleeping Car Porters* (Urbana: University of Illinois Press, 1998).

36. Flamming, *Bound for Freedom*, 8. Over time porters became more active in their demands for better wages, working conditions, and unionization; see Beth Tompkins Bates, *Pullman Porters and the Rise of Protest Politics in Black America, 1925–1945* (Chapel Hill: University of North Carolina Press, 2001).

37. Arnesen, *Brotherhoods of Color*, 2. Harry Haywood was a prominent intellectual, organizer, and communist leader who established the Maoist New Communist movement; see Walter T. Howard, ed., *Black Communists Speak on Scottsboro: A Documentary History* (Philadelphia: Temple University Press, 2008), 84–98. Benjamin E. Mays, son of a sharecropper, served as president of Morehouse College for twenty-seven years and was the first Black president of the Atlanta School Board as well as mentor to the prominent civil rights leader Martin Luther King Jr.; see Benjamin E. Mays, *Born to Rebel: An Autobiography* (Athens: University of Georgia Press, 2003), and Randal Maurice Jelks, *Benjamin Elijah Mays, Schoolmaster of the Movement: A Biography* (Chapel Hill: University of North Carolina Press, 2012). Roy Wilkins started out as assistant secretary for the NAACP, succeeded W. E. B. Du Bois as editor of the *Crisis*, and eventually succeeded Walter White as executive director; see Roy Wilkins and Tom Mathews, *Standing Fast: The Autobiography of Roy Wilkins* (New York: Da Capo Press, 1994).

38. Tye, *Rising from the Rails*, xi; Arnesen, *Brotherhoods of Color*, 2.

39. The name of the general manager that Charles B. Nixon worked for is not known and could not be determined, although lists of Texas and Pacific Railway officers and directors in Marshall, Texas, at the time can be found in the *1893 Poor's Directory of Railway Officials* (New York: Poor's Railroad Manual, 1893), 137, the *Annual Report of the Texas and Pacific Railway Company to the Stockholders for the Year Ending December 31, 1893* (New York: John C. Rankin, 1894), 3, and Waldo H. Marshall and E. N. Lewis, eds., *The Official Railway List: A Complete Directory* (Chicago: Railway Purchasing Agent Company, 1892), 237.

40. Bryson, "Progress Report," 186.

41. Conrey Bryson, *Dr. Lawrence A. Nixon and the White Primary* (El Paso, TX: Texas Western Press, 1974), 20.

42. Ibid. Bryson indicates that Nixon was three years old at the time of the move, but since he gives his birth year incorrectly as 1884 instead of 1883, then the year Lawrence Nixon left for New Orleans cannot be known for sure. The 1900 census in which Annie Lucillia Nixon is labeled as having been born in Texas (presumably in Marshall) in March 1885 and Alfaretta Sally Nixon is labeled as having been born in Louisiana (presumably in New Orleans) in March 1887 confirms the year of the move to New Orleans from Marshall (*Twelfth Census of the United States*, population schedule, Marshall, ward 2, Harrison County, TX, series T623, roll 1643, page 186B, lines 84–85). Charles J. Nixon, Lawrence's brother, was born in 1889 in Louisiana (*Fifteenth Census of the United States*, population schedule, El Paso, justice precinct 1, El Paso County, TX, series T626, roll 2328, page 104A, line 41). Charles J. Nixon died in El Paso on 22 September 1976, ten years after Lawrence; see El Paso County Clerk, Charles J. Nixon death certificate, 22 September 1976, reel no. 301, frame no. 964.

43. Donald G. Nieman, ed., *Black Southerners and the Law, 1865–1900* (Oxford, UK: Taylor and Francis, 1994), 409–10; Mark Tushnet, ed., *I Dissent: Great Opposing Opinions in Landmark Supreme Court Cases* (Boston: Beacon Press, 2008), 45–68.

44. Marcus D. Pohlmann and Linda Vallar Whisenhunt, *Student's Guide to Landmark Congressional Laws on Civil Rights* (Westport, CT: Greenwood Press, 2002), 126–27.

45. George P. Sanger, ed., *The Statutes at Large and Proclamations of the United States of America, and Treaties and Postal Conventions*, vol. 16 (Boston: Little, Brown, 1871), 140–41; George P. Sanger, ed., *The Statutes at Large and Proclamations of the United States of America, and Treaties and Postal Conventions*, vol. 17 (Boston: Little, Brown, 1873), 13.

46. The Redeemers were a loose political coalition in the post–Civil War South which consisted of prewar former slave owners, conservative Democrats, Union Whigs, and Confederate army veterans. They sought to "redeem" the South by undoing the changes brought about by the Civil War. They were committed to reducing the role of government and institutionalizing the economic and political exploitation of African Americans. The Redeemers' policies inhibited regional economic development and exacerbated the class strife and racial violence that followed the Civil War; see Eric Foner and John A. Garraty, eds., *The Reader's Companion to American History* (Boston: Houghton Mifflin Harcourt, 1991), 924, and Richard M. Valelly, *The Two Reconstructions: The Struggle for Black Enfranchisement* (Chicago: University of Chicago Press, 2004), 50, 93–94, 115–17.

47. Randolph B. Campbell, *A Southern Community in Crisis: Harrison County, Texas, 1850–1880* (Austin: Texas State Historical Association, 1983), 373.

48. *Statistics of the Population of the United States at the Tenth Census* (Washington, DC: Government Printing Office, 1881), 424.

49. Ibid.

50. Ibid., 482.

51. Campbell, *A Southern Community in Crisis*, 369, 377, 379, 384, 389, 393, 395.

52. Ibid., 392; Barry A. Crouch, *The Dance of Freedom: Texas African Americans During Reconstruction*, ed. Larry Medaris (Austin: University of Texas Press: 2007), 17–18.

53. Cary D. Wintz, forward to *Blacks in East Texas History: Selections from the East Texas Historical Journal*, ed. Bruce A. Glasrud and Archie P. McDonald (College Station: Texas A&M University Press, 2008), vii.

54. Manning Marable and Leith Mullings, *Let Nobody Turn Us Around: Voices of Resistance, Reform, and Renewal: An African American Anthology* (Lanham, MD: Rowman and Littlefield, 2009), 117–18.

55. Allen W. Trelease, *White Terror: The Ku Klux Klan Conspiracy and Southern Reconstruction* (Baton Rouge: Louisiana State University Press, 1999), 26, 51, 82–83, 420; James Michael Martinez, *Carpetbaggers, Cavalry, and the Ku Klux Klan: Exposing the Invisible Empire during Reconstruction* (Lanham, MD: Rowman and Littlefield, 2007), 10.

56. Kenneth M. Hamilton, "White Wealth and Black Repression in Harrison County, Texas: 1865–1868," *Journal of Negro History* 84.4 (1999): 340–59.

57. Randolph B. Campbell, *Grass-Roots Reconstruction in Texas, 1865–1880* (Baton Rouge: Louisiana State University Press, 1997), 111–12, 120. The abbreviation "f.m." probably stands for "freedmen." Violence against African Americans in east Texas during this time period was pervasive; see Crouch, *The Dance of Freedom*, 95–117, particularly 113n11, and 114nn15–17.

58. Campbell, *A Southern Community in Crisis*, 373. The Jefferson Division of the Texas and Pacific ran northward to Texarkana, where Charles N. Nixon (Lawrence Nixon's grandfather) lived. Charles N. Nixon would frequently visit his grandchildren in Marshall, which was about seventy-five miles from Texarkana; see Bryson, *Dr. Lawrence A. Nixon and the White Primary*, 19–20.

59. Campbell, *Grass-Roots Reconstruction in Texas*, 131, 132, 131–38. The term "carpetbagger" described Northerners who moved to the South after the Civil War and assisted or sympathized with African Americans and/or were elected as Republicans to public office. Southern Democrats accused carpetbaggers of political corruption and ineptness; see Randolph B. Campbell, "Carpetbagger Rule in Reconstruction Texas: An Enduring Myth," *Southwestern Historical Quarterly* 97.4 (1994): 587–96. Scalawags were Southern whites who were perceived to be traitors to their region and race owing to their support of Reconstruction policies; see James Alex Baggett, *The Scalawags: Southern Dissenters in the Civil War and Reconstruction* (Baton Rouge: Louisiana State University Press, 2004).

60. Campbell, *Grass-Roots Reconstruction in Texas*, 132. African Americans were not a political monolith; see Edmund L. Drago, *Hurrah for Hampton! Black Red Shirts in South Carolina During Reconstruction* (Fayetteville: University of Arkansas Press, 1998), Bernard E. Powers Jr., *Black Charlestonians: A Social History, 1822–1885* (Fayetteville: University of Arkansas Press, 1994), and Clarence E. Walker, *Deromanticizing Black History: Critical Essays and Reprisals* (Knoxville: University of Tennessee Press, 1991).

61. Campbell, *Grass-Roots Reconstruction in Texas*, 132–33.

62. James T. Gunderson, "The Rise of the Citizens Party in Post-Reconstruction Harrison County" (MA thesis, University of Houston, 2004), 14; Campbell, *Grass-Roots Reconstruction in Texas, 1865–1880*, 15–26.

63. Campbell, *A Southern Community in Crisis*, 140.

64. Alwyn Barr, "The Texas Black Uprising Scare of 1883," *Phylon* 41.2 (1980): 179–86; James N. Leiker, *Racial Borders: Black Soldiers along the Rio Grande* (College Station: Texas A&M University, 2002), 72.

65. Bryson, *Dr. Lawrence A. Nixon and the White Primary*, 21.

66. Department of the Interior, Bureau of Education, *Negro Education: A Study of the Private and Higher Education Schools for Colored People in the United States* (Washington, DC: Government Printing Office, 1917), 581.

67. David Gold, *Rhetoric at the Margins: Revising the History of Writing Instruction in American Colleges, 1873–1947* (Carbondale: Southern Illinois University Press, 2008), 24; Lloyd K. Thompson, "The Origins and Development of Black Religious Colleges in East Texas" (PhD diss., University of North Texas, 1976), 30.

68. Michael R. Heintze, *Private Black Colleges in Texas, 1865–1954* (College Station: Texas A&M University Press, 1985).

69. Dogan graduated from Rust University in 1886 and earned a PhD and DD from New Orleans University in 1910. He was a registered Republican, president of Standard American Mutual Fire Insurance Company, the National Association of Teachers in Colored Schools, the East Texas Colored Teachers' Association, and a member of the Knights of Pythias (Warmoth T. Gibbs, *President Matthew W. Dogan of Wiley College: A Biography* [Marshall, TX: Firmin-Greer, 1930], 24, 27; Frank Lincoln Mather, ed., *Who's Who of the Colored Race: A General Biographical Dictionary of Men and Women of African Descent*, vol. 1 [Chicago: Frank Lincoln Mather, 1915], 93).

70. For example, students at Bishop College and Wiley College (both located in Lawrence Nixon's hometown of Marshall) were among the first in Texas to engage in sit-ins during the early 1960s. Using Gandhi's technique of nonviolent civil disobedience that was espoused by Wiley graduate James Farmer in the early 1940s, Wiley and Bishop students R. J. Peabody, Donald J. Guinyard, Mark R. Hannon Jr., and six other students along with Dr. Doxey A. Wilkerson of Bishop unsuccessfully attempted to receive service at the F. W. Woolworth Company's lunch counter in Marshall, and days later nearly a hundred Texas Rangers would order fire hoses on dozens of students from both schools when they took over the Harrison County Courthouse. Bishop fired Wilkerson for his involvement in the protest; see "Negro Group Seeks Service in Marshall," *Abilene Reporter-News*, 27 March 1960, 2, "Marshall Tense as Fire Hoses Used on Negroes," *Del Rio News-Herald*, 31 March 1960, 1, Raymond Holbrook, "Marshall, Armed Camp, Expects New Troubles: March of Negro Students Feared," *Big Spring Daily Herald*, 1 April 1960, 1, "Bold Sit-Ins in Marshall," *Observer*, 1 April 1960, "From Chapel to Dousing," *Observer*, 8 April 1960, and Betty Swales, "Local Café Integration Demanded in 7 Days," *Texan*, 2 April 1960. On Wilkerson's life, see Maceo C. Dailey Jr. and Ernest D. Washington, "The Evolution of Doxey A. Wilkerson, 1935–45,"

Freedomways 3.1 (1985): 101–15. On the ultimate integration of higher education in Texas at the behest of African Americans, see Amilcar Shabazz, *Advancing Democracy: African Americans and the Struggle for Access and Equity in Higher Education in Texas* (Chapel Hill: University of North Carolina Press, 2004).

71. Gold, *Rhetoric at the Margins*, 22–23; Doug Rossinow, "'The Break-Through to New Life': Christianity and the Emergence of the New Left in Austin, Texas, 1956–1964," *American Quarterly* 46.3 (1994): 326, 339nn41–42.

72. African American teachers have played a critical role in inspiring students with strategies and tools to challenge oppression; see Adam Fairclough, *Teaching Equality: Black Schools in the Age of Jim Crow* (Athens: University of Georgia Press, 2001).

73. James Leonard Maximilian Farmer Sr. was the first African American in Texas to earn a PhD; see Gail K. Beil, "Sowing the Seeds of the Civil Rights Movement: Dr. J. Leonard Farmer and Wiley College, Marshall, Texas, as Case Studies of the Educational Influence on the Modern Civil Rights Leaders" (MA thesis, Stephen F. Austin State University, 1999), 2, 5. It is unknown how large Lawrence Nixon's 1902 Wiley graduating class was, but in 1903 the school had 284 students; see Henry F. Kletzing and William Henry Crogman, *Progress of a Race: The Remarkable Advancement of the Afro-American Negro from the Bondage of Slavery, Ignorance and Poverty, to the Freedom of Citizenship, Intelligence, Affluence, Honor and Trust* (Atlanta, GA: J. L. Nichols, 1903), 693.

74. Gold, *Rhetoric at the Margins*, 23.

75. Beil, "Sowing the Seeds of the Civil Rights Movement," iii. On James L. Farmer Jr., see James Farmer, *Lay Bare the Heart: An Autobiography of the Civil Rights Movement* (Fort Worth: Texas Christian University Press, 1998), and "The Higher Education of James Farmer," *Journal of Blacks in Higher Education* 18 (Winter 1997–98): 79. On Emmett J. Scott, see Maceo C. Dailey Jr., "Emmett J. Scott: The Career of a Secondary Black Leader" (PhD diss., Howard University, 1983). On the life of Melvin B. Tolson, see Robert M. Farnsworth, *Melvin B. Tolson, 1898–1966: Plain Talk and Poetic Prophecy* (Columbia: University of Missouri Press, 1984).

76. David A. Williams, *Bricks Without Straw: A Comprehensive History of African Americans in Texas* (Austin, TX: Eakin Press, 1997), 255. On Bishop College, see Emmanuel E. Egar, "Development and Termination of Bishop College between 1960 and 1988" (PhD diss., University of North Texas, 1990). "In addition to their differences, black colleges were often in competition or conflict with one another, especially across interfaith lines. Clarence Norris, a Bishop College faculty member who later became dean of St. Philip's, noted that competition between the Baptist Bishop and the Methodist Wiley, both in Marshall, was so fierce that when, in 1933, he taught as a dual appointee at the two schools to substitute for a Wiley professor on leave, he felt 'caught in the middle' between their presidents and under pressure to declare his loyalty: 'During their entire existence both colleges were very antagonistic to each other'" (Gold, *Rhetoric at the Margins*, 23).

77. Gail K. Beil, "Melvin B. Tolson: Texas Radical," in *Blacks in East Texas History*, 126–27.

78. For an analysis of the racial uprising in Longview, Texas, see William M. Tuttle, "Violence in a 'Heathen' Land: The Longview Race Riot of 1919," *Phylon* 33.4 (1972): 324–33.

79. Beil, "Melvin B. Tolson" 126–27.

80. Farmer, *Lay Bare the Heart*, 121. Farmer was one of the "big six" leaders of the 1960s civil rights movement, along with Martin Luther King Jr. (Southern Christian Leadership Conference), Asa Philip Randolph (Brotherhood of Sleeping Car Porters), Roy Wilkins (NAACP), John Lewis (Student Nonviolent Coordinating Committee), and Whitney Young (National Urban League). In 1942, Farmer cofounded the Congress for Racial Equality with Bernice Fisher, Bayard Rustin, and George Houser. Born in Marshall in January 1920, Farmer organized and participated in the freedom rides of the 1960s. On Bernice Fisher, see Mary Kimbrough and Margaret W. Dagen, *Victory without Violence: The First Ten Years of the St. Louis Committee of Racial Equality (CORE), 1947–1957* (Columbia: University of Missouri Press, 2000), 21. On Rustin, see John D'Emilio, *Lost Prophet: The Life and Times of Bayard Rustin* (Chicago: University of Chicago Press, 2004), and Bayard Rustin, *Down the Line: The Collected Writings of Bayard Rustin* (Chicago: Quadrangle Books, 1971). On George Houser, see George Houser, *No One Can Stop the Rain: Glimpses of Africa's Liberation Struggle* (Cleveland, OH: Pilgrim Press, 1989).

81. Beil, "Melvin B. Tolson," 119, 124–25, 128.

82. Ibid., 124–25; Gold, *Rhetoric at the Margins*, 14–15, 23, 28–29, 37–38, 42, 179–80.

83. Bryson, *Dr. Lawrence A. Nixon and the White Primary*, 22.

84. *Meharry Medical, Dental and Pharmaceutical Departments of Central Tennessee College, Catalogue of 1894–95 and Announcement for 1895–96* (Nashville, TN: Cumberland Presbyterian Publishing House, 1895), 5, 9; *Meharry Medical, Dental and Pharmaceutical Colleges of Walden University, Catalogue of 1907–1908 and Announcement for 1908–1909* (Nashville, TN: Marshall and Bruce, 1908), 37; *Meharry News* 1.1 (902): 1.

85. James Summerville, *Educating Black Doctors: A History of Meharry Medical College* (Tuscaloosa: University of Alabama Press, 1983), xi, 40, and 56–57. To this day, Meharry plays a vital role in educating African Americans entering the medical professions who go on to practice in medically underserved inner-city and rural areas; see Thomas C. Hunt and James C. Carper, eds., *Religious Higher Education in the United States: A Source Book* (Oxford, UK: Taylor and Francis, 1996), 468–69.

86. Nixon's original diploma is in the possession of his daughter, Edna Angela (Nixon) McIver.

87. Charles V. Roman, *Meharry Medical College: A History* (Nashville, TN: Sunday School Publishing Board of the National Baptist Convention, 1934), v.

88. *Meharry Medical, Dental and Pharmaceutical Colleges of Walden University, Catalogue of 1905–1906 and Announcement for 1906–1907* (Nashville, TN: Marshall and Bruce, 1906), 5.

89. Helen Buckler, *Doctor Dan: Pioneer in American Surgery* (Boston: Little, Brown, 1954), 75; Michael W. Williams, *The African American Encyclopedia*, vol. 6 (New York: Marshall Cavendish, 1993), 1705–7; Harriet A. Washington, *Medical Apartheid: The Dark History of Medical Experimentation on Black Americans from Colonial Times to the Present*

(New York: Doubleday, 2006), 156; Helen Buckler, *Daniel Hale Williams: Negro Surgeon* (New York: Pitman, 1968).

90. Thomas J. Ward, *Black Physicians in the Jim Crow South* (Fayetteville: University of Arkansas Press, 2003), 82; Buckler, *Doctor Dan*, 194–96, 200–201, 217, 254–55, 272; Buckler, *Daniel Hale Williams*, 200–201; Williams, *The African American Encyclopedia*, 1707; Roman, *Meharry Medical College*, 52, 71; Summerville, *Educating Black Doctors*, 44, 46.

91. Buckler, *Doctor Dan*, 201.

92. N/MFP.

93. "In Memoriam: Dr. John Henry Hale," *Journal of the National Medical Association* 34.4 (1944): 130–31; Mather, *Who's Who of the Colored Race*, 127.

94. Bryson, *Dr. Lawrence A. Nixon and the White Primary*, 22–23. During this time many Meharry students waited on tables, cleaned out laboratories, and worked on Pullman cars during their time off from classes; see Buckler, *Doctor Dan*, 200.

95. Tye, *Rising from the Rails*, 86.

96. "Meharry Commencement," *Meharry News* 4.1 (1906): 8.

97. N/MFP.

98. In 1950, A. L. Hunter was elected to serve as president of the Lone Star State Medical, Dental, and Pharmaceutical Association during its sixty-fourth annual convention held in Galveston; see "Negro Medics Elect," *San Antonio Light*, 16 June 1950, 49. For a brief history of this all-Black professional medical organization, see Alwyn Barr, "The Lone Star State Medical, Dental, and Pharmaceutical Association," *Handbook of Texas Online*, www.tshaonline.org/handbook/online/articles/sal01 (accessed 4 January 2014).

99. "Report of the Examination Held by the Board of Medicine Examiners at Their Meeting in Dallas, Texas," *Texas Medical News: A Journal of Medicine, Surgery and Hygiene* 15.10 (1906): 527–29; "Report of Examination for Licenses to Practice Medicine," *Texas State Journal of Medicine* 2.5 (1906): 141. Sources do not indicate the first names of the other two Meharry graduates who passed their examination along with Nixon. Interestingly, these two journals listed Nixon as having graduated from Meharry Medical School in 1905, while other accounts have him graduating in 1906.

100. *Meharry Medical, Dental and Pharmaceutical Colleges of Walden University, Catalogue of 1907–1908*, 39; *Meharry Medical, Dental and Pharmaceutical Colleges of Walden University, Catalogue of 1908–1909 and Announcement for 1909–1910* (Nashville, TN: Marshall and Bruce, 1909), 39.

101. Lawrence A. Nixon to Lawrence J. Nixon, 19 March 1919, N/MFP.

102. "Marriages," *Meharry News* 6.1 (1908): 5; Nixon family bible, LAWFP.

103. Lawrence A. Nixon to Lawrence J. Nixon, 19 March 1919, N/MFP.

104. Lawrence J. Nixon, obituary, memorial service program, Samuel J. Jones Funeral Home, 24 February 2006, 3, N/MFP. Lawrence Joseph Nixon died on 16 February 2006.

105. Ward, *Black Physicians in the Jim Crow South*, 99.

106. Ward, *Black Physicians in the Jim Crow South*, 99; emphasis added.

107. *Meharry Medical, Dental and Pharmaceutical Departments of Central Tennessee College, Catalogue of 1894–95*, 5, 9; *Meharry Medical, Dental and Pharmaceutical Colleges of Walden University, Catalogue of 1907–1908*, 37; *Meharry News*, 1.1 (1902): 1.

108. In 1910, there were 7,781 Blacks in Gregg County, making up 55 percent of the overall population; in Panola County, Blacks numbered 8,842, or 43 percent, of the overall population; in Smith County, they were 17,246, or 41 percent, of the overall population; in Longview there were 2,253 Blacks, representing 43.7 percent of the overall population; in Shreveport, Louisiana, Blacks totaled 13,896, or 49.6 percent, of the overall population; see *Thirteenth Census of the United States*, vol. 3 (Washington, DC, Government Printing Office: 1913), 822, 838, 842, 844, 856, and *Thirteenth Census of the United States*, vol. 2 (Washington, DC: Government Printing Office, 1913), 790.

109. *Twelfth Census of the United States*, vol. 1, pt. 1 (Washington, DC: Government Printing Office, 1901), 643.

110. Agriculture, particularly cotton, dominated Cameron's economy in the late nineteenth century, and diverse industrial interests came into play in the early twentieth century. By the turn of the century tenant farmers and sharecroppers were working 60 percent of the 5,337 farms in Milam County. In 1900 farmers planted 147,683 acres of cotton and 71,151 acres of corn, totaling 75 percent of the improved land. Cotton production rose from 10,844 bales in 1880 to 66,555 bales in 1900. Regarding coal, at the turn of the century Milam County had six mining operations that produced a total of twenty railcars of coal per day. At the peak of the mining industry in the area, between 1910 and 1920, the mines shipped as many as forty-five to fifty cars of coal each day. Most of the mine workers were immigrants from Mexico; see Vivian Elizabeth Smyrl, "Cameron, Texas," *Handbook of Texas Online*, www.tshaonline.org/handbook/online/articles/hfc01 (accessed 4 January 2014), and Cecil Harper Jr. and Vivian E. Smyrl, "Milam County," *Handbook of Texas Online*, www.tshaonline.org/handbook/online/articles/hcm13 (accessed 4 January 2014).

111. William D. Carrigan, *The Making of a Lynching Culture: Violence and Vigilantism in Central Texas, 1836–1916* (Urbana: University of Illinois Press, 2004), 148–49.

112. Bryson, *Dr. Lawrence A. Nixon and the White Primary*, 23–24.

113. *Waterloo Semi-Weekly Courier*, 8 November 1907, 8. For biography of Thomas M. Campbell, see Jesús F. de la Teja and Ty Cashion, eds., *The Human Tradition in Texas* (Wilmington, DE: SR Books, 2001), 129–44.

114. *Waterloo Semi-Weekly Reporter*, 20 December 1907, 1; *Galveston Daily News*, 17 December 1907.

115. Howard Smead, *Blood Justice: The Lynching of Mack Charles Parker* (New York: Oxford University Press, 1986), 26.

116. *Waco Weekly News*, 24 February 1893.

117. *Waco Times-Herald*, 10 August 1905. Too often the charges of rape or sexual assault of white women were levied at Black men to justify the barbaric act of lynching,

when the real culprit was self-defense, labor, and monetary disputes or a minor infraction of the racial etiquette of the day. "But chivalry in defense of imperiled white womanhood was only a rationalization, not an explanation of the epidemic of mob murder that consumed the South. Of the nearly three thousand Blacks known to have been lynched between 1889 and 1918, for example, only 19 percent were accused of rape. But in many cases what the public thought had occurred became much more important than what did happen. The public's perception of lynching, fed by the media and improved means of communication, was invariably that a sexual crime by Black men had precipitated it. As Walter White noted, 'having created the Frankenstein monster the lyncher lives in constant fear of his own creation'" (James Allen, *Without Sanctuary: Lynching Photography in America* [Santa Fe, NM: Twin Palms, 2000], 24). See also Walter F. White, *Rope and Faggot: A Biography of Judge Lynch* (New York: Knopf, 1929), 56–57, and Leon F. Litwack, *Trouble in Mind: Black Southerners in the Age of Jim Crow* (New York: Knopf, 1998).

118. *Waco Weekly Tribune*, 8 November 1902.

119. Bryson, *Dr. Lawrence A. Nixon and the White Primary*, 26. African American Cope Mills was lynched in Rosebud after an altercation with a white officer on 20 December 1909. Another Black man, Mitchell Frazier, had been lynched in Rosebud just three years earlier on 15 September 1906; see National Association for the Advancement of Colored People, *Thirty Years of Lynching in the United States, 1889–1918* (New York: NAACP, 1918), 98.

120. Those thirteen individuals lynched were Hal Wright (Harrison County, Texas, 27 April 1897), Russell Wright (Harrison County, Texas, 27 April 1897), Robert Brown (Harrison County, Texas, 27 April 1897), Walker Davis (Marshall, Texas, 1 October 1903), James Hodges, (Marshall, Texas, 27 April 1909), Matthew Chase (Marshall, Texas, 30 April 1909), "Pie" Hill, (Marshall, Texas, 30 April 1909), "Mose" Creole (Marshall, Texas, 30 April 1909); unidentified Black man (Marshall, Texas, 29 October 1911), George Saunders (Marshall, Texas, 13 February 1912), Mary Jackson (Marshall, Texas, 13 February 1912), Anderson (Marshall, Texas, 25 February 1913), and Charles Jones (Marshall, Texas, 22 August 1917) (National Association for the Advancement of Colored People, *Thirty Years of Lynching in the United States*, 96–99; Ralph Ginzburg, *100 Years of Lynchings* [New York: Lancer Books, 1962], 269–70).

121. *Denton Record-Chronicle*, 30 April 1909, 1; *Grand Rapids Tribune*, 5 August 1908.

122. Avery, *Up from Washington*, 36, 203–4nn2–4.

123. Ward, *Black Physicians in the Jim Crow South*, 99.

124. I borrow the phrase "sharpen his oyster knife" from the Harlem Renaissance writer Zora Neale Hurston, who remarked "No, I do not weep at the world—I am too busy sharpening my oyster knife" in describing her refusal to wallow in self-pity over being a Black woman in a sexist, racist, and patriarchal society; see Valerie Boyd, *Wrapped in Rainbows: The Life of Zora Neale Hurston* (New York: Simon and Schuster, 2003), 172–73.

Chapter 2. The Lure of El Paso, 1910–1919

1. The epigraph to this chapter is quoted in Bobby L. Lovett, *The African-American History of Nashville, Tennessee* (Fayetteville: University of Arkansas Press, 1999), 240.

2. Drusilla Elizabeth Nixon, interview no. 194 (11 December 1975), 18, IOH-UTEP; Conrey Bryson, *Dr. Lawrence A. Nixon and the White Primary* (El Paso, TX: Texas Western Press, 1974), 26.

3. Ibid., 26.

4. "El Pasoan Ends Medical Career," *El Paso Herald-Post*, 24 July 1963, 6.

5. Bryson, *Dr. Lawrence A. Nixon and the White Primary*, 20. Nixon's uncle's name is unknown. No person with the last name Engledow is listed in the 1880, 1900, or 1910 U.S. Census for El Paso, Texas. In addition, Engledow is not listed in the El Paso city directories for the 1880s, 1890s, or early 1900s.

6. *Texas Almanac and State Industrial Guide* (Dallas, TX: Belo, 1910), 183–84. In 1904 El Paso County had geographically become the largest in the state; see *Texas Almanac and State Industrial Guide* (Galveston, TX: Clarke and Courts, 1904), 257–58. Today El Paso is the largest United States city on the Mexican border, the sixth largest city in Texas, and the twenty-first largest city in the United States; see Eric Peterson, *Frommer's Texas* (Hoboken, NJ: Wiley, 2007), 338.

7. Donald E. Chipman, *Spanish Texas, 1519–1821* (Austin: University of Texas Press, 1997), 63–70.

8. Ramón Eduardo Ruiz, *On the Rim of Mexico: Encounters of the Rich and Poor* (Boulder, CO: Westview Press, 1998), 35.

9. Guadalupe Santiago Quijada, *Propiedad de la tierra en Ciudad Juárez, 1888 a 1935* (Tijuana, México: UACJ, 2002), 37n58. Today Ciudad Juárez is the largest populated city on México's northern border.

10. For more information on the French intervention in Mexico, also known as the Maximilian Affair or the Franco-Mexican War, see Enrique Krauze, *Mexico, Biography of Power: A History of Modern Mexico, 1810–1996* (New York: Harper Collins, 1997), 152–204. On the life of Benito Pablo Juárez García, see Michael S. Werner, ed., *Concise Encyclopedia of Mexico* (London: Taylor and Francis, 2001), 311–14.

11. Ruiz, *On the Rim of Mexico*, 35; Oscar J. Martínez, *Border Boom Town: Ciudad Juárez since 1848* (Austin: University of Texas Press, 1978), 16, 17, 176nn23–24; Floyd S. Fierman, *The Schwartz Family of El Paso: The Story of a Pioneer Jewish Family in the Southwest* (El Paso: Texas Western Press, 1980), 11.

12. Ken Hudnall and Connie Wang, *Spirits of the Border*, vol. 2, *The History and Mystery of Fort Bliss, Texas* (El Paso, TX: Omega Press, 2003), 11–20. Historian Monica Perales asserts that El Paso military installations were "crucial components of national defense," particularly during World War I and II, as well as the Cold War (*Smeltertown: Making and Remembering a Southwest Border Community* [Chapel Hill: University of North Carolina Press, 2010], 310n10).

13. Perry Jamieson, "A Survey History of Fort Bliss, 1890–1940," *Historic and Natural Resources*, report no. 5, Cultural Resources Management Program (Fort Bliss, TX: U.S. Army Air Defense Artillery Center, 1993).

14. Zachary Taylor, *Letters of Zachary Taylor, from the Battle-Fields of the Mexican War* (Alcester, UK: Read Books, 2008), xii–xiii; Samuel R. Curtis, *Mexico Under Fire* (Fort Worth: Texas Christian University Press, 1994), 267n14.

15. William Wallace Mills, *Forty Years at El Paso, 1858–1898: Recollections of War, Politics, Adventure, Events, Narratives, and Sketches* (El Paso, TX: W. W. Mills, 1901), 38–39; see also Dale Baum, "Pinpointing Apparent Fraud in the 1861 Texas Secession Referendum," *Journal of Interdisciplinary History* 22.2 (1991): 206, 218.

16. Kristine Navarro and Maceo C. Dailey Jr., eds., *Wheresoever My People Chance to Dwell: Oral Interviews with African American Women of El Paso* (Baltimore, MD: Black Classic Press, 2000), 13.

17. Martin Hardwick Hall, "Negroes with Confederate Troops in West Texas and New Mexico," *Password* 13.1 (1968): 11–12. Hall cites the eighth U.S. census.

18. Wilbert H. Timmons, "El Paso, TX," *Handbook of Texas Online*, www.tshaonline.org/handbook/online/articles/hde01 (accessed 4 January 2014); Conrey Bryson, "El Paso County," *Handbook of Texas Online*, www.tshaonline.org/handbook/online/articles/hce05 (accessed 4 January 2014).

19. Jerry D. Thompson, ed., *Civil War in the Southwest: Recollections of the Sibley Brigade* (College Station: Texas A&M University Press, 2001), xxi; Ralph A. Wooster, "Texas in the Southern War for Independence," in *The Texas Military Experience: From the Texas Revolution through World War II*, ed. Joseph G. Dawson III (College Station: Texas A&M University Press, 1995), 76–77; *Harper's New Monthly Magazine*, vol. 25 (New York: Harper and Brothers Publishers, 1862), 838.

20. Francis Edward Abernethy, ed., *Legendary Ladies of Texas* (Denton: University of North Texas Press, 1994), 133–40; see also H. Gordon Frost, *The Gentlemen's Club: The Story of Prostitution in El Paso* (El Paso, TX: Mangan Books, 1983), 33, 72.

21. For a recent history of these three railways, see Richard N. Griffith, "Empire, Progress, and the American Southwest: The Texas and Pacific Railroad, 1850–1882" (PhD diss., University of Southern Mississippi, 2001), Richard J. Orsi, *Sunset Limited: The Southern Pacific Railroad and the Development of the American West, 1850–1930* (Berkeley: University of California Press, 2005), Pamela Berkman, *The History of the Atchison, Topeka and Santa Fe* (New York: Smithmark, 1994), and James H. Ducker, *Men of the Steel Rails: Workers on the Atchison, Topeka and Santa Fe Railroad, 1869–1900* (Lincoln: University of Nebraska Press, 1994).

22. Eugene C. Barker, Ernest W. Winkler, and Francis W. Johnson, eds., *A History of Texas and Texans*, vol. 2 (Chicago: American Historical Society, 1914), 1056. For a brief biography of the Galveston, Harrisburg and San Antonio Railway Company, see George C. Werner, "Galveston, Harrisburg and San Antonio," *Handbook of Texas Online*, www.tshaonline.org/handbook/online/articles/eqg06 (accessed 4 January 2014).

23. Rudolf Eickemeyer, *Letters from the Southwest* (New York: J. J. Little, 1894), 10, 20.

24. Ibid., 10, 18, 49. For more on Afro-Mexicans in the Southwest, see Laura E. Gómez, *Manifest Destinies: The Making of the Mexican American Race* (New York: New York University Press, 2007), and Martha Menchaca, *Recovering History, Constructing Race: The Indian, Black, and White Roots of Mexican Americans* (Austin: University of Texas Press, 2001).

25. Barker, Winkler, and Johnson, *A History of Texas and Texans*, 1056.

26. Cadwell Walton Raines, *Year Book for Texas*, vol. 2 (Austin, TX: Gammel-Statesman, 1903), 388.

27. Michael R. Haines and Richard H. Steckel, eds., *A Population History of North America* (New York: Cambridge University Press, 2000), 625n16; also see Fred W. Powell, *The Railroads of Mexico* (Boston: Stratford Company, 1921), 127–31, and John M. Hart, *Revolutionary Mexico: The Coming and Process of the Mexican Revolution* (Berkeley: University of California Press, 1987), 124, 133, 146, 149, 269.

28. Perales, *Smeltertown*, 27. Nixon had Mexican and Mexican American patients in the historic community of Smeltertown. There is a handwritten prescription in Spanish by Nixon for a Ms. Mendoza, a patient residing at 12M-Smeltertown, in an unprocessed and unnamed collection at the El Paso County Historical Society.

29. Mario T. García, *Desert Immigrants: The Mexicans of El Paso, 1880–1920* (New Haven, CT: Yale University Press, 1981), 14, 16, 17.

30. Ibid., 15.

31. H. H. Windsor, ed., "Elephant Butte Dam in New Hydroelectric Project," *Popular Mechanics*, April 1921, 568; Arthur Powell Davis, *Irrigation Works Constructed by the United States Government* (New York: John Wiley, 1917), 237–51; Paul Ganster and David E. Lorey, *The U.S.-Mexican Border into the Twenty-First Century* (Lanham, MD: Rowman and Littlefield, 2008), 43.

32. Timmons, "El Paso"; Bryson, "El Paso County."

33. Larry Tye, *Rising from the Rails: Pullman Porters and the Making of the Black Middle Class* (New York: Henry Holt, 2004), 86.

34. Charlotte Ivy, "Forgotten Color: Black Families in Early El Paso," *Password* 35.1 (1990): 7.

35. Ibid., 7.

36. Gerald Horne, *Black and Brown: African Americans and the Mexican Revolution, 1910–1920* (New York: New York University Press, 2005), 5. For more detailed accounts of the Mexican Revolution and its different dimensions and major figures, see Friedrich Katz, *The Life and Times of Pancho Villa* (Stanford, CA: Stanford University Press, 1998), Samuel Brunk, *Emiliano Zapata: Revolution and Betrayal in Mexico* (Albuquerque: University of New Mexico Press, 1995), Friedrich Katz, ed., *Riot, Rebellion, and Revolution: Rural Social Conflict in Mexico* (Princeton, NJ: Princeton University Press, 1988), and Friedrich Katz, *The Secret War in Mexico: Europe, the United States, and the Mexican Revolution* (Chicago: University of Chicago Press, 1981). El Paso's relationship to the Mexican Revolution is detailed in Charles H. Harris and Louis R. Sadler, *The Secret War in El Paso: Mexican Revolutionary Intrigue, 1906–1920* (Albuquerque: University of New Mexico Press, 2009).

37. John F. Worley, ed., *Worley's 1911 City Directory of El Paso, Texas* (Dallas, TX: John F. Worley, 1911), 376–77, 557; Bryson, *Dr. Lawrence A. Nixon and the White Primary*, 28; John F. Worley, ed., *El Paso City Directory, 1917* (Dallas, TX: John F. Worley, 1917), 376, 554.

38. Gloria López-Stafford, *A Place in El Paso: A Mexican-American Childhood* (Albuquerque: University of New Mexico Press, 1996), 7–8.

39. *Thirteenth Census of the United States*, population schedule, El Paso, justice precinct 1, El Paso County, TX, series T624, roll 1548, page 164A, line 13. On Wolf's life, see Drusilla E. (Tandy) Nixon, interview no. 194 (11 December 1975), 29–30, IOH-UTEP, Eugene O. Porter, *Lord Beresford and Lady Flo* (El Paso: Texas Western Press, 1970), Maceo C. Dailey Jr., "Florida J. Wolfe (c.1867–1913)," *BlackPast.org: An Online Reference Guide to African American History*, www.blackpast.org/?q=aaw/wolfe-florida-j-c-1867-1913 (accessed 4 January 2014).

40. *Fourteenth Census of the United States*, population schedule, El Paso, ward 2, precinct 2, El Paso County, TX, series T625, roll 1798, page 199B, line 95. On Flipper's life, see Don Cusic, *The Trials of Henry Flipper: The First Black Graduate of West Point* (Jefferson, NC: McFarland, 2009).

41. López-Stafford, *A Place in El Paso*, 7–8.

42. Ibid., 8.

43. Mike Romo, interview no. 215 (1976), IOH-UTEP; Pratt and Pickett, eds., *The American Heritage Guide to Contemporary Usage and Style*, 90.

44. Maceo C. Dailey Jr., ed., *I'm Building Me a Home: El Paso's African American Community, 1539–1998* (El Paso: Chase Bank of Texas, 1998), 15.

45. Emmanuel Campbell, *The Development of Negro Education in El Paso* (El Paso, TX: El Paso Public Schools, 1945), 6.

46. Ibid., 4, 7–10. Olalee McCall died 14 September 1957; see El Paso County Clerk, Olalee McCall death certificate, 14 September 1957, reel no. 0486, frame 1625. On William O. Bundy, see *Fifteenth Census of the United States*, population schedule, El Paso, justice precinct 1, El Paso County, TX, series T626, roll 2328, page 269A, lines 2–8, and "4 Pioneer E.P. Blacks Are Profiled," *El Paso Herald-Post*, 13 February 1976, 18. On Alfred C. Murphy, see *Twelfth Census of the United States*, population schedule, El Paso, justice precinct 1, El Paso County, TX, series T623, roll 1631, page 112A, lines 37–42. On Emmanuel Campbell, see "Emmanuel Campbell, Principal of Douglass School, Resigns," *El Paso Times*, 21 May 1952, 1, "School Principal Quits," *El Paso Herald-Post*, 21 May 1952, 9, and "Principals Discuss High School Openings," *El Paso Herald-Post*, 16 August 1951, 17. On Edwin W. Mangram, see "Name New Principal," *El Paso Herald-Post*, 18 June 1952, 3.

47. Campbell, *The Development of Negro Education in El Paso*, 9. Nixon hunted with Bundy and others on at least one excursion to the Santa Fe and Taos region of New Mexico. On another occasion, Nixon hunted in the Sierra Diablo area of New Mexico; see Lawrence A. Nixon to Drusilla E. (Tandy) Attwell, 26 September 1932, N/MFP.

48. Dailey, "I'm Building Me a Home," 15. Douglass served as an important venue for community activities, providing, for example, a meeting place for the Rio Grande Chapter, no. 2, for Colored Disabled Veterans; see "Capt. Broaddus To Speak," *El Paso Herald-Post*, 30 April 1932, 3. See also "Douglass," *El Paso Herald-Post*, 9 March 1938, 4.

49. "Negro Poet To Appear," *San Antonio Express*, 8 April 1932, 6; Arnold Rampersad, ed., *The Collected Works of Langston Hughes* (Columbia: University of Missouri Press, 2001), 91.

50. Bruce A. Glasrud and Merline Pitre, eds., *Black Women in Texas History* (College Station: Texas A&M University Press, 2008), 119.

51. Bernice Love Wiggins, *Tuneful Tales* (Lubbock: Texas Tech University Press, 2002); Lorraine Elena Roses and Ruth Elizabeth Randolph, *The Harlem Renaissance and Beyond: Literary Biographies of 100 Black Women Writers, 1900–1945* (Boston: G.K. Hall, 1990), 347–48.

52. *Howard University Catalogue, 1919–1920* (Washington, DC: Howard University, 1920), 251, 257, 259, 292, 294. According to this catalogue, Clarence B. Friday (1896–1958) was from El Paso (298) and San Antonio (272). Friday lived in Seguin, Texas, became a physician, was involved in the NAACP (1939–1958), and served as president of the Lone Star State Medical, Dental, and Pharmaceutical Association (ca. 1950s); see Nathalie Gross Collection, 1948–1975, no. 815, Civil Rights 2 box, Civil Rights–Texas folder, "To Secure These Rights" program, 8 January 1950, EPPL-SW, and "Professional News: Deaths," *Journal of the National Medical Association* 51.2 (March 1959): 157–58.

53. Coleman was a member of the El Paso NAACP, the National Association of Teachers in Colored Schools, Texas Colored Teachers' Association, Knights of Pythias, Knights Templar, Odd Fellows, and a registered Republican. He was also a thirty-second degree Royal Arch Mason, Shriner, grand lecturer of Negro Masons in Texas, and grand director for the Court of Heorines of Jericho (Frank L. Mather, *Who's Who of the Colored Race: A General Biographical Dictionary of Men and Women of African Descent* [Chicago: Frank L. Mather, 1915], 73).

54. Oddly—considering his father's own politics—the junior Nixon was very active in the ultraright wing "Lyndon LaRouche Political Organization and made frequent trips to Harrisburg, PA and Washington, D.C. to support" this group's many causes; see Lawrence J. Nixon obituary, memorial service program, Samuel J. Jones Funeral Home, 24 February 2006, 3, and "Texas Lawyer Pays up NAACP Life Membership," *Pittsburgh Courier*, 26 September 1942, 18.

55. Andrew Bunie, *Robert L. Vann of the* Pittsburgh Courier*: Politics and Black Journalism* (Pittsburgh, PA: University of Pittsburgh Press, 1974); Charles A. Simmons, *The African American Press: A History of News Coverage during National Crises with Special Reference to Four Black Newspapers, 1827–1965* (Jefferson, NC: McFarland, 1998), 43–50.

56. "Capt. Broaddus To Speak," *El Paso Herald-Post*, 30 April 1932, 3; "Douglass," *El Paso Herald-Post*, 9 March 1938, 4.

57. "Debate to Be Held in Douglass Hall," *El Paso Herald-Post*, 19 March 1935, 7.

58. Hobart Jarrett, "Adventures in Interracial Debates," *Crisis* 42.8 (1935): 240. The Tolson team beat USC, not Harvard as the Denzel Washington movie *The Great Debaters* (2007) presents it. Washington donated one million dollars to Wiley College so it could reestablish its debate team; see Jamie Stengle, "Inspired by Movie, Wiley College has a New Debate Team," *Dallas Morning News*, 2 January 2009, and Gail K.

Beil, "Tolson, Farmer Intertwined by Wiley Debate Team," *Marshall News Messenger*, web.archive.org/web/20090606055052/http://www.marshallnewsmessenger.com/featr/content/features/greatdebaters/farmer_tolson.html (accessed 26 January 2014).

59. David Levering Lewis, *W. E. B. Du Bois: Biography of a Race, 1868–1919* (New York: Henry Holt, 1993); University of Massachusetts Special Collections and University Archives at the Du Bois Library, *Du Bois Central: Resources on the Life and Legacy of W.E.B. Du Bois*, www.library.umass.edu/spcoll/dubois/ (accessed 4 January 2014).

60. W. E. B. Du Bois, "I Go A-Talking," *Crisis* 6.3 (1913): 130–32; W. E. B. Du Bois, "The Great Northwest," *Crisis* 6.5 (1913): 237–40. For more on Du Bois's trip to the West, see *Crisis* 6.4 (1913): 192–95, Lonnie G. Bunch, "A Past Not Necessarily Prologue: The Afro-American in Los Angeles," in *20ᵗʰ Century Los Angeles: Power, Promotion, and Social Conflict* (Claremont, CA: Regina Books, 1990), 101, and Albert Broussard, *Black San Francisco: The Struggle for Racial Equality in the West, 1900–1954* (Lawrence: University Press of Kansas, 1993), 73.

61. *Denver Post*, June 24, 1925, quoted in Quintard Taylor, *In Search of the Racial Frontier: African Americans in the American West, 1528–1990* (New York: Norton, 1998), 17.

62. *Seattle Daily Intelligencer*, 28 May 1879, quoted in Taylor, *In Search of the Racial Frontier*, 17.

63. *Thirteenth Census of the United States*, vol. 3 (Washington, DC, Government Printing Office, 1913), 816, 817.

64. Monroe N. Work, *Negro Year Book and Annual Encyclopedia of the Negro* (Tuskegee, AL: Negro Year Book Publishing Company, 1916), 387.

65. "Negro May Get Drunk in El Paso Circus Day," *El Paso Herald*, 28 September 1911, 3. In 1910 Adrian Pool was a Texas-born single thirty-three-year-old white male lawyer, who was a "roomer" at 207 San Antonio Avenue. By 1930, Pool was still a "lodger" and an attorney who lived on West Franklin Avenue in El Paso. He eventually became an El Paso County court judge, although the exact year is unknown (*Thirteenth Census of the United States*, population schedule, El Paso, justice precinct 1, El Paso County, TX, series T624, roll 1549, page 41B, line 93; *Fifteenth Census of the United States*, population schedule, El Paso, justice precinct 1, El Paso County, TX, series T626, roll 2329, page 206B, line 77; *Southwestern Reporter*, vol. 190 [St. Paul: West Publishing Company, 1917], 522, 542; Adrian Pool, "Good Roads," Thirty-Fifth Annual Convention, May 27–29, 1919, Convention Proceedings, *The Texas Bankers Record*, 8.10 (1919): 57–58; J. Morgan Broaddus Jr., *The Legal Heritage of El Paso* [El Paso: Texas Western College Press, 1963], 156, 177).

66. William L. Katz, *The Black West* (Garden City: Doubleday, 1971), 50, 54, 284.

67. Garna L. Christian, *Black Soldiers in Jim Crow Texas, 1899–1917* (College Station: Texas A&M University Press, 1995), 46–68, 92–96; Taylor, *In Search of the Racial Frontier*, 176–77; United States Senate, "Summary of Discharge or Mustering Out of Regiments or Companies," 60th Congress, 1st Session, Document No. 402, pt. 1, 353.

68. *El Paso Herald*, 1 November 1911, quoted in David D. Romo, *Ringside Seat to a Revolution: An Underground Cultural History of El Paso and Juárez: 1893–1923* (El Paso, TX: Cinco Puntos Press, 2005), 205.

69. Romo, *Ringside Seat to a Revolution*, 203.

70. *El Paso Daily Times*, 10 October 1893, 7, and *El Paso Daily Times*, 18 October 1893, 7, quoted in Marilyn T. Bryan, "The Economic, Political, and Social Status of the Negro in El Paso," *Password* 13.3 (1968): 86nn89–91; *El Paso Evening Tribune*, 9 October 1893, quoted in Horne, *Black and Brown*, 9.

71. The term "lyceum" has its origins in Greek culture. The site of Aristotle's Peripatetic school in Athens 336 BCE, the lyceum was one of the main public gymnasia in the city, named after the sanctuary dedicated to Apollo—the Greek version of the African Netcher Heru—and Asclepius, the Greek name for the African scholar Imhotep. In the fourth and fifth centuries BCE various Sophists, as well as Socrates, lectured in the Lyceum; see Angela G. Ray, *The Lyceum and Public Culture in the Nineteenth Century United States* (East Lansing: Michigan State University Press, 2005), 3–6, Nigel Guy Wilson, ed., *Encyclopedia of Ancient Greece* (London: Routledge, 2006), 431, and Anthony T. Browder, *Nile Valley Contributions to Civilization: Exploding the Myths*, vol. 1 (Washington, DC: Institute of Karmic Guidance, 1998), 126, 155–56.

72. Ray, *The Lyceum and Public Culture in the Nineteenth Century United States*, 21, 30–32, 34, 36–39, 42, 116, 132, 134, 155, 175.

73. Jeffrey B. Perry, *Hubert Harrison: The Voice of Harlem Radicalism, 1883–1918* (New York: Columbia University Press, 2009), 70; Nina Mjagkij, ed., *Organizing Black America: An Encyclopedia of African American Associations* (London: Taylor and Francis, 2001), 89, 312, 328, 330, 525; Ray, *The Lyceum and Public Culture in the Nineteenth Century United States*, 113–42, 119, 176–77.

74. Miriam DeCosta-Willis, ed., *The Memphis Diary of Ida B. Wells: An Intimate Portrait of the Activist as a Young Woman* (Boston: Beacon Press, 1995), 22, 34, 51, 110, 121, 129, 145. Recent books on Ida B. Wells include Mia Bay, *To Tell the Truth Freely: The Life of Ida B. Wells* (New York: Hill and Wang, 2009), and Paula Giddings, *Ida: A Sword among Lions: Ida B. Wells and the Campaign against Lynching* (New York: Amistad, 2008). Pinckney Benton Stewart Pinchback was the grandfather of well-known Harlem Renaissance writer Jean Toomer, author of *Cane* (1923). During Reconstruction Pinchback served as Louisiana state senator and lieutenant governor prior to becoming governor for one month (December 1872–January 1873) and then was elected to the United States House of Representatives and United States Senate but prevented from serving by Democrats (James Haskins, *Pinckney Benton Stewart Pinchback* [New York: Macmillan, 1973]; Nicholas Lemann, *Redemption: The Last Battle of the Civil War* [New York: Macmillan, 2007], 196–99).

75. Officers of EPLCIS included Jasper B. Williams (president), Frank D. Burdett (vice president), LeRoy White (secretary), Jerry B. Baldwin (corresponding secretary), William Coleman (treasurer), William M. Sublett (sergeant at arms), and Mack H. Carmichael (musical director). Jasper Williams, who is listed as the only "colored" druggist in the 1923 city directory, was also the president of the El Paso NAACP. He subsequently became a farmer in New Mexico, cultivating 640 acres near Las Cruces after moving there in the mid-to-late 1920s. While in Las Cruces, Jasper became a member of the Las Cruces NAACP (*Hudspeth's 1923 El Paso City Directory* [El Paso:

Hudspeth Directory Company, 1923], 848, 891; Bruce A. Glasrud, ed., *African American History in New Mexico: Portraits from Five Hundred Years* [Albuquerque: University of New Mexico Press, 2013], 7, 16, 162; *Fourteenth Census of the United States*, population schedule, El Paso, voting precinct 6, El Paso County, TX, series T625, roll 1798, page 120, lines 65–68). Jerry B. Baldwin was born and raised in Louisiana and at the time of the 1920 census was a thirty-eight-year-old barber (*Fourteenth Census of the United States*, population schedule, El Paso, voting precinct 10, El Paso County, TX, series T625, roll 1798, page 223A, lines 6–7). William M. Sublett was a thirty-eight-year-old African American from Texas who was a "lodger" on Tays Street and was employed as a letter carrier for the United States Post Office (*Fourteenth Census of the United States*, population schedule, El Paso, voting precinct 6, El Paso County, TX, series T625, roll 1798, page 138, line 17). Mack H. Carmichael, a thirty-six-year-old African American from Texas, was a lodger with Sublett on Tays Street and was employed as a music teacher, focusing on the piano. Presumably Carmichael was working for himself, as the census does not indicate if he was affiliated with an institution such as Douglass School (*Fourteenth Census of the United States*, population schedule, El Paso, voting precinct 6, El Paso County, TX, series T625, roll 1798, page 138, line 16). No additional information could be found on Frank D. Burdett.

76. Jerry B. Baldwin to W. E. B. Du Bois, November 27, 1913, LOCMD, NAACP Papers, pt. 1, Branch Files: El Paso, Texas, 1913–1925, box G-202, folder 2.

77. Lewis, *W. E. B. Du Bois*, 390.

78. Roberta Senechal de la Roche, *In Lincoln's Shadow: The 1908 Race Riot in Springfield, Illinois* (Carbondale: Southern Illinois University Press, 2008).

79. Lewis, *W. E. B. Du Bois*, 386–407.

80. Stephen R. Fox, *The Guardian of Boston: William Monroe Trotter* (New York: Atheneum, 1970).

81. Information on both of these important civil rights organizations can be found in Fox, *The Guardian of Boston*, 81–114, and Mjagkij, *Organizing Black America*, 456–57, 523–25.

82. W. E. B. Du Bois, *Dusk of Dawn: An Essay Toward an Autobiography of a Race Concept* (Edison, NJ: Transaction, 1984), 72–73; Fox, *The Guardian of Boston*, 179–85; Christine A. Lunardini, "Standing Firm: William Monroe Trotter's Meetings with Woodrow Wilson, 1913–1914," *Journal of Negro History* 64.3 (1979): 244–64; William Harrison, "Phylon Profile IX: William Monroe Trotter—Fighter," *Phylon* 7.3 (1946): 237–45.

83. Manfred Berg, *"The Ticket to Freedom:" The NAACP and the Struggle for Black Political Integration* (Gainesville: University of Florida Press, 2005), xiv–xv.

84. Abby A. Johnson and Ronald M. Johnson, *Propaganda and Aesthetics: The Literary Politics of African American Magazines in the Twentieth Century* (Amherst: University of Massachusetts Press, 1979), 32–33, 35.

85. Berg, *"The Ticket to Freedom,"* xv.

86. Jerry B. Baldwin to W. E. B. Du Bois, 27 November 1913, LOCMD, NAACP Papers, pt. 1, Branch Files: El Paso, Texas, 1913–1925, box G-202, folder 2.

87. NAACP to Jerry B. Baldwin, 5 December 1913, LOCMD, NAACP Papers, pt. 1, Branch Files: El Paso, Texas, 1913–1925, box G-202, folder 2.

88. LeRoy White to May Childs Nerney of the NAACP, 15 June 1914, LOCMD, NAACP Papers, pt. 1, Branch Files: El Paso, Texas, 1913–1925, box G-202, folder 2. In the 1930 census, John Kelley was described as a fifty-year-old janitor for a shoe parlor (*Fifteenth Census of the United States*, population schedule, El Paso, justice precinct 1, El Paso County, TX, series T626, roll 2328, page 105, lines 71–73). Sylvester M. Collins was an African American mail carrier for the post office (*Fourteenth Census of the United States*, population schedule, El Paso, voting precinct 6, El Paso County, TX, series T625, roll 1798, page 116, lines 13–17). Joseph Donnell is listed in the 1910 census as a forty-three-year-old porter at a bank (*Thirteenth Census of the United States*, population schedule, El Paso, justice precinct 1, El Paso County, Texas, series T624, roll 1548, page 86, lines 8–10).

89. Lewis, *W. E. B. Du Bois*, 513.

90. Michael Bieze, *Booker T. Washington and the Art of Self-Representation* (New York: Peter Lang, 2008), 5–6. This publication is among many others that have begun to reexamine Booker T. Washington and complicate the conventional wisdom that Washington was simply an accommodationist who did more harm than good; see Maceo C. Dailey Jr., "Neither 'Uncle Tom' nor 'Accommodationist': Booker T. Washington, Emmett Jay Scott, and Constructionalism," *Atlanta History* 38.4 (1995): 20–33, Andrew Zimmerman, *Alabama in Africa: Booker T. Washington, the German Empire, and the Globalization of the New South* (Princeton, NJ: Princeton University Press, 2010), Michael B. Boston, *The Business Strategy of Booker T. Washington: Its Development and Implementation* (Gainesville: University Press of Florida, 2010), David H. Jackson, *Booker T. Washington and the Struggle against White Supremacy: The Southern Educational Tours, 1908–1912* (New York: Palgrave Macmillan, 2009), Robert J. Norrell, *Up From History: The Life of Booker T. Washington* (Cambridge, MA: Belknap Press of Harvard University Press, 2009), Raymond Smock, *Booker T. Washington: Black Leadership in the Age of Jim Crow* (Chicago: Ivan R. Dee, 2009), Michael R. West, *The Education of Booker T. Washington: American Democracy and the Idea of Race Relations* (New York: Columbia University Press, 2008), Lee H. Walker, Diane C. Bast, and T. S. Karnick, *Booker T. Washington: A Re-Examination* (Chicago: Heartland Institute, 2008), and Kenneth M. Hamilton, "Booker T. Washington: America's Early Memory of a National Icon" (forthcoming).

91. Wilson Jeremiah Moses, *Creative Conflict in African American Thought: Frederick Douglass, Alexander Crummell, Booker T. Washington, W. E. B. Du Bois, and Marcus Garvey* (New York: Cambridge University Press, 2004), 152.

92. *El Paso Herald*, 25 September 1911, 8.

93. Nixon is the only "colored" doctor listed in the business section under the heading for physicians in the 1911 El Paso city directory (Worley, *Worley's 1911 City Directory of El Paso, Texas*). Prince S. Gathings, an African American physician who graduated from Meharry Medical College the same year as Lawrence A. Nixon, practiced medicine in El Paso for about two years, from 1907 to 1909, before moving

to Oklahoma (*Meharry Medical, Dental and Pharmaceutical Colleges of Walden University Catalogue of 1907–1908 and Announcement for 1908–1909* [Nashville: Marshall and Bruce, 1908], 39; *Meharry Medical, Dental and Pharmaceutical Colleges of Walden University Catalogue of 1908–1909 and Announcement for 1909–1910* [Nashville: Marshall and Bruce, 1909], 39; *Thirteenth Census of the United States,* population schedule, Lawton, ward 4, Comanche County, OK, series T624, roll 1248, page 269A, line 4; *Fourteenth Census of the United States*, population schedule, Lawton, ward 1, Comanche County, OK, series T625, roll 1458, page 100, lines 85–87). Also, Black doctor George Andrew Lewis practiced in El Paso during this same period at 406 San Antonio and 207 South Kansas (John F. Worley, ed., *El Paso Directory for 1907* [Dallas, TX: John F. Worley, 1906], 607; John F. Worley, ed., *El Paso Directory for 1908* [Dallas, TX: John F. Worley, 1907), 344, 382). No mention is made of Dr. George A. Lewis in the 1909 or 1910 *El Paso Directory*. Sterling Langdon Smith was an African American physician and surgeon who also practiced in El Paso, although when is not known (Dailey, "I'm Building Me a Home," 35). For other Black doctors during this era, see Geraldine Rhoades Beckford, *Biographical Dictionary of American Physicians of African Ancestry, 1800–1920* (Cherry Hill, NJ: Africana Homestead Legacy Publishers, 2013), 120, 129, 197, 239, 339).

94. *Meharry News* 4.1 (1906): 3.

95. Lawrence A. Nixon to Drusilla E. (Tandy) Attwell, 9 May 1934, N/MFP.

96. Daniel C. Thompson, *The Negro Leadership Class* (Englewood Cliffs, NJ: Prentice-Hall, 1963), 44, 68–70, 74–76. For a brief definition of the three types of Black leadership, see Rufus Burrow Jr., *James H. Cone and Black Liberation Theology* (Jefferson, NC: McFarland, 1994), 227n130.

97. Ward, *Black Physicians in the Jim Crow South*, 273.

98. The idea of race men did not admit of the possibility that black women might participate in civil rights activism. Hazel Carby gives an excellent critique of it in *Race Men* (Cambridge, MA: Harvard University Press, 2000), 1–8.

99. "Booker Washington Discusses the Negro in South and His Need," *El Paso Herald*, 25 September 1911, 8; "Noted Negro Speaks Here," *El Paso Morning Times*, 25 September 1911, 5.

100. "Noted Negro Speaks Here," *El Paso Morning Times*, 25 September 1911, 5. On the issue of race, racism, Booker T. Washington, and the temperance movement, see Doris M. Provine, *Unequal Under Law: Race in the War on Drugs* (Chicago: University of Chicago Press, 2007), 49–58, and Hanes Walton Jr. and James E. Taylor, "Blacks and the Southern Prohibition Movement," *Phylon* 32.3 (1971): 247–59.

101. *El Paso Herald*, 25 September 1911, 8. Reverend Henry R. Wilson resided at 509 Tays and Second Baptist Church was located at 401 S. Virginia; see "The Texas Capital: Regular Correspondence of *The Age*," *New York Age*, 7 September 1911, *Thirteenth Census of the United States*, population schedule, El Paso, justice precinct 1, El Paso County, TX, series T624, roll 1548, page 173A, lines 4–7, and Worley, *Worley's 1911 City Directory of El Paso, Texas*.

102. Jackson, *Booker T. Washington and the Struggle Against White Supremacy*, 132. "Book-erite" is a phrase used to describe those who endorsed Washington's particular strategy of racial advancement.

103. *El Paso Herald*, 10 February 1906, and *El Paso Herald*, 27 February 1907, quoted in Cynthia F. Haines, *Showtime! From Opera Houses to Picture Palaces in El Paso* (El Paso: Texas Western Press, 2006), 38–39, 40, 122. On the racial makeup of the attendees and financers of the rental space, see "Booker T. Washington Ends Tour of Texas," *New York Age*, 12 October 1911, 1. On the location and managers of the theater, see Worley, *Worley's 1911 City Directory of El Paso Texas*, 215. Washington often spoke to both Blacks and white audiences; see "Dr. Washington Tours Arkansas: Both Negroes and Whites Turn Out In Large Numbers to Greet Nation's Greatest Citizen," *Afro-American Ledger*, 21 September 1911, 1.

104. It was the activism of Emory Douglass Williams, one of the El Pasoans on the platform at Washington's speech, that convinced the management of a Las Cruces movie theater to "refrain from showing the film." Williams had moved from El Paso to Las Cruces in 1896, where he became a significant real estate owner. He was a member of the Mesilla Valley Chamber of Commerce, president of the Doña Ana County NAACP, and was appointed deputy game warden by the governor of New Mexico. Despite not living in El Paso, he nevertheless became an early member of its NAACP chapter. Williams and Lawrence A. Nixon were good friends ("Still Fighting The Film," *Crisis* 12.2 [1916]: 87; "Emory Williams Died Thursday; Funeral Pending," *Las Cruces Sun-News*, 9 December 1949, 1; "Last Rites For Emory Williams Will Be Tuesday," *Las Cruces Sun-News*, 12 December 1949, 1; "Owner Denies Price Holdup," *Las Cruces Sun-News*, 26 November 1940, 1; *NAACP Papers*, LOCMD, box G-128, Las Cruces, New Mexico folder).

105. *El Paso Herald*, 25 September 1911, 8. The El Paso Theater stage was thirty-six feet deep and seventy-five feet wide, and the proscenium arch was twenty-nine feet high and thirty-six feet wide; see *El Paso Herald*, 27 February 1907, quoted in Haines, *Showtime!*, 39.

106. *El Paso Herald*, 25 September 1911, 8; Jackson, *Booker T. Washington and the Struggle Against White Supremacy*, 133.

107. Lovett, *The African-American History of Nashville, Tennessee*, 239.

108. On Washington visiting Ciudad Juárez, see *El Paso Herald*, 25 September 1911, 8. On Washington visiting Ciudad Juárez and meeting with Alvarez, see "Noted Negro Speaks Here," *El Paso Morning Times*, 25 September 1911, 5, and Jackson, *Booker T. Washington and the Struggle against White Supremacy*, 133–34. On Guillermo Alvarez, see Armando B. Chávez Montañez, *Sesenta años de gobierno municipal: Jefes políticos del distrito bravos y presidentes del municipio de Juárez, 1897–1960* (México: Gráfica Cervantina, 1959), 61–65, "Alvarez Will Resign," *El Paso Herald*, 10 November 1911, 1, and *El Paso Herald*, 7 November 1911, 11.

109. "Washington Visited Juárez Yesterday," *El Paso Morning Times*, 26 September 1911, 5. For Gaston O. Sanders's occupation, race, employer, employer address,

and residence, see Worley, *Worley's 1911 City Directory of El Paso, Texas*, 436, and John F. Worley, ed., *Worley's Directory of El Paso, Texas, 1912* (Dallas, TX: John F. Worley, 1912), 422.

110. Kenneth Mason, *African Americans and Race Relations in San Antonio, Texas, 1867–1937* (New York: Garland, 1998), 212; Ramona Houston, "The NAACP State Conference in Texas: Intermediary and Catalyst for Change, 1937–1957," *Journal of African American History* 94.4 (2009): 510; Michael L. Gillette, "The NAACP in Texas, 1937–1957" (PhD diss., University of Texas–Austin, 1984), 1. While Mason, Houston, and Gillette all indicate that El Paso was the first Texas city to establish a NAACP chapter, they also state that the chapter was founded in 1915, which is incorrect. Some believe Houston was the first city in Texas to found an NAACP chapter; see Melvin James Banks, "The Pursuit of Equality: The Movement for First Class Citizenship Among Negroes in Texas, 1920–1950" (PhD diss., Syracuse University, 1962), 178, and Alwyn Barr, *Black Texans: A History of African Americans in Texas, 1528–1995* (Norman: University of Oklahoma Press, 1996), 144. But in the NAACP 1917 annual report, the El Paso branch was the only chapter in the state mentioned (Mason, *African Americans and Race Relations in San Antonio*, 212; Houston, "The NAACP State Conference in Texas," 510; Gillette, "The NAACP in Texas, 1937–1957," 1). It is surprising that bigger cities in Texas, with much larger Black populations, did not already have established branch chapters of this nationally well-known civil rights organization. When one considers prominent cities with sizable Black communities in Dallas, Austin, Houston, San Antonio, Marshall, and Galveston this fact becomes even more perplexing.

111. Jim Crow laws, which ironically had their origins in the North, instituted state-sponsored, state-sanctioned racial apartheid (Comer Vann Woodward, *The Strange Career of Jim Crow* [New York: Oxford University Press, 1956], 13–21, 25–29; Comer Vann Woodward, "Strange Career Critics: Long May They Persevere," *Journal of American History* 75.3 (1988): 857–68; Michael J. Pfeifer, "Review of Comer Vann Woodward's *The Strange Career of Jim Crow: A Commemorative Edition*," *H-Net Reviews*, May 2003, www.h-net.org/reviews/showrev.php?id=7561 [accessed 4 January 2014]).

112. Lawrence A. Nixon to Drusilla E. (Tandy) Attwell, 4 and 27 August 1933, N/MFP. Hayes was born in 1887 to poor Black parents in Curryville, Georgia. He attended Fisk and ultimately became a renowned singer in German, French, and Italian; see Roland Hayes, "Thine Own Self," *Crisis* 40.6 (1933): 127, MacKinley Helm, *Angel Mo' and Her Son, Roland Hayes* (Boston: Little, Brown, 1942), "Roland Hayes: A Lifetime on the Concert Stage," *Ebony*, September 1962, 42–46, and Herbert Aptheker, ed., *The Correspondence of W. E. B. Du Bois*, vol. 1 (Amherst: University of Massachusetts Press, 1973), 328–29. Famed poet Langston Hughes may have encountered Nixon when he visited El Paso in April 1932; see "Negro Poet to Appear," *San Antonio Express*, 8 April 1932, 6.

113. Rampersad, *The Collected Works of Langston Hughes*, 91; "Negro Poet to Appear," *San Antonio Express*, 8 April 1932, 6.

114. Thomas J. Sugrue, *Sweet Land of Liberty: The Forgotten Struggle for Civil Rights in the North* (New York: Random House, 2008), 139.

115. Frances Hills, interview no. 751 (12 October 1985), 5, IOH-UTEP. See also Drusilla E. Nixon, interview no. 194 (11 December 1975), 10, IOH-UTEP, and Navarro and Dailey, *Wheresoever My People Chance to Dwell*, 91.

116. Haines, *Showtime!*, 129. The Plaza Theater had special screenings of its regular movie fare for Black El Pasoans at midnight. Many segregated movie theaters throughout the nation engaged in this practice, which they often termed "midnight rambles"; see Haines, *Showtime!*, 129, and S. Torriano Berry and Venise T. Berry, *Historical Dictionary of African American Cinema* (Lanham, MD: Scarecrow Press, 2007), xxix. See also "Negroes Seek Desegregation in E.P. Theaters," *El Paso Herald-Post*, 17 August 1956, 20.

117. *El Paso Herald*, 9 November 1911, 5. Dr. Magruder's full name is not listed in the advertisement, simply his initials "H. A. Magruder," which is similar to his 1910 census entry, yet his 1920 census entry lists his first name as "Arthur" and his middle initial as "H." In both census entries he is described as a dentist; see *Fourteenth Census of the United States*, population schedule, El Paso, voting precinct 38, El Paso County, TX, series T625, roll 1799, page 95A, lines 10–16.

118. "Restrictions Running with the Land in Lafayette Place," quoted in Dailey, "I'm Building Me a Home," 30.

119. Ronald C. Tobey, *Technology as Freedom: The New Deal and the Electrical Modernization of the American Home* (Berkeley: University of California Press, 1996), 199, 198–200, 259n10. Racially restrictive covenants "became widespread after 1917," when the Supreme Court invalidated racially exclusionary zoning laws that segregated Blacks into certain neighborhoods. The courts enforced the covenants by "permitting homeowners to sue to enjoin neighbors from voluntarily selling" to Black buyers. In 1948, in *Shelley v. Kraemer*, the "Court killed all racially restrictive covenants by ruling that they are judicially unenforceable"; see Jethro K. Lieberman, *A Practical Companion to the Constitution: How the Supreme Court Has Ruled on Issues from Abortion to Zoning* (Berkeley: University of California Press, 1999), 428.

120. "By 1920 El Paso had the second largest (next to San Antonio) Mexican population of any American City and was the only major southwestern metropolis with more Mexicans than Americans" (García, *Desert Immigrants*, 36, 244n10).

121. *El Paso Herald*, 2 June 1914; Romo, *Ringside Seat to a Revolution*, 206. On the Gold Dust Twins, see John Strausbaugh, *Black Like You: Blackface, Whiteface, Insult and Imitation in American Popular Culture* (New York: Jeremy P. Tarcher, 2007), 275, 279.

122. *El Paso Herald*, 20 February 1919, 7. See also Marilyn Kern-Foxworth, *Aunt Jemima, Uncle Ben, and Rastus: Blacks in Advertising, Yesterday, Today, and Tomorrow* (Westport, CT: Greenwood Press, 1994), 61, 83,107, and Kenneth W. Goings, *Mammy and Uncle Mose: Black Collectibles and American Stereotyping* (Bloomington: Indiana University Press, 1994), xiii, 1, 88.

123. Eickemeyer, *Letters from the Southwest*, 48; emphasis in original. Eickemeyer may have been referring to Mexican/Mexican American or light-skinned African American students. It is doubtful that Anglos in El Paso sent their children to Douglass School, a predominately if not all-Black school.

124. On Jim Crow and prostitution, see Frost, *The Gentlemen's Club*, 140, 189, 234–25, and Alecia P. Long, *The Great Southern Babylon: Sex, Race, and Respectability in New Orleans, 1865–1920* (Baton Rouge: Louisiana State University Press, 2005), 192. On the absurdity of segregated courtroom Bibles, see Carl N. Degler, *Out of Our Past: The Forces that Shaped Modern America* (New York: HarperCollins, 1984), 253, and Shane K. Bernard, *The Cajuns: Americanization of a People* (Jackson: University Press of Mississippi, 2003), 53.

125. Susan Borreson, "The Good Fight: Lacking in Experience and Money, Fred Knollenberg Takes on the All-White Primary in Texas," *Texas Lawyer* 15.40 (1999): 26.

126. James Allen, *Without Sanctuary: Lynching Photography in America* (Santa Fe, NM: Twin Palms, 2000), 12, 24–25. Jim Crow promoted the idea among some whites that Blacks, as an undifferentiated group, were criminal, violent, dirty, ignorant, lazy, loud, unsanitary, oversexed, carefree, and unambitious, notions that many middle-class Blacks—including those in El Paso—spent most of their lives trying to dispel. Jim Crow came with a humiliating price for many Blacks in some parts of the South: a muted critique of institutional racism, a neglect of political organization and demands, and at times a strict adherence to a racial etiquette that demanded the perpetuation of absurd societal norms, including not looking at whites in the eye, stepping to the side on sidewalks so whites could pass unfettered, and deferentially calling whites "Sir," "Miss," "Ma'am," "Boss," and "Captain" and in exchange tolerating "Boy," "Uncle," "Aunt," "Mammy," and other derogatory phrases. Of course, this was a throwback to the antebellum period, as southern whites sought to revive a romantic nostalgic idea of Black's perceived submissiveness and servility; see Jennifer Lynn Ritterhouse, *Growing up Jim Crow: How Black and White Southern Children Learned Race* (Chapel Hill: University of North Carolina Press, 2006), 25, 30, 31, 37, and David M. Oshinsky, *Worse Than Slavery: Parchman Farm and the Ordeal of Jim Crow Justice* (New York: Simon and Schuster, 1997), 122–27.

127. *Freeing America: Seventh Annual Report of the National Association for the Advancement of Colored People* (New York: NAACP, 1917), 15–22, 18. See also Frances Hills, interview no. 751 (12 October 1985), 17–19, IOH-UTEP.

128. Mason, *African Americans and Race Relations in San Antonio*, 215. On the decline of NAACP memberships in Texas see, Steven A. Reich, "Soldiers of Democracy: Black Texans and the Fight for Citizenship, 1917–1921," *Journal of American History* 82.4 (1996): 1501, 1503.

129. The total population in El Paso County was 101,877, which meant that Blacks constituted 1.5 percent of the overall population; see *Fourteenth Census of the United States*, vol. 2 (Washington, DC, Government Printing Office, 1922), 1363. In 1930, the "Negro" population in El Paso county increased by 422 to 1,970, remaining 1.5 percent of the overall population within the county; see *Fifteenth Census of the United States*, vol. 3, pt. 2 (Washington, DC, Government Printing Office, 1932), 1064.

130. Nixon family Bible, LWFP.

131. Mark R. Henry, *The U.S. Army of World War I* (New York: Osprey, 2003), 6.

132. 1918 military registration, card 3153, draft 1827, Local Board 1, El Paso, Texas, 12 September 1918.

133. El Paso County Clerk, Esther J. Calvin Nixon death certificate, 21 February 1919, file 6695; Lawrence A. Nixon to Lawrence J. Nixon, 19 March 1919, N/MFP. Two days earlier, 19 February 1919, Carrie C. Calvin (Esther J. Nixon's mom) had died in El Paso from unknown complications. "Historians have also attempted to find correlations between vulnerability to influenza and such variables as class, race, gender, and ethnicity. Of these, class and gender seem most likely. Women generally suffered higher mortalities, perhaps because pregnant women were especially vulnerable, or because women (as the primary caregivers themselves) were less likely to receive nursing care when they fell ill. Arguments linking influenza mortality to race and class in the United States have been inconclusive. African Americans suffered low mortality, American Indians high mortality, yet both were economically poor groups" (Jo N. Hays, *Epidemics and Pandemics: Their Impacts on Human History* [Santa Barbara: ABC-CLIO, 2005], 394). Esther was nearing her thirty-sixth birthday when she fell ill and died (Lawrence A. Nixon to Lawrence J. Nixon, 19 March 1919, N/MFP).

134. Jenny Nixon is listed as living with her son Lawrence in both the 1920 and 1930 U.S. census; see *Fourteenth Census of the United States*, population schedule, El Paso, precinct 17, El Paso County, TX, series T625, roll 1799, page 113, lines 64–66, and *Fifteenth Census of the United States*, population schedule, El Paso, justice precinct 1, El Paso County, TX, series T626, roll 2328, page 104, lines 40–42. Lawrence A. Nixon (twenty-seven years old) is listed in the 1910 census, although surprisingly not in El Paso, but in Marshall, Texas, along with his father Charles Nixon (fifty-two-year-old "head of household"), Jennie Nixon (forty-five-year-old wife), Charlie Nixon (twenty-one-year-old son), Alfaretta Nixon (twenty-three-year-old daughter), Annie Richardson (twenty-five-year-old daughter), J. H. Richardson (thirty-five-year-old son-in-law), Alfaretta Richardson (three-year-old granddaughter), Charles Richardson (one-year-old grandson), and Lucy Patterson (sixty-five-year-old mother). An explanation for Lawrence Nixon's presence in Marshall in April 1910 when the census enumerator arrived was probably due to him wanting to spend time with his family, particularly his father, who may have been ill and ultimately would die on July 7, 1910, less than three months later; see *Thirteenth Census of the United States*, population schedule, Marshall, precinct 11, ward 2, Harrison County, TX, series T624, roll 1562, page 138, lines 18–27. Alfaretta Nixon is listed as "colored" in the 1912 city directory boarding at 517 E. Fannin Street and Jennie V. Nixon is listed as a "laundress" in the 1914 city directory; see *R. L. Polk's 1912 City Directory for Marshall, Texas* (Detroit, MI: Ralph Lane Polk, 1912), 146, and *R. L. Polk's 1914 City Directory for Marshall, Texas* (Detroit, MI: Ralph Lane Polk, 1914), 148. These two directories were found in the archives of the Harrison County Genealogical Society, 117 East Bowie Street, Marshall, TX.

135. Charles B. Nixon died on July 7, 1910; see Nixon family Bible, LWFP.

136. John M. Barry, *The Great Influenza: The Story of the Deadliest Pandemic in History* (New York: Penguin, 2005), 4.

137. Ibid., 4–5. The correlation between U.S. Army troop increases and the spread of influenza is well documented. El Paso had a large presence of troops in the city during this time, which undoubtedly encouraged the spread of influenza. Carol R. Byerly takes this correlation into account and documents other Texas military bases and cities, yet she makes no mention of El Paso's Fort Bliss or El Paso itself; see her *Fever of War: The Influenza Epidemic in the U.S. Army during World War I* (New York: New York University Press, 2005), 18, 53, 56, 79, 154, 159, 175.

138. Bradford Luckingham, *Epidemic in the Southwest, 1918–1919* (El Paso: Texas Western Press, 1984), 7, 8, 9, 17. For an analysis of how El Paso reacted to other medical concerns such as tuberculosis, infant mortality, and venereal diseases in a racialized manner during this era, see Ann R. Gabbert, "Defining the Boundaries of Care: Local Responses to Global Concerns in El Paso Public Health Policy, 1881–1941" (PhD diss., University of Texas–El Paso, 2006).

Chapter 3. Bullets and Ropes: Wading in Bloody Waters, 1919–1924

1. The epigraph to this chapter is quoted in Mark Ellis, "'Closing Ranks' and 'Seeking Honors': W. E. B. Du Bois in World War I," *Journal of American History* 79.1 (1992): 100.

2. The *Crisis* had nearly a hundred thousand subscribers by the end of 1919; by the end of 1920 it had less than sixty-five thousand subscribers. By 1930, it had under thirty thousand, by 1944, it had thirty-one thousand (Johnson, *Propaganda and Aesthetics*, 35; "Along the N.A.A.C.P. Battlefront," *Crisis* 51.2 [1944]: 51).

3. Bernice Love Wiggins, *Tuneful Tales* (El Paso, TX: [n.p.], 1925), 38–39; Bernice Love Wiggins, *Tuneful Tales* (Lubbock: Texas Tech University Press, 2002), 38–39.

4. 1918 military registration, card 3153, draft 1827, Local Board 1, El Paso, Texas, 12 September 1918.

5. Herbert Aptheker, *A Documentary History of the Negro People in the United States, 1933–1945*, vol. 2 (Secaucus, NJ: Citadel Press, 1974), 243.

6. Gerald Horne, *Black and Brown: African Americans and the Mexican Revolution, 1910–1920* (New York: New York University Press, 2005), 87; Steven A. Reich, ed., *The Great Black Migration: A Historical Encyclopedia of the American Mosaic* (Santa Barbara, CA: ABC-CLIO, 2014), 144–47, 55–60.

7. James N. Leiker, *Racial Borders: Black Soldiers along the Rio Grande* (College Station: Texas A&M University Press, 2002), 116, 212n43. Between 275,000 and 750,000 southern Blacks migrated between 1916 and 1918.

8. Gerald W. Patton, *War and Race: The Black Officer in the American Military, 1915–1941* (Westport, CT: Greenwood Press, 1981), 27.

9. *Thirteenth Census of the United States*, vol. 3 (Washington, DC: Government Printing Office, 1913), 816–17.

10. *Fourteenth Census of the United States*, vol. 2 (Washington, DC: Government Printing Office, 1922), 1363; "El Paso's Population," *Fort Worth Star-Telegram*, 14 February 1916, 4.

11. *Fifteenth Census of the United States*, volume 3, pt. 2 (Washington, DC: Government Printing Office, 1932), 1064.

12. Nia Woods Haydel and Kijua Sanders-McMurtry, "Thirty Years of Lynching in the United States: 1889–1919," in *Encyclopedia of American Race Riots*, ed. Walter Rucker and James Nathaniel Upton (Westport, CT: Greenwood Press, 2007), 637.

13. "The Case of Mr. Shillady," *Crisis* 18.6 (1919): 300–301; *Mobbing of John R. Shillady, Secretary of the National Association for the Advancement of Colored People, at Austin, Texas, Aug. 22, 1919* (New York: NAACP, 1919); Mark R. Schneider, *"We Return Fighting": The Civil Rights Movement in the Jazz Age* (Boston: Northeastern University Press, 2002), 39.

14. Schneider, *"We Return Fighting,"* 30.

15. For other injustices against Black troops during World War I, see Vincent Mikkelsen, "Coming from Battle to Face a War: The Lynching of Black Soldiers in the World War I Era" (PhD diss., Florida State University, 2007).

16. For an account of alleged and actual socialist and communist sympathies within the African American community during this era, see Theodore Kornweibel Jr., *Seeing Red: Federal Campaigns against Black Militancy, 1919–1925* (Bloomington: Indiana University Press, 1998).

17. The position of county judge was more like county executive in that county judge served as "budgeting officer of the county" and handled "numerous duties pertaining to elections" (Dick Smith, "County Judge," *Handbook of Texas Online*, www.tshaonline.org/handbook/online/articles/muc09 [accessed 4 January 2014]).

18. *Tenth Annual Report of the National Association for the Advancement of Colored People for the Year 1919* (New York: NAACP, 1920), 33.

19. Charles F. Kellogg, *NAACP: A History of the National Association for the Advancement of Colored People* (Baltimore, MD: Johns Hopkins Press, 1967), 230.

20. Kellogg, *NAACP*, 240.

21. Sondra K. Wilson, ed., *In Search of Democracy: The NAACP Writings of James Weldon Johnson, Walter White, and Roy Wilkins* (New York: Oxford University Press, 1999), 11, 9–17. Cary D. Wintz and Paul Finkelman, eds., *Encyclopedia of the Harlem Renaissance* (New York: Taylor and Francis, 2004), 862.

22. *Crisis* 6.1 (1913): 26–29, quoted in Horne, *Black and Brown*, 80. The Austin branch had 75 members, Beaumont, 94, Dallas, 169, El Paso, 75, Fort Worth, 166, Galveston, 141, Gonzales, 50, Houston, 414, Orange, 182, San Antonio, 1,228, and Silsbee, 8.

23. *Eighth and Ninth Annual Reports: A Summary of Work, Auditing, Report of the National Association for the Advancement of Colored People for the Years 1917 and 1918* (New York: NAACP, 1919), 86–87.

24. Reich, "Soldiers of Democracy: Black Texans and the Fight for Citizenship, 1917–1921," *Journal of American History* 82.4 (1996): 1503 and 1501. Reich's extensive list of 1918 to 1921 NAACP branches in Texas includes thirty-three branches, but oddly he makes no mention in the article of El Paso's May 1914 formal beginnings and activism during these years.

25. On Lowry's goal to flee into México, see "Anxiety to Hear from Home Cause of Negro's Death," *Memphis Press*, 26 January 1921, 1, and Horne, *Black and Brown*, 74.

26. "They Fed before They Killed," *New York Times*, 27 January 1921, 1, quoted in Schneider, *"We Return Fighting,"* 145. See also Todd E. Lewis, "Mob Justice in the 'American Congo': 'Judge Lynch' in Arkansas during the Decade after World War I," *Arkansas Historical Quarterly* 52.2 (1993): 156–84.

27. Henry Lowry's exact age is unknown; however, William Pickens—the NAACP field secretary who investigated Lowry's murder—estimated that "Lowry was a man of forty years or more" ("The American Congo—Burning of Henry Lowry," *Nation*, 23 March 1921, 426–28). Pickens's 1921 account became a stinging indictment of U.S. southern culture and civilization and the exploitative economic system it fostered (*Negro Star*, 1 April 1921, 1; Nancy Clara Cunard and Hugh D. Ford, eds., *Negro: An Anthology* [New York: Continuum, 1934], 21–23). Nodena is a hamlet in Mississippi County, near the town of Wilson, in northeast Arkansas, twenty-nine miles north of Memphis, Tennessee, and only fourteen miles southwest of Fort Pillow (Lauderdale County, Tennessee), site of the Civil War's Fort Pillow massacre that occurred on 12 April 1864. The Confederate victory saw Union soldiers, most of whom were African American, surrender and then immediately murdered under the command of the infamous Confederate Major General Nathan Bedford Forrest, the first grand wizard of the Ku Klux Klan (Andrew Ward, *River Run Red: The Fort Pillow Massacre in the American Civil War* [New York: Viking, 2005]).

28. Bonnie Thornton Dill and Tallese Johnson, "Between a Rock and a Hard Place: Mothering, Work, and Welfare in the Rural South," in *Sister Circle: Black Women and Work*, ed. in Sharon Harley and the Black Women and Work Collective (New Brunswick, NJ: Rutgers University Press, 2002), 72; Earl Black and Merle Black, *Politics and Society in the South* (Cambridge, MA: Harvard University Press, 1989), 163–65.

29. Books and newspaper accounts give Craig's name as simply O. T. Craig. However, the 1920 census reveals his name to be Osben T. Craig, a sixty-eight-year-old white farmer, head of the household, who lived with his sixty-two-year-old wife (Mary), two daughters, ages twenty-eight (Elizabeth) and twenty-one (Margret), and three sons, ages thirty-two, twenty-four (Richard), and nineteen (*Fourteenth Census of the United States*, population schedule, Troy, Mississippi County, AR, series T625, roll 73, page 246, lines 22–28). Unfortunately, there is no listing in this census for Henry Lowry or his wife Callie Lowry, despite their 1918 move to Arkansas from Mississippi.

30. Nan Elizabeth Woodruff, *American Congo: The African American Freedom Struggle in the Delta* (Cambridge, MA: Harvard University Press, 2003), 110. Lucy Oliver's brother married Henry Lowry's daughter; see Woodruff, *American Congo*, 249n1. Harsh treatment of Blacks by whites was not unusual during this period. Historian Leon Litwack summarizes it this manner: "Some thirty years after emancipation, between 1890 and 1920, in response to perceptions of a New Negro born in freedom, undisciplined by slavery, and unschooled in proper racial etiquette, and in response to growing doubts that this new generation could be trusted to stay in its place without legal and

extra-legal force, the white South denied Blacks a political voice, imposed rigid patterns of racial segregation (Jim Crow), sustained an economic system—sharecropping and tenantry—that left little room for ambition or hope, refused Blacks equal educational resources, and disseminated racial caricatures and pseudo-scientific theories that reinforced and comforted whites in their racist beliefs and practices" ("Hellhounds," in *Without Sanctuary: Lynching Photography in America*, ed. James Allen (Santa Fe, NM: Twin Palms, 2000), 11.

31. Edward C. Royce, *The Origins of Southern Sharecropping* (Philadelphia: Temple University Press, 1993), 181–82, 184–85, 186–222.

32. Woodruff, *American Congo*, 110.

33. Schneider, *"We Return Fighting,"* 146.

34. Pickens, "The American Congo," 427; Cunard and Ford, *Negro*, 22.

35. Woodruff, *American Congo*, 111.

36. Ibid., 111, 249n4. Williams's first name is unknown.

37. "Negro, Hunted by Arkansas Mob, Tells El Paso Detective of Slaying Two Men on Farm," *El Paso Herald*, 19 January 1921, 4.

38. Woodruff, *American Congo*, 111, 113. On the history and influence of the Masons and Odd Fellows in the Black community see Anne S. Butler, "Black Fraternal and Benevolent Societies in Nineteenth-Century America," in *African American Fraternities and Sororities: The Legacy and the Vision*, ed. Tamara L. Brown, Gregory Parks, and Clarenda M. Phillips (Lexington: University Press of Kentucky, 2005), 75–81, and William A. Muraskin, *Middle-Class Blacks in a White Society: Prince Hall Freemasonry in America* (Berkeley: University of California Press, 1975). After the Lowry lynching, local Black benevolent and fraternal organizations attracted negative attention from authorities for having aided Lowry's flight; see "Arkansans Propose to Break up Negro Fraternal Lodges," *Anniston Star*, 28 January 1921, 1, "Order Restored After Lynching," *Emporia Gazette*, 27 January 1921, 1, and "Negro Burning; More Blacks Held," *Evening Gazette*, 27 January 1921, 1.

39. Schneider, *"We Return Fighting,"* 146. For a map of the Segundo Barrio/Second Ward neighborhood in El Paso, see Kristine Navarro and Maceo C. Dailey Jr., *Wheresoever My People Chance to Dwell: Oral Interviews with African American Women of El Paso* (Baltimore, MD: Black Classic Press, 2000), 14.

40. Lowry writes of not having the $10 fee to cross over into Mexico and estimates that the train fare for his wife, Callie, to go to El Paso would be $41. The letter was postmarked 11 January 1921 and signed under the alias S. M. Thompson; the letter is reprinted in its entirety in Aptheker, *A Documentary History of the Negro People in the United States*, 316–77.

41. Lowry astutely addressed his letter to his comrade Morris Jenkins in Turrell, Arkansas, because he knew Richard Osben was the postmaster. The city of Turrell is about twenty-seven miles southwest of Nodena in neighboring Crittenden County. In the letter, Lowry asks Jenkins to personally deliver the correspondence to his good friend J. T. Williams, who knew his wife's whereabouts. Yet for unknown reasons

Jenkins failed to follow these important instructions, opting instead to mail the letter to Williams, which resulted in its seizure by Osben, who in turn notified the local sheriff and probably began to assemble the lynch mob to avenge the untimely deaths of his sister and father, as well as the injuries to his brothers.

42. "Negro, Hunted by Arkansas Mob, Tells El Paso Detective of Slaying Two Men on Farm," *El Paso Herald*, 19 January 1921, 4; "Negro Arrested in Murder of Two," *Fort Worth Star-Telegram*, 19 January 1921, 4. The *Herald* indicates that "Capt. Smith will claim for the detective department a reward of $1,000 offered for the arrest" of Henry Lowry; see "Negro Will Answer Charges of Killing Two and Wounding One," *El Paso Herald*, weekend edition, 22–23 January 1921, 17.

43. Herbert Shapiro, *White Violence and Black Response: From Reconstruction to Montgomery* (Amherst: University of Massachusetts Press, 1988), 177; Schneider, *"We Return Fighting,"* 146.

44. The precise date when Frederick Charles Knollenberg became a member of the local NAACP is unknown, but two years later—August 1923—he clearly was a paying dues member of the El Paso branch; see line item no. 47 in "Memberships of the El Paso Branch," Jerry B. Baldwin, secretary of El Paso branch, to NAACP secretary, 27 August 1923, *NAACP Papers*, LOCMD, pt. 1, Branch Files: El Paso, box G-202. Le Roy Washington was a founding member of the El Paso branch and served in other capacities with the organization including as secretary and as a member of its initial executive committee. He became president of the El Paso branch of the NAACP between 1918 and 1920 (there are no letters between 1918 and 1923 that would indicate definitively when exactly he became branch president) and remained in that office until his death in May 1941 ("Along the NAACP Battlefront: News from the Branches and Youth Councils," *Crisis* 48.6 [1941]: 200).

45. Schneider, *"We Return Fighting,"* 146.

46. The Thomas Chipman McRae Papers are housed in the special collections of the University of Arkansas Libraries in Fayetteville. Jeannie M. Whayne, past chair of the History Department at the University of Arkansas–Fayetteville, examined these papers for any mention of Lawrence Nixon, Le Roy Washington, Fred Knollenberg, or Henry Lowry, but she reported that the papers "are very skimpy. There isn't much in the correspondence files at all and they skip about eight months (Nov. 1920 to June 1921 are blank)" (Jeannie M. Whayne, e-mail to Will Guzmán, 12 February 2005).

47. Frederick Knollenberg to Thomas McRae, 20 January 1921, Le Roy Washington to Elias C. Morris, 20 January 1921, and telegraph from Thomas McCrae to Frederick Knollenberg, 23 January 1921, quoted in Schneider, *"We Return Fighting,"* 146, 422n6; Woodruff, *American Congo*, 111–12, 250n5. Elias C. Morris, the first president of the National Baptist Convention, was one of the most prominent Black Baptists in the nation. For a brief biography of Morris, see Todd E. Lewis, "Elias Camp Morris (1855–1922)," *Encyclopedia of Arkansas History and Culture*, www.encyclopediaofarkansas .net/encyclopedia/entry-detail.aspx?search=1&entryID=433 (accessed 4 January 2014).

48. "Negro, Alleged Slayer, Captured by El Paso Police for Crime Committed in Arkansas, Is Wrested from Officers on Train in Mississippi by Armed Mob Which Conveys Prisoner into Woods and Disappears," *El Paso Herald*, 26 January 1921, 1; "Armed Men Take Accused Negro from Deputies," *Fort Worth Star-Telegram*, 26 January 1921, 2. The first names of the detectives are not given in newspaper accounts.

49. Timothy Paul Donovan, Willard B. Gatewood, and Jeannie M. Whayne, eds., *The Governors of Arkansas: Essays in Political Biography* (Fayetteville: University of Arkansas Press, 1995), 160. On McRae's tenure as governor, see Calvin R. Ledbetter Jr., "Thomas C. McRae: National Forests, Education, Highways, and *Brickhouse v. Hill*," *Arkansas Historical Quarterly* 59.1 (2000): 1–29.

50. Nodena is nearly 175 miles northeast of Little Rock.

51. "Mississippi Mob Makes away with Arkansas Negro," *Fayetteville Democrat*, 26 January 1921, 1; *San Antonio Express*, 28 January 1921, 10; *Fourteenth Census of the United States*, population schedule, Blytheville, ward 2, Mississippi County, AR, series T625, roll 72, page 230, lines 78–82.

52. "Mob Burns Negro Who Was Arrested Here On Charge of Murdering Arkansans," *El Paso Herald*, 27 January 1921, 2.

53. "Negro, Alleged Slayer, Captured by El Paso Police for Crime Committed in Arkansas, Is Wrested From Officers on Train in Mississippi by Armed Mob Which Conveys Prisoner into Woods and Disappears," *El Paso Herald*, 26 January 1921, 1; "Mob Burns Negro Who Was Arrested Here on Charge of Murdering Arkansans," *El Paso Herald*, 27 January 1921, 2; Woodruff, *American Congo*, 111–12.

54. "Mob Burns Negro Who Was Arrested Here on Charge of Murdering Arkansans," *El Paso Herald*, 27 January 1921, 2; "Negro Burned at Stake Should Think of Torture He Misses by Being in U.S. instead of China," *El Paso Herald*, 28 January 1921, 6. The *El Paso Times* condemned the lynching of Henry Lowry; see Schneider, *"We Return Fighting,"* 147, 422n10.

55. "Negro Burned at Stake Should Think of Torture He Misses by Being in U.S. instead of China," *El Paso Herald*, 28 January 1921, 6.

56. "Mob Burns Negro Who Was Arrested Here on Charge of Murdering Arkansans," *El Paso Herald*, 27 January 1921, 2; "Arkansas Governor Says Burning of Negro State's Most Disreputable Deed," *Fort Worth Star-Telegram*, 27 January 1921, 7.

57. "They Fed before They Killed," *New York Times*, 27 January 1921, 1; "Mob Burns Negro Who Was Arrested Here on Charge of Murdering Arkansans," *El Paso Herald*, 27 January 1921, 2. Victims of lynch mobs were often forced to confess to their alleged crime after having been beaten and tortured; see Amy Louise Wood, *Lynching and Spectacle: Witnessing Racial Violence in America, 1890–1940* (Chapel Hill: University of North Carolina Press, 2009), 61–62.

58. "A NAACP Crisis Timeline," *Crisis* 106.4 (1999): 40; James Weldon Johnson, quoted in Christopher Waldrep, *African Americans Confront Lynching: Strategies of Resistance from the Civil War to the Civil Rights Era* (Lanham, MD: Rowman and Littlefield, 2009), 166.

59. Woodruff, *American Congo*, 112; Cunard and Ford, *Negro*, 21–23.

60. Woodruff, *American Congo*, 112.

61. "Negroes Want Pool at Washington Park; It Won't Do—Mayor," *El Paso Herald*, 18 April 1924, newspaper clipping, Richard Moberley Dudley Scrapbook, no. 559 (4 March 1924–30 September 1924), 47, EPPL-SW. This scrapbook was compiled by deputy city clerk George N. Gorham and donated to the public library by Frances "Fannie" Dudley, Mayor Dudley's wife.

62. Holman Taylor, ed., "Miscellaneous: El Paso," *Texas State Journal of Medicine* 17.12 (1922): 585.

63. "CWA Projects Totaling $75,000 Asked by City," *El Paso Herald-Post*, 22 December 1933, 5; "Money Is Donated to Help Establish Negro Center Here," *El Paso Times*, 12 May 1934, 6. The Civil Works Administration was established a month earlier by an executive order of FDR. I have been unable to find any records that suggest the city did indeed fulfill their promise to the Black community and actually build an all-Black pool; see "Swimming Pool at Park for Negroes Is Planned," *El Paso Herald-Post*, 14 April 1934, 2, "Negro Pool Chance Considered Slight," *El Paso Herald-Post*, 17 May 1937, 2, "U.S. Projects Good Business, Harlan Says," *El Paso Herald-Post*, 8 April 1938, 18; *El Paso Herald-Post*, Tuesday 24 May 1938, 2; "$10,000 More Asked to Repair Pool," *El Paso Herald-Post*, 12 January 1939, 5, "Negroes Ask $3,000," *El Paso Herald-Post*, 11 May 1939, 14, and "E.P. Negroes Ask Swimming Pool," *El Paso Times*, 19 July 1940, 16.

64. "Negroes Want Pool at Washington Park; It Won't Do—Mayor," *El Paso Herald*, 18 April 1924, newspaper clipping, Richard Moberley Dudley Scrapbook, no. 559 (4 March 1924–30 September 1924), 47, EPPL-SW.

65. Jerry B. Baldwin to Robert W. Bagnall, March 7, 1923, LOCMD, NAACP Papers, pt. 1, Branch Files: El Paso, Texas, 1913–1925, box G-202, folder 2. In this letter Baldwin wrote to Bagnall regarding NAACP matters on the letterhead of Elite Barber Shop and Cigar Store. Baldwin had scratched out the name "C. O. Borcherding" as proprietor and handwritten his own name in its place.

66. *Fourteenth Census of the United States*, population schedule, El Paso, precinct 5, El Paso County, TX, series T625, roll 1798, page 57B, lines 52–53.

67. On Andrew B. Poe, see *Fourteenth Census of the United States*, population schedule, El Paso, precinct 20, El Paso County, TX, series T625, roll 1799, page 156B, lines 84–87. On Harvey P. Jackson, see *Fourteenth Census of the United States*, population schedule, El Paso, precinct 20, El Paso County, TX, series T625, roll 1799, page 206A, lines 16–20.

68. "Negroes Want Pool at Washington Park," *El Paso Herald*, 18 April 1924.

69. Dailey, "I'm Building Me a Home," 15. The Douglass School moved to the corner of Fourth and Kansas in south El Paso (Chihuahuita) in 1889. For the 1920 boundaries of Chihuahuita neighborhood, see maps 2 and 3, in Mario T. García, *Desert Immigrants: The Mexicans of El Paso, 1880–1920* (New Haven, CT: Yale University Press, 1981), 128–29.

70. "Dudley Draws Color Line on Park Bathing," *El Paso Times*, 19 April 1924, newspaper clipping, Richard Moberley Dudley Scrapbook, no. 559 (4 March 1924–30 September 1924), 47, EPPL-SW.

71. On car ownership among African Americans during this era, see Kathleen Franz, "The Open Road": Automobility and Racial Uplift in the Interwar Years," in *Technology and the African-American Experience: Needs and Opportunities for Study*, ed. Bruce Sinclair (Cambridge, MA: MIT Press, 2004), 131–54.

72. Jeff Wiltse, *Contested Waters: A Social History of Swimming Pools in America* (Chapel Hill: University of North Carolina Press, 2007), 88. According to Wiltse, in 1925, for example, Los Angeles operated fifteen indoor and only three outdoor pools, although during the next five years eight more outdoor pools were constructed. Spokane operated no municipal pools before 1919 but then opened three outdoor facilities during the 1920s. Fort Worth, Texas, likewise had no municipal pools before 1920, but opened four between 1921 and 1927, including a segregated pool for Blacks. Dallas opened three outdoor pools during the 1920s, one of which was assigned for African American use. Throughout the 1920s Jim Crow pools were also opened in Atlanta and New Orleans, giving many urban Blacks in the South access to public pools (90–91).

73. Ibid., 88; William H. Timmons, *El Paso: A Borderlands History* (El Paso: Texas Western Press, 1990), 236.

74. Wiltse, *Contested Waters*, 92; García, *Desert Immigrants*, 86, 96, 107.

75. Wiltse, *Contested Waters*, 92; García, *Desert Immigrants*, 209–11, 217, 221.

76. Wiltse, *Contested Waters*, 88.

77. Timmons, *El Paso*, 238; Christopher C. Burt and Mark Stroud, *Extreme Weather: A Guide and Record Book* (New York: Norton, 2007), 33.

78. Wiltse, *Contested Waters*, 148.

79. Ibid., 124.

80. Ibid., 132–33. Arguably, white men were not just anxious about Black men viewing the relatively scantily clad bodies of white women at public pools and interacting with them in such "intimate and erotic public spaces" but about all men. In June 1923 El Paso city councilman Andrew Poe advised against the installation of any more lights for the wading basins at Florence and Seventh because women were "coming to bathe in the pool with such thin things on," adding that "as it is now one can see but not too well." In other words, he preferred inadequate lighting, which could potentially lead to injuries and perhaps even crime over more lighting that would make the bodies of women more visible to males ("No More Lights Needed In City's Swimming Basin," *El Paso Herald*, 20 June 1923, newspaper clipping, Richard Moberley Dudley Scrapbook, no. 558 [23 April 1923–3 March 1924], 49, EPPL-SW).

81. Wiltse, *Contested Waters*, 124–25, 134–35, 156; Gail Bederman, *Manliness and Civilization: A Cultural History of Gender and Race in the United States, 1880–1917* (Chicago: University of Chicago Press, 1995), 8, 11–31, 170–215.

82. "Negroes Want Pool at Washington Park; It Won't Do—Mayor," *El Paso Herald*, 18 April 1924 newspaper clipping, Richard Moberley Dudley Scrapbook, no. 559 (4 March 1924–30 September 1924), 47, EPPL-SW. Dudley became the only mayor of El Paso to be elected without opposition when he ran for a second term. Dudley was sworn in 16 April 1925 but died two weeks later in an El Paso hospital after undergoing

ulcer surgery (Arthur H. Leibson, "Dudley, Richard M.," *Handbook of Texas Online*, www .tshaonline.org/handbook/online/articles/fdu55 [accessed 4 January 2014]).

83. "Dudley Draws Color Line on Park Bathing," *El Paso Times*, 19 April 1924.

84. Taylor, "Miscellaneous," 581; "Negroes Want Pool at Washington Park; It Won't Do—Mayor," *El Paso Herald*, 18 April 1924, newspaper clipping, Richard Moberley Dudley Scrapbook, no. 559 (4 March 1924–30 September 1924), 47, EPPL-SW.

85. However, during his second term in the state legislature in 1923 he became involved in a bitter city campaign against the Ku Klux Klan. The KKK was increasing its membership throughout the state, including in El Paso, where it controlled the local school board. As the anti-Klan mayoral candidate, Dudley was elected with his entire alderman slate, causing a setback for the local KKK from which it never politically recovered (Leibson, "Dudley, Richard M."; Shawn Lay, ed., *The Invisible Empire in the West: Toward a New Historical Appraisal of the Ku Klux Klan of the 1920s* [Urbana: University of Illinois Press, 1992], 88–90).

86. "Dudley Draws Color Line on Park Bathing," *El Paso Times*, 19 April 1924; emphasis added.

87. Sondra K. Wilson, ed., *The Selected Writings of James Weldon Johnson: The New York Age Editorials, 1914–1923* (New York: Oxford University Press, 1995), 53; Jan Voogd, *Race Riots and Resistance: The Red Summer of 1919* (New York: Peter Lang, 2008); see also William M. Tuttle, *Race Riot: Chicago in the Red Summer of 1919* (Urbana: University of Illinois Press, 1996), William Tuttle, "Violence in a 'Heathen' Land: The Longview Race Riot of 1919," *Phylon* 33.4 (1972): 324–33, Jan Voogd, "Longview (Texas) Riot of 1919," in *Encyclopedia of American Race Riots*, 369–71, Robert Whitaker, *On the Laps of Gods: The Red Summer of 1919 and the Struggle for Justice That Remade a Nation* (New York: Random House, 2008); Grif Stockley Jr., *Blood in Their Eyes: The Elaine Race Massacre of 1919* (Fayetteville: University of Arkansas Press, 2001), and Alfred L. Brophy, *Reconstructing the Dreamland: The Tulsa Riot of 1921: Race, Reparations, and Reconciliation* (New York: Oxford University Press, 2003).

88. Monte Akers, *Flames after Midnight: Murder, Vengeance, and the Desolation of a Texas Community* (Austin: University of Texas Press, 1999).

89. For borderland reports on the "race war" in Florida, see "Six Slain in Race Rioting; Help Rushed: Florida Trouble beyond Control," *San Antonio Express*, 5 January 1923, 1, "22 Dead in Florida Race Riot," *San Antonio Evening News*, 5 January 1923, 1, "Races in a Gory War," *Santa Fe New Mexican*, 5 January 1923, 1, "Five Dead Result of Fla. Race Riot," *Wichita Daily Times*, 5 January 1923, 7, "Florida Race War Dead Five," *Port Arthur News*, 5 January 1923, 1; "Officers Control Florida Race War," *San Antonio Express*, 6 January 1923, 4, "Quiet Follows Racial Clash in Florida Towns," *Brownsville Herald*, 6 January 1923, 1, "Florida Negro Taken to Side of Newly-Dug Graves and There Shot," *Galveston Daily News*, 7 January 1923, 17, and "Negro Shot Down at Grave of Mother Also Slain by Mob," *San Antonio Express*, 7 January 1923, 1, 3.

90. "Dudley Draws Color Line on Park Bathing," *El Paso Times*, 19 April 1924.

91. Frances Hills, interview no. 751 (12 October 1985), 15, 23–24, IOH-UTEP.

92. *El Paso Herald-Post*, 12 October 1953, 20; "'More Sensitive Than Schools': The Struggle to Desegregate Municipal Swimming Pools," in Wiltse, *Contested Waters*, 154–80.

93. "Let Negroes Use Pool," *El Paso Herald-Post*, 28 July 1933, 9.

94. "Ask Negro Swin [*sic*] Pool," *El Paso Herald-Post*, 6 October 1933, 11. The names and ethnicity of the 123 people on this petition are not known.

95. Mitchell A. Kachun, *Festivals of Freedom: Memory and Meaning in African American Emancipation Celebrations, 1808–1915* (Amherst: University of Massachusetts Press, 2003), 97–146; Francis E. Abernethy, Carolyn F. Satterwhite, Patrick B. Mullen, and Alan B. Govenar, eds., *Juneteenth Texas: Essays in African American Folklore* (Denton: University of North Texas Press, 1996), 5.

96. "Negroes Prefer Jan. 1 for Celebrating Day of Slaves' Freedom," *El Paso Herald*, 19 June 1918, 4; Kachun, *Festivals of Freedom*, 254, 302n44.

97. Kachun, *Festivals of Freedom*, 254.

98. "Emancipation Day Observed in City by Negro Colony," *El Paso Times*, 20 June 1923, newspaper clipping, Richard Moberley Dudley Scrapbook, no. 558 (23 April 1923–3 March 1924), 49, EPPL-SW.

99. Thomas L. Purvis, *A Dictionary of American History* (Cambridge, UK: Blackwell, 1997), 383; Ian Stuart-Hamilton, *An Asperger Dictionary of Everyday Expressions* (Philadelphia: Jessica Kingsley, 2004), 203.

100. "Emancipation Day Observed in City by Negro Colony," *El Paso Times*, 20 June 1923, newspaper clipping, Richard Moberley Dudley Scrapbook, no. 558 (23 April 1923–3 March 1924), 49, EPPL-SW.

101. Ibid.

102. See chapter 4 for more about these three individuals. On their memberships into the El Paso NAACP, see "Membership Report," 27 June 1929, Viola E. Washington, El Paso branch secretary, to NAACP New York headquarters, NAACP Papers, LOCMD, pt. 1, Branch Files: El Paso box G-202, folder 4. See also "Memberships of the El Paso Branch," Jerry B. Baldwin, El Paso branch secretary, to NAACP secretary, 27 August 1923, NAACP Papers, LOCMD, Part I, Branch Files: El Paso, box G-202.

Chapter 4. Nixon, the NAACP, and the Courts, 1924–1934

1. "El Paso Negro Doctor to Fight Again for Vote," *El Paso Herald-Post*, 4 August 1932. The epigraph to this chapter is quoted in Susan Borreson, "The Good Fight: Lacking in Experience and Money, Fred Knollenberg Takes on the All-White Primary in Texas," *Texas Lawyer* 15.40 (1999): 26.

2. Berg, *"The Ticket to Freedom": The NAACP and the Struggle for Black Political Integration* (Gainesville: University of Florida Press, 2005), 264.

3. Ibid., 251.

4. On *Nixon v. McCann*, see Darlene Clark Hine, "The Elusive Ballot: The Black Struggle against the Texas Democratic White Primary, 1932–1945," in *The African American*

Experience in Texas: An Anthology, ed. Bruce A. Glasrud and James M. Smallwood (Lubbock: Texas Tech University Press, 2007), 284–86, and *Nixon v. McCann*, NAACP Papers, LOCMD, pt. 1, Legal File, 1910–40, Cases Supported, boxes D-63 and D-92.

5. Robert W. Mickey, "The Beginning of the End for Authoritarian Rule in America: *Smith v. Allwright* and the Abolition of the White Primary in the Deep South, 1944–1948," *Studies in American Political Development* 22.2 (2008): 152–54.

6. Allen W. Trelease, *White Terror: The Ku Klux Klan Conspiracy and Southern Reconstruction* (Baton Rouge: Louisiana State University Press, 1999), 3, 173–74; Wyn Craig Wade, *The Fiery Cross: The Ku Klux Klan in America* (New York: Oxford University Press, 1998), 109–10.

7. John Hope Franklin and Alfred A. Moss Jr., *From Slavery to Freedom: A History of African Americans* (New York: McGraw-Hill, 1994), 275, 384.

8. Rory McVeigh, *The Rise of the Ku Klux Klan: Right-Wing Movements and National Politics* (Minneapolis: University of Minnesota Press, 2009), 20; Anthony Slide, *American Racist: The Life and Films of Thomas Dixon* (Lexington: University Press of Kentucky, 2004), 83–84; John Milton Cooper, *Woodrow Wilson: A Biography* (New York: Knopf, 2009), 3, 13, 33, 121–39; Wyn C. Wade, *The Fiery Cross: The Ku Klux Klan in America* (New York: Simon and Schuster, 1987), 126–27; Melvyn Stokes, *D. W. Griffith's The Birth of a Nation: A History of "The Most Controversial Motion Picture of All Time"* (New York: Oxford University Press, 2007), 207.

9. Stephen A. Brown, "'A Thing So Illogical' in Georgia: Reconsidering Race, Myth, and the Lynching of Leo Frank," in *The Southern Albatross: Race and Ethnicity in the American South*, ed. Philip D. Dillard and Randal L. Hall (Macon, GA: Mercer University Press, 1999), 163–94.

10. McVeigh, *The Rise of the Ku Klux Klan*, 20.

11. James Michael Martinez, *Carpetbaggers, Cavalry, and the Ku Klux Klan: Exposing the Invisible Empire during Reconstruction* (Lanham, MD: Rowman and Littlefield, 2007), 251.

12. Stokes, *D. W. Griffith's The Birth of a Nation*, 233, 235; McVeigh, *The Rise of the Ku Klux Klan*, 23.

13. McVeigh, *The Rise of the Ku Klux Klan*, 7.

14. Ibid.

15. Ibid., 8.

16. John M. Mecklin, *The Ku Klux Klan: A Study of the American Mind* (New York: Russell and Russell, 1963), 107–8; Frank Tannenbaum, *Darker Phases of the South* (New York: G. P. Putnam's Sons, 1924), 24–34, quoted in Norman D. Brown, *Hood, Bonnet, and Little Brown Jug: Texas Politics, 1921–1928* (College Station: Texas A&M University Press, 1984), 50, 446n5.

17. Shawn Lay, ed., *The Invisible Empire in the West: Toward a New Historical Appraisal of the Ku Klux Klan of the 1920s* (Urbana: University of Illinois Press, 1992), 67.

18. Franklin and Moss, *From Slavery to Freedom*, 385.

19. Bernadette Pruitt, *The Other Great Migration: The Movement of Rural African Americans to Houston, 1900–1941* (College Station: Texas A&M University Press, 2013), 160; Brian R. Farmer, "The Ku Klux Klan in Texas," in *Texas Politics Today*, ed. Earl M. William,

Ernest Crain, and Adolfo Santos (Boston: Cengage, 2011), 37; Tyina L. Steptoe, "Dixie West: Race, Migration, and the Color Lines in Jim Crow Houston" (PhD diss.: University of Wisconsin–Madison, 2008), 60; James M. SoRelle, "Race Relations in 'Heavenly Houston,' 1919–45," in *Black Dixie: Afro-Texan History and Culture in Houston*, ed. Howard Beeth and Cary D. Wintz (College Station: Texas A&M University Press, 2000), 178; McVeigh, *The Rise of the Ku Klux Klan*, 102.

20. McVeigh, *The Rise of the Ku Klux Klan*, 15.

21. Mario T. García, *Desert Immigrants: The Mexicans of El Paso, 1880–1920* (New Haven, CT: Yale University Press, 1981), 36 and 244n10.

22. McVeigh, *The Rise of the Ku Klux Klan*, 103.

23. Richard Maxwell Brown, *Strain of Violence: Historical Studies of American Violence and Vigilantism* (Oxford: Oxford University Press, 1975), 284.

24. Lay, *The Invisible Empire in the West*, 69–70.

25. McVeigh, *The Rise of the Ku Klux Klan*, 136.

26. Francisco Arturo Rosales, *Pobre Raza! Violence, Justice, and Mobilization among México Lindo Immigrants, 1900–1936* (Austin: University of Texas Press, 1999), 72.

27. Lay, *The Invisible Empire in the West*, 83, 86.

28. William L. Strickland, "Remembering Malcolm: A Personal Critique of Manning Marable's Non-Definitive Biography of Malcolm X," *Black Scholar* 42.1 (2012): 33.

29. McVeigh, *The Rise of the Ku Klux Klan*, 25; Farmer, "The Ku Klux Klan in Texas," 37.

30. Brown, *Hood, Bonnet, and Little Brown Jug*, 52.

31. McVeigh, *The Rise of the Ku Klux Klan*, 102. Race and immigration concerned many; see Frank Bohn, "The Future World of Six Great Nations," *New York Times*, 30 March 1924, xx4.

32. Charles V. Porras, interview no. 212 (18 November 1975), 1, 3, IOH-UTEP.

33. *General Laws of the State of Texas, 38th Legislature* (Austin, TX: A. C. Baldwin and Sons, 1923), 74–75; Brown, *Hood, Bonnet, and Little Brown Jug*, 151.

34. Dorothy J. Blodgett, Terrell Blodgett, and David L. Scott, *The Land, the Law, and the Lord: The Life of Pat Neff* (Austin, TX: Home Place Publications, 2007), 138.

35. Charles L. Zelden, *The Battle for the Black Ballot: Smith v. Allwright and the Defeat of the Texas All-White Primary* (Lawrence: University Press of Kansas, 2004), 15.

36. Strong sentiments in favor of the implementation of a poll tax were ignored by the majority at the Texas Constitutional Convention of 1876, which granted almost unlimited male suffrage (Charles W. Ramsdell, "Reconstruction in Texas" [PhD diss.: Columbia University, 1910], 176–80, 225–28, 251–57).

37. Michael J. Klarman, *From Jim Crow to Civil Rights: The Supreme Court and the Struggle for Racial Equality* (New York: Oxford University Press, 2004), 31, 52, 141–42.

38. Zelden, *The Battle for the Black Ballot*, 36.

39. Lewis L. Gould, *Alexander Watkins Terrell: Civil War Soldier, Texas Lawmaker, American Diplomat* (Austin: University of Texas Press, 2004).

40. Donald Strong, "The Poll Tax: The Case of Texas," *American Political Science Review* 38.4 (1944): 693–94; Dick Smith, "Texas and the Poll Tax," *Southwestern Social Science Quarterly* 45.2 (1964): 167–68.

41. Gould, *Alexander Watkins Terrell*, 74.

42. Lawrence D. Rice, *The Negro in Texas, 1874–1900* (Baton Rouge: Louisiana State University, 1971), 136.

43. *General Laws of the State of Texas, 28th Legislature* (Austin, TX: Von Roeckmann-Jones, 1903), 133–59.

44. Blodgett, Blodgett, and Scott, *The Land, the Law, and the Lord*, 33–43.

45. Darlene Clark Hine, *Black Victory: The Rise and Fall of the White Primary in Texas* (Columbia: University of Missouri Press, 1979), 85.

46. *General Laws of the State of Texas, 28th Legislature*, 150.

47. "Begins Fight To Test Vote Law in South: Disfranchisement the Main Question," *Chicago Defender*, 11 April 1925, 2.

48. NAACP, eds., *NAACP: Celebrating a Century; 100 Years in Pictures* (Layton, UT: Gibbs Smith, 2008), 62–64. On the Houston uprising of 1917, see "Campaign For Signatures To Petition for 24th Infantrymen an Overwhelming Success," *Crisis* 27.4 (1924): 165–67, Garna L. Christian, *Black Soldiers in Jim Crow Texas, 1899–1917* (College Station: Texas A&M University Press, 1995), 145–72, and Brian D. Behnken, "Houston (Texas) Mutiny of 1917," in *Encyclopedia of American Race Riots*, ed. Walter Rucker and James Nathaniel Upton (Westport, CT: Greenwood Press, 2007), 280–89.

49. NAACP, *NAACP*, 62.

50. Claudine L. Ferrell, *Nightmare and Dream: Anti-Lynching in Congress, 1917–1922* (New York: Garland, 1986), 94, 166, 298–300, 374, 390; Marilyn K. Howard, "Dyer, Leonidas C. (1871–1952)," in *Encyclopedia of American Race Riots*, 182–84.

51. Hine, *Black Victory*, 113.

52. Borreson, "The Good Fight," 26.

53. Hine, *Black Victory*, 113.

54. Poll tax receipt no. 3496, El Paso County, TX, precinct 9, 24 January 1924, N/MFP and LANP-LBJL.

55. Ronald W. Walters, *Black Presidential Politics in America: A Strategic Approach* (Albany: State University of New York Press, 1988), 10.

56. Lawrence A. Nixon to Walter F. White, NAACP executive secretary, 25 February 1952, N/MFP, reprinted in Conrey Bryson, "Progress Report: A Letter from Dr. L. A. Nixon to the NAACP, 1952," *Password* 32.4 (1987), 186.

57. Walters, *Black Presidential Politics in America*, 10. Afro-Texan Norris Wright Cuney is a poignant exception to the Republican Party's neglect of its Black constituency in Texas prior to 1900. In 1873 Cuney was appointed secretary of the Republican State Executive Committee and presided at the state convention of Black leaders at Brenham. Cuney became inspector of customs of the port of Galveston and revenue inspector at Sabine Pass in 1872, special inspector of customs at Galveston in 1882, and finally collector of customs of the port of Galveston in 1889. From his appointment as the first assistant to the sergeant at arms of the Twelfth Legislature in 1870, he went on to serve as a delegate to every national Republican convention from 1872 to 1892. In 1883, Cuney was elected alderman on the Galveston City Council from

the Twelfth District, and in 1886, he became Texas national committeeman of the Republican party. According to scholar Merline Pitre, this was "the most important political position given to an African American of the South in the nineteenth century" ("Norris Wright Cuney (1846–1898)," *Handbook of Texas Online*, www.tshaonline.org/handbook/online/articles/fcu20 [accessed 4 January 2014]).

58. Jeffrey B. Perry, *Hubert Harrison: The Voice of Harlem Radicalism, 1883–1918* (New York: Columbia University Press, 2009), 270; Rebecca Carroll, *Uncle Tom or New Negro? African Americans Reflect on Booker T. Washington and Up From Slavery One Hundred Years Later* (New York: Random House, 2006), 3, 153.

59. Sheldon Avery, *Up From Washington: William Pickens and the Negro Struggle for Equality, 1900–1954* (Wilmington: University of Delaware Press, 1989), 147–49. Despite his progressive and socialist credentials, a Black nationalist he was not—as a "Committee of Eight" member, Pickens was a leading proponent of the "Garvey Must Go" campaign; see Robert A. Hill, ed., *The Marcus Garvey and Universal Negro Improvement Association Papers*, vols. 9 and 10 (Berkeley: University of California Press, 1995–2006), 9: 553, 556n2; 10: lxxiii–lxxiv, 128n2.

60. Frederick Douglass's often cited words (from the 1872 Black worker convention in New Orleans) on why Blacks remained with the Republicans were that "the Republican party is the deck, all else is the sea" (Matthew R. Rees, *From the Deck to the Sea: Blacks and the Republican Party* [Wakefield, NH: Longwood Academic, 1991], 1).

61. Stephen R. Fox, *The Guardian of Boston: William Monroe Trotter* (New York: Atheneum, 1970), 11–13.

62. Ibid.

63. Ibid., 17.

64. Hine, *Black Victory*, 115; *New York Times*, 4 April 1925, 13.

65. Ibid.

66. "Local Negro Vote Case in High Court," *El Paso Times*, 5 January 1927, 1.

67. "Court Upholds Texas Negro Can Vote," *Brownsville Herald*, 7 March 1927, 1; Bryson, *Dr. Lawrence A. Nixon and the White Primary*, 40, 45; "Lawyers Disagree on Primary Ruling," *New York Times*, 9 March 1927, 6.

68. "Topics of The Times," *New York Times*, 16 March 1927, 24.

69. Gloria Garrett Samson, *The American Fund for Public Service: Charles Garland and Radical Philanthropy, 1922–1941* (Westport, CT: Greenwood Press, 1996), 152. The cost for *Nixon v. Herndon* was $2,909.31, for *Nixon v. Condon* $2,879.92, and for *Nixon v. McCann* $750; see Steven F. Lawson, *Black Ballots: Voting Rights in the South, 1944–1969* (Lanham, MD: Lexington Books, 1999), 360n36. A $10,000 figure was published by a local newspaper reporter; see Marshall Hail, "El Paso Negro Doctor to Fight Again for Vote," *El Paso Herald-Post*, 4 August 1932, 1. The *Chicago Whip* and *Pittsburgh Courier* believed the NAACP was "acting fraudulently, that on the pretense of raising money for the [Ossian] Sweet defense, it was in fact using it to develop other cases [*Nixon v. Herndon*]"; see Kenneth Robert Janken, *White: The Biography of Walter White, Mr. NAACP* (New York: New Press, 2003), 77–78.

70. J. R. Reynolds, dean of Haven Teachers College, to Lawrence A. Nixon, 9 March 1927, N/MFP. Haven Teachers College and Conservatory of Music was a Methodist Episcopal institution in Meridian, Mississippi, that operated from 1921 to 1930.

71. "Ruling Gratifies Negroes Here," *New York Times*, 8 March 1927, 6.

72. "Negro Vote Decision Surprises Caraway," 7 March 1927, 1, newspaper clipping, box 2, "Legal Docs, Notes, Correspondence, Clippings," folder, document no. 46, LANP-LBJL.

73. "Plan New Party Rules in Texas," *New York Times*, 8 March 1927, 6.

74. "Demands Negroes Vote in Primary," 13 July 1927, 1, newspaper clipping, box 2, "Legal Docs., Notes, Correspondence, Clippings," folder, document no. 790, LANP-LBJL.

75. Ibid.

76. Hine, *Black Victory*, 120.

77. Ibid., 140.

78. "Allred Is Leading in Texas Returns," *New York Times*, 29 July 1934, 25.

79. Michael J. Klarman, "The White Primary Rulings: A Case Study in the Consequences of Supreme Court Decision Making," *Florida State University Law Review* 29.1 (2001): 58.

80. Sanford N. Greenberg, "White Primary," *Handbook of Texas Online*, www.tshaonline .org/handbook/online/articles/wdw01 (accessed 5 January 2014). Moody became governor after defeating Miriam "Ma" Ferguson (1925–1927 and 1932–1935); see "'Ma' Challenges, Moody Accepts," *New York Times*, 24 May 1926, 21.

81. *Journal of the House of Representatives*, vol. 40 (Austin, TX: A. C. Baldwin, 1927), 300, 302.

82. Klarman, "The White Primary Rulings," 58–59.

83. Lawrence A. Nixon to W. L. Thornton, 7 July 1928, N/MFP.

84. Hine, *Black Victory*, 80.

85. "Primary Bar before U.S. Supreme Court," *New York Amsterdam News*, 5 August 1931, 2.

86. James Marshall, chairman of the New York State Republican Advisory Committee, was elected to the NAACP Board of Directors in 1931; see "Join Board of Negro Aid Group," *New York Times*, 11 November 1931, 2.

87. "Party Power to Bar Negro Held Illegal," *Mexia Weekly Herald*, 6 May 1932, 3.

88. "Texas Negro Wins His Damage Suit," *El Paso Herald-Post*, 17 October 1932, 1; "Negro Is Victor in Election Suit," *Evening Independent* (Massillon, Ohio), 17 October 1932, 2; "Negro, Refused Ballot Right, Wins Damage Suit," *Lima News*, 17 October 1932, 10; "Negro Wins Vote Suit," *Oshkosh Daily Northwestern*, 17 October 1932, 1; "Dr. L. A. Nixon Is Again Winner in Vote Tilt in Tex.," *Chicago Courier*, 22 October 1932, 1.

89. Benjamin N. Cardozo and Abraham L. Sainer, *Law Is Justice: Notable Opinions of Mr. Justice Cardozo* (Union, NJ: Lawbook Exchange, 1999), 317. On the decision to reargue, see "Will Review Capital Slaying," *New York Times*, 19 January 1932, 3.

90. "Texas Negro Exclusion Law Held Invalid," *El Paso Herald-Post*, 2 May 1932, 1; "Court Rules Texas Democratic Chiefs Can't Bar Negroes," *Big Spring Herald*, 6 May 1932, 2.

91. "Voids Ban on Negro in Texas Primary," *New York Times*, 3 May 1932, 2; "To Test Texas Primary Laws," *New York Times*, 20 October 1931, 50.

92. H. L. Hunnicutt to Charles Elmore Cropley, clerk, United States Supreme Court, 16 March 1932, in *Lawrence A. Nixon v. James Condon and Charles H. Kolle* 286 U.S. 73 (1932), no. 265, file 36079, NARA-DC. For more Hunnicutt rants, see "Anything Wrong In Wanting White Grandchildren?," flier (ca. 1957), and H. L. Hunnicutt to Virgil Blossom, Little Rock superintendent, racist plea for continued segregation, 13 July 1957, in Virgil Blossom Papers MC 1364, box 6, file 8, Land of (Unequal) Opportunity Collection, University of Arkansas Libraries, and H. L. Hunnicutt to Herbert L. Thomas opposing the "Arkansas Plan" for school integration, 10 April 1958, Herbert Thomas Papers MC 437, box 4, file 3, Land of (Unequal) Opportunity Collection, University of Arkansas Libraries.

93. "Be it resolved that all white citizens of the state of Texas who are qualified to vote under the constitution and laws of the state shall be eligible to membership in the Democratic party and as such entitled to participate in its deliberations" ("Allred Backs Democrat Ban on Negro Vote," *El Paso Herald-Post*, 12 July 1934, 1).

94. Klarman, "The White Primary Rulings," 59.

95. Irvin S. Taubkin, "Texas Negroes Fail to Gain By Decision: Cardozo Ruling Came Too Late to Give Voice in Democratic Primary," *New York Times*, 8 May 1932, E-6; Irvin S. Taubkin, "Nation Politics Muddled in Texas," *New York Times*, 29 July 1928, N-8.

96. "Bars Voting by Mexicans: Texas Democratic Committee Says They Are Not of 'White Race,'" *New York Times*, 27 July 1934, 6.

97. "Negro Vote Suit Called for Trial," *El Paso Herald-Post*, 31 January 1934, 1, newspaper clipping, LOCMD, NAACP Papers, pt. 1, Legal Files, Cases Supported—Texas Primary, box D92, folder no. 1, January–March 1934; "Starts Third Suit for Negro Voters," *El Paso Herald-Post*, 1 June 1933, 10. Three years later, election judge George L. McCann ran for local elected office; see "Candidate for Alderman Held Wide Range of Jobs," *El Paso Herald-Post*, 9 December 1936, 5.

98. "El Paso Negro Wins Suit for Voting Rights," *El Paso Times*, 7 February 1934, 1; "Negro Vote Suit Called for Trial," *El Paso Herald-Post*, 31 January 1934, 1; "Thinks Negroes Still Barred," *El Paso Herald-Post*, 9 February 1934, 5; "House Votes against Negroes at Convention," *El Paso Herald-Post*, 15 October 1935, 1.

99. "Allred Backs Democrat Ban on Negro Vote," *El Paso Herald-Post*, 12 July 1934, 1; "Judges Told Not to Permit Negro Voting," *El Paso Herald-Post*, 13 July 1934, 2. For details on Allred's life and politics, see "James V. Allred of U.S. Bench, 60; Federal Judge for South Texas Dies," *New York Times*, 25 September 1959.

100. Hine, *Black Victory*, 145.

101. "Houston Editor Sues for Right to Vote," *El Paso Herald-Post*, 13 July 1934, 2.

102. "Allred Is Leading in Texas Returns," *New York Times*, 29 July 1934, 25.

103. *Houston Defender*, 20 April 1935, newspaper clipping, LOCMD, NAACP Papers, pt. 1, "Texas Primary: Undated News Clipping, 1935" folder.

104. James Weldon Johnson to Lawrence A. Nixon, 11 June 1928; a copy of original letter can be found in Dailey, "I'm Building Me a Home," 57. See also "Texas Lawyer Pays up NAACP Life Membership," *Pittsburgh Courier*, 26 September 1942, 18. Nixon was not the only member of the El Paso NAACP who demanded suffrage for African Americans. Black women in El Paso also asserted themselves in their advocacy for voting rights. On 26 March 1918, women in Texas had won the right to vote in primary elections (Rosalyn Terborg-Penn, *African American Women in the Struggle for the Vote, 1850–1920* [Bloomington: Indiana University Press, 1998], 105). Maud Edith Sampson, as president of the El Paso Colored Woman's Club, attempted to apply for membership to the Texas Equal Suffrage Association. Like Lawrence Nixon, she and her husband, Edward P. Sampson, were members of the El Paso NAACP ("Membership Report," Viola E. Washington, El Paso branch secretary, to NAACP New York headquarters, 27 June 1929, NAACP Papers, LOCMD, pt. 1, Branch Files: El Paso, box G-202, folder 4). In June 1918, Maud Sampson sent a letter applying for membership in the National American Woman Suffrage Association (NAWSA) on behalf of the El Paso Colored Woman's Club. The NAWSA had no individual club members, as membership was through state associations only, and the matter was referred back to Texas (Ruthe Winegarten, ed., *Black Texas Women: A Sourcebook: Documents, Biographies, Timeline* [Austin: University of Texas Press, 1996], 187, 291). A response came from the president, Carrie Chapman Catt, longtime women's advocate and founder of the League of Women Voters (Sara Hunter Graham, *Woman Suffrage and the New Democracy* [New Haven, CT: Yale University Press, 1996], 24–25). Chapman Catt wrote to state chapter president Mrs. Edith Hinkle League, suggesting that League "write Mrs. Sampson and tell her that you will be able to get the vote for women more easily if they do not embarrass you by asking for membership and that you are getting it for colored women as well as for white women and appeal to her interest in the matter to subside" (Winegarten, *Black Texas Women*, 188–89; Ruthe Winegarten, ed., *Black Texas Women: 150s Years of Trial and Triumph* [Austin: University of Texas Press, 1995], 209). On the NAWSA, see Mari Jo Buhle and Paul Buhle, eds., *The Concise History of Woman Suffrage: Selections from History of Woman Suffrage* (Urbana: University of Illinois Press, 2005). On the Texas suffrage movement, see A. Elizabeth Taylor, "The Woman Suffrage Movement in Texas," *Journal of Southern History* 17.2 (1951): 194–215, Mary S. Cunningham, *The Woman's Club of El Paso: Its First Thirty Years* (El Paso: Texas Western Press, 1978), and Judith N. McArthur, *Texas through Women's Eyes* (Austin: University of Texas Press, 2010), 29–30.

105. Also meeting Nixon in Denver as official delegates for El Paso's NAACP were Reverend and Mrs. H. A. Rogers. NAACP El Paso branch president LeRoy Washington was not able to attend due to illness within his family. In a letter addressed to Walter White, Washington regretted "not to come in contact with you men who are giving

your very lives to such a worthy cause as is the N.A.A.C.P" (11 June 1925, NAACP Papers, LOCMD, pt. 1, Branch Files: El Paso, box G-202).

106. Lee Sartain, *Invisible Activists: Women of the Louisiana NAACP and the Struggle for Civil Rights, 1915–1945* (Baton Rouge: Louisiana State University Press, 2007), 38.

107. "Membership Report," Viola E. Washington, El Paso branch secretary, to NAACP New York headquarters, 27 June 1929, NAACP Papers, LOCMD, pt. 1, Branch Files: El Paso, box G-202, folder 4. Rudolph López was a thirty-five-year-old Black man who taught manual training at Douglass School, and Mary López was a thirty-six-year-old maid for a local family (*Fifteenth Census of the United States*, population schedule, El Paso, justice precinct 1, El Paso County, TX, series T626, roll 2328, page 1B, lines 86–87; "4 Pioneer E.P. Blacks Are Profiled," *El Paso Herald-Post*, 13 February 1976, B-6; "Here's List of Teachers and Assignments for Schools," *El Paso Herald-Post*, 1 September 1934, 2). Frances Hills, longtime African American El Paso resident, remembers Rudolph López as "one of the leaders in [the] Pullman car." López may have had another career after teaching at Douglass School either as a Pullman porter or as a union representative for their Brotherhood of Sleeping Car Porters union (Frances Hills, interview no. 751 [12 October 1985] 21, IOH-UTEP, 21). The forty-year-old López remarried twenty-three-year-old Georgia Louise Brown in September 1935; see "Vital News: Marriage Licenses," *El Paso Herald-Post*, 13 September 1935, 14.

108. "4 Pioneer E.P. Blacks Are Profiled," *El Paso Herald-Post*, 13 February 1976, B-6.

109. "Nixon," *El Paso Herald-Post*, 8 March 1966, 21.

110. "Memberships of the El Paso Branch," Jerry B. Baldwin, El Paso branch secretary, to NAACP secretary, 27 August 1923, NAACP Papers, LOCMD, pt. 1, Branch Files: El Paso, box G-202.

111. James R. Murphy, *El Paso, 1850–1950* (Charleston, SC: Arcadia Publishing, 2009), 45. Louis Laskin was born in Russia in 1887 and his wife, Celia, was born in Russia in 1895. Both Celia and Louis became naturalized citizens in 1908 and Russian was their mother tongue (*Fourteenth Census of the United States*, population schedule, El Paso, precinct 36, El Paso County, TX, series T625, roll 1799, page 72A, lines 24–26). Laskin was an "annual member" of the Jewish Publication Society, a scholarly organization that published Jewish works in English. In 1918, throughout the United States, this organization had nearly fifty thousand members, which included sixty-four in El Paso and nearly three hundred across Texas (Samson D. Oppenheim, ed., *The American Jewish Year Book, Volume 20* [Philadelphia: The Jewish Publication Society of America, 1918], 424, 578. Cyrus Adler, Mayer Sulzberger, and Solomon Solis-Cohen created the Jewish Publication Society in 1888 and the American Jewish Historical Society in 1892, both based in Philadelphia, to promote serious Jewish scholarship throughout the United States (Stephen H. Norwood and Eunice G. Pollack, eds., *Encyclopedia of American Jewish History* [Santa Barbara: ABC-CLIO, 2008], 31, 142).

112. A brief history of Jews in El Paso can be found in H. Ava Weiner, *Jewish Stars in Texas: Rabbis and Their Works* (College Station: Texas A&M University Press, 1999), 102–19. On Jewish sympathies with the plight of African Americans, see Hasia R. Diner,

In the Almost Promised Land: American Jews and Blacks, 1915–1935 (Westport, CT: Greenwood Press, 1977), 12, 23, 28, 35, 71, 154, 229, and Rafael Medoff, *Jewish Americans and Political Participation: A Reference Handbook* (Santa Barbara, CA: ABC-CLIO, 2002), 89.

113. Leonard C. Schlup and Donald W. Whisenhunt, eds., *It Seems to Me: Selected Letters of Eleanor Roosevelt* (Lexington: University Press of Kentucky, 2001), 29.

114. "Branch News," *Crisis* 42.4 (1935): 121.

115. The Women's City Government Club was a predominately white civic local organization; see Judith N. McArthur, *Creating the New Woman: The Rise of Southern Women's Progressive Culture in Texas, 1893–1918* (Urbana: University of Illinois Press, 1998), 77. Roth's parents were born in Hungary, as he too was originally from Hungary, arriving in the United States in 1903 (*Fifteenth Census of the United States*, population schedule, El Paso, justice precinct 1, El Paso County, TX, series T626, roll 2329, page 159A, lines 45–50). The German-speaking Rabbi Zielonka arrived in the United States in 1898 and his father was born in Poland and his mother was born in Germany (*Twelfth Census of the United States*, population schedule, Quincy, ward 4, precinct 15, Adams County, IL, series T623, roll 236, page 131A, lines 38–43).

116. Knollenberg was born in Quincy, Illinois, in January 1877 to parents who had roots in Germany and Britain. Knollenberg's father was in the merchant milling business (*Twelfth Census of the United States*, population schedule, Quincy, ward 4, precinct 15, Adams County, IL, series T623, roll 236, page 131A, lines 38–43). He earned his law degree from the University of Michigan in 1901 (*University of Michigan, Department of Law, Catalogue of Students for 1899–1900 and Annual Announcement, 1900–1901* [Ann Arbor: University of Michigan, 1900], 35, 40, 43; *University of Michigan, General Catalogue of Officers and Students, 1837–1911* [Ann Arbor: University of Michigan, 1912], 485, 1031). In 1902, he moved to Missouri to practice law and eventually made his way to New Mexico—Silver City and Alamogordo—where he practiced between 1907 and 1910. In 1910, he moved to El Paso, where he was admitted to the Texas Bar and soon after became a member of the Bar Association of El Paso County (J. Morgan Broaddus Jr., *The Legal Heritage of El Paso* [El Paso: Texas Western College Press, 1963], 171, 177, 178, 223) and established a law partnership with his fellow 1903 Michigan Law School alumnus Charles R. Loomis ("News from the Classes," *Michigan Alumnus* 22 [October 1915–August 1916]: 251). In October 1916, Knollenberg became a member of the newly formed Tri-State Bar Association (which consisted of attorneys and judges from west Texas, New Mexico, and Arizona), and after the Bar Association of El Paso County disbanded, he became a member of the newly created El Paso Bar Association in August 1919, two months after its inception (Broaddus, *The Legal Heritage of El Paso*, 177–78, 181). In 1941, Chief Justice Charles Evans Hughes appointed Knollenberg to serve as the southwestern representative for the American Law Institute, a national governing body with restricted membership. Knollenberg died at the age of seventy-four in El Paso on June 11, 1951 ("Death Takes Well Known Attorney," *El Paso Times*, 12 June 1951, A-1).

117. Fred C. Knollenberg to William R. Stansbury, clerk, U.S. Supreme Court, 1 December 1925 and 23 February 1927, in *Nixon v. Herndon*, 273 U.S. 536 (1927), no. 480

and no. 117, file 31199, NARA-DC. On gold teeth and personality, see Borreson, "The Good Fight," 26.

118. Borreson, "The Good Fight," 26.

119. LeRoy W. Washington, El Paso NAACP president, to Walter White, NAACP secretary, 25 January 1932, NAACP Papers, LOCMD, pt. 1, Branch Files: El Paso, box G-202, folder 4.

120. William B. Hixson Jr., *Moorfield Storey and the Abolitionist Tradition* (New York: Oxford University Press, 1972), 138, 233n64.

121. Robert Dallek, *Lone Star Rising: Lyndon Johnson and His Times, 1908–1960* (New York: Oxford University Press, 1991), 316.

122. Michael J. Klarman, "Is the Supreme Court Sometimes Irrelevant? Race and the Southern Criminal Justice System in the 1940s," *Journal of American History* 89.1 (2002): 149.

123. Lawrence A. Nixon to Walter F. White, NAACP executive secretary, 25 February 1952, N/MFP, reprinted in Bryson, "Progress Report," 186.

124. David Lublin, *The Republican South: Democratization and Partisan Change* (Princeton, NJ: Princeton University Press, 2004), 116.

Chapter 5. Optimism and Rejection, 1925–1962

1. The epigraph to this chapter is quoted in *Social and Physical Conditions of Negroes in Cities* (Atlanta, GA: Atlanta University Press, 1897), 44.

2. Barbara Bates, *Bargaining for Life: A Social History of Tuberculosis* (Philadelphia: University of Pennsylvania Press, 1992), 1.

3. Ibid., 4.

4. Harriet A. Washington, *Medical Apartheid: The Dark History of Medical Experimentation on Black Americans from Colonial Times to the Present* (New York: Doubleday, 2006), 29, 326. Today, in the developing world, many deaths from AIDS are due to the tuberculosis that accompanies it. Furthermore, in the United States, half of incarcerated TB sufferers are not only Black "but also homeless and many have a history of mental illness, alcohol and drug abuse, or all of the above risk factors" (Washington, *Medical Apartheid*, 326).

5. Samuel K. Roberts Jr., *Infectious Fear: Politics, Disease, and the Health Effects of Segregation* (Chapel Hill: University of North Carolina Press, 2009), 34–35, 234n20.

6. Ibid., 4, 64–65.

7. Ronald L. Braithwaite and Sandra E. Taylor, *Health Issues in the Black Community* (Chichester, UK: John Wiley, 2009), 29.

8. Roberts, *Infectious Fear*, 4, 64–65.

9. Ibid.; Anthony P. Mora, *Border Dilemmas: Racial and National Uncertainties in New Mexico, 1848–1912* (Durham, NC: Duke University Press, 2011), 353n29.

10. Booker T. Washington and Albon L. Holsey, *Booker T. Washington's Own Story of His Life and Work* (Atlanta: J. L. Nichols, 1915), 427. In 1921, in order to honor the memory of Washington, who had died on 14 November 1915, the initiative was switched from

January to the week of his birthday, 5 April, just eleven months after the launch of the first Negro Health Week (Braithwaite and Taylor, *Health Issues in the Black Community*, 29).

11. "Hold Health Meeting," *El Paso Herald-Post*, 7 April 1933, 10; "Negro Health Week Program Tomorrow," *El Paso Herald-Post*, 7 April 1937, 10. For more details on National Negro Health Week, including Monroe N. Work antecedents, see Susan L. Smith, *Sick and Tired of Being Sick and Tired: Black Women's Health Activism in America, 1890–1950* (Philadelphia: University of Pennsylvania Press, 1995), 35–39.

12. Washington, *Medical Apartheid*, 156.

13. Susan L. Smith, "National Medical Association," in *Organizing Black America: An Encyclopedia of African American Associations*, ed. Nina Mjagkij (London: Taylor and Francis, 2001), 468–70.

14. Henry S. Plummer, clinical section, Mayo Clinic, to Lawrence A. Nixon, 25 May 1926, N/MFP.

15. Edward Starr Judd, surgical section, Mayo Clinic, to Lawrence A. Nixon, 1 June 1926, N/MFP.

16. Roberts, *Infectious Fear*, 4; Bates, *Bargaining for Life*, 293.

17. Lawrence A. Nixon to Kendall Emerson, National Tuberculosis Association, 12 December 1933, letter, N/MFP.

18. "Proposed Hospital for Treatment of Tuberculosis at El Paso Promises to Be One of Most Useful and Largest Negro Projects," *El Paso Herald-Post*, 19 May 1934, 5.

19. Lawrence A. Nixon to Kendall Emerson, National Tuberculosis Association, 12 December 1933N/MFP; emphasis added.

20. Holman Taylor, "A Tuberculosis Sanatorium for Negroes," *Texas State Journal of Medicine* 16.10 (1921): 419–20; Dorothy J. Blodgett, Terrell Blodgett, and David L. Scott, *The Land, the Law, and the Lord: The Life of Pat Neff* (Austin, TX: Home Place Publications, 2007), 100.

21. Roberts, *Infectious Fear*, 287n34; "Why a Negro Sanatorium in Texas?," *Journal of the Outdoor Life*, May 1921, 172.

22. Washington, *Medical Apartheid*, 326.

23. Lieutenant Colonel Albert A. King to Lawrence A. Nixon, 20 May 1926, N/MFP.

24. "I am instructed to say that the Salvation Army is prepared to accept $10,000 cash down payment with 7% interest on the balance, and a principal payment of $2,500 semi-annually plus interest. If the full amount of purchase price is paid within twelve months, it is my opinion that the Salvation Army would consider waiving the interest payment for that period in order to assist your worthy project" (Major Albert E. Baynton, assistant property secretary, Salvation Army, to Lawrence A. Nixon, 7 July 1926, N/MFP).

25. Lawrence A. Nixon to Kendall Emerson, National Tuberculosis Association, 12 December 1933, N/MFP.

26. "Loan to Build Hospital for Negroes Asked," *El Paso Herald-Post*, 22 December 1933, 5.

27. Frederick C. Knollenberg to Lawrence A. Nixon, 28 August 1934, N/MFP.

28. Ishmael Flory, "Envision Beautiful Tubercular Hospital Rising on Texas Site: Nationally Known Group to Seek Government Funds, Project Calls for Millions," *Chicago Defender*, 28 April 1934, 11; "Proposed Hospital for Treatment of Tuberculosis at El Paso Promises to Be One of Most Useful and Largest Negro Projects," *El Paso Herald-Post*, 19 May 1934, 5. George S. Schuyler spoke at Second Baptist Church in El Paso on December 4, 1931 under auspices of the NAACP El Paso branch; see "Texas State News," *Chicago Defender*, 28 November 1931, 21.

29. "Loan to Build Hospital for Negroes Asked," *El Paso Herald-Post*, 22 December 1933, 5; and Lawrence A. Nixon to Drusilla E. (Tandy) Attwell, 21 July 1933, N/MFP.

30. Vanessa N. Gamble, *Making a Place for Ourselves: The Black Hospital Movement, 1920–1945* (New York: Oxford University Press, 1995), 22.

31. Drusilla and Nixon had two children: Drusilla Ann Nixon was born with Down syndrome on 19 April 1937 and Edna Angela Nixon was born 18 January 1939 ("Dursilla [*sic*] Ann Nixon," *El Paso Times*, obituary section, 7 December 1994; "Edna Angela Nixon," birth indexes, birth records, El Paso County Clerk, www.epcounty.com/publicrecords/birthrecords/BirthRecordSearch.aspx [accessed 7 January 2014]).

32. Drusilla E. (Tandy) Nixon, interview no. 194 (11 December 1975), 20, IOH-UTEP, 20.

33. Ibid; "Four E.P. Hospitals on Approved List," *El Paso Herald-Post*, 9 October 1933, 10.

34. "Negroes, Whites Segregated Here," *El Paso Herald-Post*, 29 June 1937, 8.

35. Barbara Funkhouser, *The Caregivers: El Paso's Medical History, 1898–1998* (El Paso: Sundance Press, 1999), 243; Conrey Bryson, *Dr. Lawrence A. Nixon and the White Primary* (El Paso, TX: Texas Western Press, 1974), 27.

36. Drusilla E. (Tandy) Nixon, interview no. 194 (11 December 1975), 20, IOH-UTEP.

37. Lawrence A. Nixon to Franklin D. Roosevelt, 6 March 1934, N/MFP.

38. Horatio B. Hackett, assistant administrator, Federal Emergency Administration of Public Works, to Lawrence A. Nixon, 11 June 1935, N/MFP.

39. Gamble, *Making a Place for Ourselves*, xvi.

40. Ibid., 61.

41. Ibid., 102–3.

42. Marshall Hail, "Is Southern Conference for Human Welfare a Red Front?" *El Paso Herald-Post*, 22 January 1948, 1. The most recent definitive work on the SCHW is Linda Reed, *Simple Decency and Common Sense: The Southern Conference Movement, 1938–1963* (Bloomington: Indiana University Press, 1991).

43. Marshall Hail, "El Paso Negro Doctor to Fight Again for Vote," *El Paso Herald-Post*, 4 August 1932, 1.

44. One the bureau's biggest concerns was the El Paso SCHW's multiracial composition. In its January 1947 report, the FBI special agent notes that SCHW socials and meetings are held twice per month and "are attended by both Negroes and whites." The agent further notes that "it is definitely against the customs prevailing in El Paso,

Texas, for Negroes and whites to mingle socially." The agent, most likely an individual who had lived in El Paso for some time, suggests that El Paso is less of a western city and more southern culturally and socially as it relates to race relations. LeRoy White was described by the FBI as someone "colored" who "had been a pastor of a Negro church in El Paso for a number of years. He has, for many years, been a strong advocate of immediate Negro equality—an equality in every way. As an example of this, several years ago White refused to lend assistance in getting a theater built because the theater proposed, as is the custom in this section, to have a reserved space for Negroes. Rev. White objected to this advising that a Negro should be able to sit any place in the theater and for that reason refused to lend his assistance" ("SCHW," internal security-C reports, prepared by Special Agent Frederick A. Johns, El Paso file no. 100-338, 27 January 1947, pages 1–2, FOIPA no. 1128189-000, USDJ-FBI-DC).

45. Ibid., page 1.

46. Ibid.

47. "SCHW," internal security-C reports, prepared by Special Agent John E. Keane, El Paso file no. 100-338, 20 November 1946, pages 2, 5, FOIPA no. 1128189-000, USDJ-FBI-DC; Nathalie Gross Collection, 1948–1975, no. 819, Mexican-Americans box 1, Mexican-Americans—El Paso folder, "Southern Conference for Human Welfare, El Paso Chapter," bulletin, ca. 1946–1947, EPPL-SW.

48. "SCHW," internal security-C reports, prepared by Special Agent Frederick A. Johns, El Paso file no. 100-338, 27 January 1947, page 9, FOIPA no. 1128189-000, USDJ-FBI-DC.

49. Ibid.

50. Thomas A. Krueger, *And Promises To Keep: The Southern Conference For Human Welfare, 1938–1948* (Nashville: Vanderbilt University Press, 1967), 148.

51. Marshall Hail, "Is Southern Conference for Human Welfare a Red Front?" *El Paso Herald-Post*, 22 January 1948, 1; Martin B. Duberman, *Paul Robeson* (New York: New Press, 2005), 259.

52. Warren Ashby, *Frank Porter Graham: A Southern Liberal* (Winston-Salem, NC: J. F. Blair, 1980); Julian M. Pleasants and Augustus M. Burns, *Frank Porter Graham and the 1950 Senate Race in North Carolina* (Chapel Hill: University of North Carolina Press, 1990); James Clotfelter, *Frank Porter Graham: Service to North Carolina and the Nation* (Greensboro: North Carolina Service Project, 1993); John Ehle and Charles Kuralt, *Dr. Frank: Life with Frank Porter Graham* (Chapel Hill, NC: Franklin Street Books, 1993); John Wilson, Charles Kuralt, and Martin Clark, producer and director, *Dr. Frank the Life and Times of Frank Porter Graham*, documentary (Research Triangle Park: North Carolina Public Television, 1994).

53. "Discussion of 'Vital Issues of the Day,'" *El Paso Herald-Post*, 31 October 1947, 25.

54. "SCHW," internal security-C reports, prepared by Special Agent Frederick A. Johns, El Paso file no. 100-338, 16 December 1947, page 3, FOIPA no. 1128189-000, USDJ-FBI-DC.

55. Ibid.; "Senator Taylor Flies to New York," *El Paso Herald-Post*, 3 November 1947, 3; *El Paso Times*, 2 November 1947.

56. Thomas A. Krueger, *And Promises To Keep: The Southern Conference for Human Welfare, 1938–1948* (Nashville, TN: Vanderbilt University Press, 1967), 146–47; Ann Fagan Ginger and David Christiano, eds., *The Cold War against Labor: An Anthology* (Berkeley, CA: Meiklejohn Civil Liberties Institute, 1987), 592–600.

57. El Paso Vertical File—Clubs: R-S, SCHW, "Southern Conference for Human Welfare: El Paso Chapter," bulletin, vol. 1, no. 1, 28 September 1946, page 2, EPPL-SW.

58. Humberto Silex Sr., obituary, newspaper clipping, CVF—Humberto Silex Sr. folder, EPPL-SW.

59. Monica Perales, *Smeltertown: Making and Remembering a Southwest Border Community* (Chapel Hill: University of North Carolina Press, 2010), 119, 127, 132–33; Frank Macomber, "Unions Widen Organization of Plant Employees," *El Paso Herald-Post*, 25 November 1941, 5. For more on Silex union organizing activities in El Paso, see "Brick Company Employes [*sic*] Ignore Order to Work," *El Paso Herald-Post*, 29 April 1943, 1, 16, Frank Macomber, "AFL and CIO Battle for Control of E.P. Labor," *El Paso Herald-Post*, 25 November 1941, 5, "CIO Makes Progress in El Paso During Year," *El Paso Herald-Post*, 7 September 1942, 14, "Smelter Ordered to Reinstate Employe [*sic*]," *El Paso Herald-Post*, 28 May 1942, 8, "Smelter Union Seeks Settlement," *El Paso Herald-Post*, 13 May 1946, 1, "Toledano Asks Juarez Workers to Support Aleman for President," *El Paso Herald-Post*, 1 May 1946, 1, "Union Opposes Deportation," *El Paso Herald-Post*, 21 October 1946, 16, *El Paso Herald-Post*, 11 October 1947, quoted in "Ten Years Ago," *El Paso Herald-Post*, 11 October 1957, 22, "Ten Years Ago," *El Paso Herald-Post*, 24 December 1957, 4, "Ten Years Ago," *El Paso Herald-Post*, 24 December 1956, 12, and "Union to Ask $300,000 Here," *El Paso Herald-Post*, 23 December 1946, 1.

60. "Peace Bond Issued," *El Paso Herald-Post*, 10 October 1945, 9; "Woman Refuses to Say in Court If She Is Commie," *El Paso Herald-Post*, 6 October 1949, 1; *El Paso Herald-Post*, 1 March 1947, 6.

61. "The Attack on Humberto Silex," flier, CVF—Humberto Silex Sr. folder, EPPL-SW.

62. El Paso Vertical File—Clubs: R-S, SCHW, "Southern Conference for Human Welfare: El Paso Chapter," bulletin, vol. 1, no. 1, 28 September 1946, page 2, EPPL-SW.

63. "E.P. Labor Leader Receives Pardon," *El Paso Herald-Post*, 16 September 1946, 1.

64. "Nicaraguan Faces Deportation Action," *El Paso Herald-Post*, 25 March 1957, 1; "Judge Clears Way for Labor Man's Citizenship," *El Paso Herald-Post*, 23 December 1947, 1.

65. El Paso Vertical File—Clubs: R-S, SCHW, "Southern Conference for Human Welfare: El Paso Chapter," bulletin, vol. 1, no. 1, 28 September 1946, pages 1–2, EPPL-SW. On New Mexico senator Dionisio Chavez and the FEPC, see Matthew Gritter, *Mexican Inclusion: The Origins of Anti-Discrimination Policy in Texas and the Southwest* (College Station: Texas A&M University Press, 2012), 91–97, 108–9.

66. Ibid; "OPA Studies Rent Hike Proposal," *El Paso Herald-Post*, 14 November 1946, 15.

67. El Paso Vertical File—Clubs: R-S, SCHW, "Southern Conference for Human Welfare: El Paso Chapter," bulletin, vol. 1, no. 1, 28 September 1946, pages 1–2, EPPL-SW.

68. Nathalie Gross Collection, 1948–1975, no. 819, Mexican-Americans box 1, Mexican-Americans—El Paso folder, "Southern Conference for Human Welfare, El Paso Chapter: 'Last Weeks [*sic*] Meeting Well Attended,'" bulletin, vol. 1, no. 8, 18 January 1947, and "Southern Conference for Human Welfare, El Paso Chapter: 'Meeting Notice!,'" bulletin, vol. 1, no. 7, 9 January 1947, EPPL-SW.

69. Marshall Hail, "Is Southern Conference For Human Welfare a Red Front?," *El Paso Herald-Post*, 22 January 1948, 1.

70. "Report on Southern Conference for Human Welfare: Investigation of Un-American Activities in the United States," Committee on Un-American Activities, House of Representatives, Eightieth Congress, first session, House Report no. 592, 1; John Edgar Hoover, FBI Director to Alice O'Donnell, "Houston Organization Committee of the Southern Conference for Human Welfare, Houston, Texas," 23 April 1948, FOIPA no. 1128189-000, USDJ-FBI-DC.

71. Walter Gellhorn, "Report on a Report of the House Committee on Un-American Activities," *Harvard Law Review* 60.8 (1947): 1234. The Dies Committee, a precursor to the HUAC, publicly dismissed the idea that the ACLU had any "Communist taint."

72. Ibid., 1233. Walter Gellhorn's sister was the highly regarded Martha Ellis Gellhorn, whose coverage of the Spanish Civil War, Second World War, and the Vietnam War earned her a reputation as one of the greatest foreign reporters of the twentieth century.

73. "El Paso Herald," *Portal to Texas History*, texashistory.unt.edu/explore/collections/EPHD/ (accessed 13 January 2014); "El Paso Herald," *Chronicling America: Historic American Newspapers*, Library of Congress, chroniclingamerica.loc.gov/essays/196/ (accessed 13 January 2014).

74. "SCHW," internal security-C reports, prepared by Special Agent Frederick A. Johns, El Paso file no. 100-338, 27 January 1947, page 7, FOIPA no. 1128189-000, USDJ-FBI-DC.

75. Gloria Garrett Samson, *The American Fund for Public Service: Charles Garland and Radical Philanthropy, 1922–1941* (Westport, CT: Greenwood Press, 1996), 186–87.

76. "SCHW," internal security-C reports, prepared by Special Agent Frederick A. Johns, El Paso file no. 100–338, 16 December 1947, page 6, FOIPA no. 1128189-000, USDJ-FBI-DC.

77. Ibid.

78. "Civic Club Members Invited to Meeting," *El Paso Herald-Post*, 14 November 1946, 12; "Pattern for a Police State, U.S.A." *El Paso Herald-Post*, 11 May 1948, 13.

79. Ibid.

80. Ibid.; Rebecca Woodham, "Southern Conference for Human Welfare (SCHW)," *Encyclopedia of Alabama*, www.encyclopediaofalabama.org/face/Article.jsp?id=h-1593 (accessed 13 January 2014).

81. "SCHW," internal security-C reports, prepared by Special Agent Frederick A. Johns, El Paso file no. 100-338, 16 March 1949, pages 1, 3, FOIPA no. 1128189-000, USDJ-FBI-DC.

82. Linda Reed, "Southern Conference Movement: The Southern Conference for Human Welfare and the Southern Conference Educational Fund," in *The Eleanor Roosevelt Encyclopedia*, ed. Maurine H. Beasley, Holly C. Shulman, and Henry R. Beasley (Westport, CT: Greenwood Press, 2001), 487.

83. Drusilla E. (Tandy) Nixon, interview no. 194 (11 December 1975), 13–14, IOH-UTEP. Nixon, who was born in July 1899, was a member of the Phyllis Wheatley Club in El Paso for over forty years, and at one time she served as its president. In 1935, she organized the Black Girl Reserves of the YWCA in El Paso, which emphasized service, spirit, health, and knowledge (Ruthe Winegarten, ed., *Black Texas Women: A Sourcebook: Documents, Biographies, Timeline* [Austin: University of Texas Press, 1996], 298; Jacqueline M. Moore, *Leading the Race: The Transformation of the Black Elite in the Nation's Capital, 1880–1920* [Charlottesville: University of Virginia Press, 1999], 174; Nancy Marie Robertson, *Christian Sisterhood, Race Relations, and the YWCA, 1906–1946* [Urbana: University of Illinois Press, 2007]). Drusilla also was the first Black woman in El Paso to serve on the YWCA board, after having been a general member of the organization since the age of fourteen. In 1955, she represented the El Paso YWCA as a delegate to the organization's Centennial Celebration in New York City. The El Paso Commission for Women inducted Nixon posthumously as an honorary member of the El Paso Hall of Fame (Mary Margaret David, "Widow of El Paso Civil Rights Pioneer Dies in Albuquerque," *El Paso Times*, 11 May 1990, B-1; *Albuquerque Journal*, 11 May 1990; Clara Duncan-Adams, "El Paso Hall of Fame Members (as of 9/9/08)," *El Paso Commission for Women*, elpasowomen.org/HallOfFame.htm [accessed 13 January 2014]; "Drusilla Nixon Helped Bring Change," *El Paso Times*, 23 February 2009; Will Guzmán, "Drusilla Elizabeth Tandy Nixon," *Handbook of Texas Online*, www.tshaonline.org/handbook/online/articles/fni18 [accessed 5 January 2014]).

84. Rodolfo Rosales, *The Illusion of Inclusion: The Untold Political Story of San Antonio* (Austin: University of Texas Press, 2000), 71; Ronnie Dugger, "Gonzalez of San Antonio," pt. 3, *Texas Observer*, 9 May 1980, 15–24.

85. Thomas R. Cole, *No Color Is My Kind: The Life of Eldrewey Stearns and the Integration of Houston* (Austin: University of Texas Press, 1997), 44, 56; William H. Kellar, *Make Haste Slowly: Moderates, Conservatives, and School Desegregation in Houston* (College Station: Texas A&M University Press, 1999), 117; F. Kenneth Jensen, "The Houston Sit-In Movement of 1960–61," in *Black Dixie: Afro-Texan History and Culture in Houston*, ed. Howard Beeth and Cary D. Wintz (College Station: Texas A&M University Press, 2000), 211–22; David Perman, producer and director, *The Strange Demise of Jim Crow:*

How Houston Desegregated Its Public Accommodations, 1959–1963, documentary (Galveston: Institute for the Medical Humanities, University of Texas–Medical Branch, 1997).

86. Cole, *No Color Is My Kind*, 53.

87. Ibid., 60.

88. Perman, *The Strange Demise of Jim Crow*.

89. Ibid.

90. Cole, *No Color Is My Kind*, 93.

91. *Austin American Statesman*, 7 November 2001.

92. *Austin American Statesman*, 2 April 1994.

93. Richard Stephenson, "Race in the Cactus State," *Crisis* 61.4 (1954): 198–99.

94. George Long, "How Albuquerque Got Its Civil Rights Ordinance," *Crisis* 60.11 (1953): 524.

95. Thomas Lark, ed., *History of Hope: The African American Experience in New Mexico* (Albuquerque, NM: Albuquerque Museum, 1996), 6.

96. *Daily Texan*, 23 October 1963, in Winegarten, *Black Texas Women*, 211.

97. "Council Okays Integration," *El Paso Herald-Post*, 7 June 1962, 1, 2.

98. Mario T. García, *The Making of a Mexican American Mayor: Raymond L. Telles of El Paso* (El Paso: Texas Western Press, 1999), 1, 108–9.

99. Ibid., 109.

100. Ibid., 108–9.

101. Oscar J. Martínez, *The Chicanos of El Paso: An Assessment of Progress* (El Paso: Texas Western Press, 1980), 6.

102. García, *The Making of a Mexican American Mayor*, 110.

103. *United States Census Population: 1960*, vol. 1 (Washington, DC: Government Printing Office, 1961), 45–671; *United States Census Population: 1970*, vol. 1 (Washington, DC: Government Printing Office, 1972), 45–1267.

104. Martínez, *The Chicanos of El Paso*, 6.

105. For population figures on the Chinese and other Asians in El Paso, see Nancy Farrar, *The Chinese in El Paso* (El Paso: Texas Western Press, 1972), 44.

106. Albert Schwartz interview, conducted by Denika Rose, 15 September 1997, videotape cassette, African American Studies Department, University of Texas–El Paso; "El Paso Passes Anti-Bias Law," *Pittsburgh Courier*, 7 July 1962, 6.

107. Albert Schwartz interview, conducted by Denika Rose, 15 September 1997, videotape cassette, African American Studies Department, University of Texas–El Paso.

108. Obra Lee Malone interview, conducted by Charlotte Ivy, 16 June 1987.

109. *El Paso Times*, 1 February 1994. Robin E. L. Washington was also a former major in the army and past president of Black El Paso Democrats.

110. "Integration Ordinance Vetoed by Seitsinger," *El Paso Times*, 20 June 1962, 1.

111. Ibid.; *El Paso Times*, 16 June 1962.

112. "Integration Ordinance Vetoed by Seitsinger," *El Paso Times*, 20 June 1962, 1.

113. "Mayor Seitsinger Wants Voluntary Integration," *El Paso Herald-Post*, 20 June 1962, 1, 11.

114. "Integration: 100% in El Paso," *Newsweek*, 2 July 1962, 17.

115. "Integration Ordinance Vetoed by Seitsinger," *El Paso Times*, 20 June 1962, 1.

116. "El Paso Passes Anti-Bias Law," *Pittsburgh Courier*, 7 July 1962, 6.

117. "Integration Okayed over Mayor's Veto," *El Paso Herald-Post*, 21 June 1962, 1, 2. On San Martín de Porres (1579–1639), see Carlos Parra, "San Martín de Porres," in *Africana: The Encyclopedia of the African American Experience*, ed. Kwame A. Appiah and Henry L. Gates (New York: Basic Civitas Books, 1999), 1540–41.

118. "El Paso Passes Anti-Bias Law," *Pittsburgh Courier*, 7 July 1962, 6.

119. Robert James Branham and Stephen J. Hartnett, *Sweet Freedom's Song: "My Country 'Tis of Thee" and Democracy in America* (New York: Oxford University Press, 2002).

120. "Mayor Hints Veto of Ordinance," *El Paso Herald-Post*, 14 June 1962, 1, s2.

121. "Integration: 100% in El Paso," *Newsweek*, 2 July 1962, 17.

122. Drusilla E. (Tandy) Nixon, interview no. 194 (11 December 1975), 13–14, IOH-UTEP.

123. Nixon added that although El Paso was never a racial utopia, "it was the first city to desegregate its schools after the Supreme Court [1954] ruling" ("El Paso Passes Anti-Bias Law," *Pittsburgh Courier*, 7 July 1962, 6). El Paso Public Schools desegregated in the fall of 1955. The Ysleta Independent School District desegregated in the fall of 1956. The Clint School Board and the Fabens Independent School District desegregated in the summer of 1956 ("Negroes Seek Desegregation in E.P. Theaters," *El Paso Herald-Post*, 17 August 1956, 20).

124. "Integration: 100% in El Paso," *Newsweek*, 2 July 1962, 17.

125. Wilbert H. Timmons, *El Paso: A Borderlands History* (El Paso: Texas Western Press, 1990), 251.

126. "Integration Law Goes into Effect," *El Paso Herald-Post*, 22 June 1962, 1.

Coda

1. Other doctors honored at the convention that year were G. P. A. Ford of Houston, Arthur Q. Shirley of San Antonio, and Peter G. Byrd and E. S. Craven of Beaumont (Robert J. Robertson, *Fair Ways: How Six Black Golfers Won Civil Rights in Beaumont, Texas* [College Station: Texas A&M University Press, 2005], 36–37, 190n18).

2. Dick Landsheft to Lawrence A. Nixon, 30 July 1963, N/MFP.

3. "Youth Thrown from Scooter, Injured," *El Paso Herald-Post*, 1 March 1966, 20; Edna Angela (Nixon) McIver, telephone interview with Will Guzmán, 13 April 2010; El Paso County Clerk, Lawrence Aaron Nixon death certificate, reel no. 0017, frame no. 0246, reel no. 0508, frame no. 1781; "Dr. Nixon of *Nixon v. Herndon*," *Crisis* 73.7 (1966): 378–79; "Nixon," *El Paso Herald-Post*, 7 March 1966, 21; "Nixon," *El Paso Herald-Post*, 8 March 1966, 21. Lawrence Nixon's interment was in Concordia Cemetery in El Paso; see "Obsequies for Dr. Lawrence A. Nixon," 9 March 1966, N/MFP. Nixon's

death certificate suggests his body was taken to Fairview Memorial Park Crematory in Albuquerque, NM, and possibly cremated.

4. *Albuquerque Journal*, 11–15 May 1990; "Widow of El Paso Civil Rights Pioneer Dies in Albuquerque," *El Paso Times*, 11 May 1990, B-1.

5. Richard C. White, Congress of the United States, House of Representatives, 16th District, to Drusilla E. Nixon, 11 March 1966; John B. Connally Jr., governor of Texas, to Drusilla E. Nixon, 14 March 1966; William H. Fort, assistant to the director, Office of Development, Meharry Medical College to Drusilla E. Nixon, 14 September 1966, N/MFP.

6. "Nixon," *El Paso Herald-Post*, 7 March 1966, 21; "Nixon," *El Paso Herald-Post*, 8 March 1966, 21.

7. *Fourteenth Census of the United States*, population schedule, El Paso, voting precinct 12, El Paso County, TX, series T625, roll 1799, page 50B, lines 94–96; *Fifteenth Census of the United States*, population schedule, El Paso, justice precinct 1, El Paso County, TX, series T626, roll 2328, page 235B, lines 69–76. By 1976 the Arredondo family had fifteen pharmacists in their family, for which they received the Outstanding Pharmacy Family of the Year award from the National Association of Retail Druggists and Scherling Corporation ("Obituaries: Arredondo," *El Paso Herald-Post*, 21 November 1977, D-2).

8. Drusilla E. (Tandy) Nixon, interview no. 194 (11 December 1975), 20, IOH-UTEP.

9. Lawrence A. Nixon to Drusilla E. (Tandy) Attwell, 9 May 1934, N/MFP.

10. "Black Doctor Honored in Hometown," *Los Angeles Sentinel*, 15 January 1987, A-10.

11. Matthew C. Whitaker, *Race Work: The Rise of Civil Rights in the Urban West* (Lincoln: University of Nebraska Press, 2005), 154.

12. Lawrence A. Nixon to Drusilla E. (Tandy) Attwell, 9 May 1934, N/MFP.

13. Bruce A. Glasrud, Paul H. Carlson, and Tai D. Kreidler, eds., *Slavery to Integration: Black Americans in West Texas* (Buffalo Gap, TX: State House Press, 2008), 22.

14. John Hope Franklin and Alfred A. Moss Jr., *From Slavery to Freedom: A History of African Americans* (New York: McGraw-Hill, 1994), 120.

15. Lawrence A. Nixon to Drusilla E. (Tandy) Attwell, 9 May 1934, N/MFP; emphasis in original.

16. Ibid.

Index

WILL GUZMÁN is an associate professor of history and African American studies at Florida A&M University. He is a coauthor of *Landmarks and Legacies: A Guide to Tallahassee's African American Heritage*.

The University of Illinois Press
is a founding member of the
Association of American University Presses.

_____

University of Illinois Press
1325 South Oak Street
Champaign, IL 61820-6903
www.press.uillinois.edu